本书由"中国—东盟命运共同体研究中心"资助出版

大学生思想道德教育双语专题十二讲

徐秦法　陈牧　吴昊　编译

新华出版社

图书在版编目（CIP）数据

大学生思想道德教育双语专题十二讲 / 徐秦法，陈牧，吴昊编译 . -- 北京：新华出版社，2022.9

ISBN 978-7-5166-6399-8

Ⅰ . ①大… Ⅱ . ①徐… ②陈… ③吴… Ⅲ . ①思想修养－教学研究－高等学校 Ⅳ . ① G641.6

中国版本图书馆 CIP 数据核字 (2022) 第 159506 号

大学生思想道德教育双语专题十二讲

编　译：徐秦法　陈　牧　吴　昊

责任编辑：蒋小云　　　　　　　　　　封面设计：优盛文化

出版发行：新华出版社

地　　址：北京石景山区京原路 8 号　　邮　　编：100040

网　　址：http://www.xinhuapub.com

经　　销：新华书店、新华出版社天猫旗舰店、京东旗舰店及各大网店

购书热线：010-63077122　　　　　中国新闻书店购书热线：010-63072012

照　　排：优盛文化

印　　刷：石家庄汇展印刷有限公司

成品尺寸：185mm×260mm

印　　张：14.5　　　　　　　　　　字　　数：260 千字

版　　次：2022 年 9 月第一版　　　　印　　次：2022 年 9 月第一次印刷

书　　号：ISBN 978-7-5166-6399-8

定　　价：88.00 元

前　言

　　本书的目的是解决高校《思想道德与法律》双语思政课教学参考资料空缺问题。

　　本书立足《思想道德与法律》，根据中国教育国际化、中国留学生日益增多以及中国日益走近世界舞台中央的需要，采取中英文双语形式编译而成，从另一个侧面创新研究高校思政课教育教学，以培养国际化双语型马克思主义思想政治理论教育教学应用人才。本书从大学生的人生追求、大学生的理想信念、大学生的价值取向、大学生的人生梦想、大学生的中国传统美德继承、大学生的中国精神弘扬、大学生的爱国主义情怀、大学生的价值准则、大学生的改革创新、大学生的道德规范、大学生的道德品格、大学生的社会主义核心价值观践行等十二个方面进行了大学生思想道德教育方面的双语编译，从双语教学视阈创新高校《思想道德与法律》思政课教育，集政治性、时代性、针对性和创新性于一体。本书反映了《思想道德与法律》思政课双语教学改革创新过程中编译者们实践经验的总结和思考。

　　本书所有专题都由广西大学马克思主义学院徐秦法院长统稿后进行校对、修改、审核，最终定稿，第二作者陈牧主任和第三作者吴昊博士协助徐秦法院长校对、修改、审核。其中，专题三由华侨大学外国语学院2019级外国语言文学专业硕士研究生吴晓涵和广西大学马克思主义学院2020级思想政治教育专业硕士研究生严勇俊提供初稿，专题十一由湖南大学外国语学院2019级翻译专业硕士研究生段永俊和梧州学院马克思主义学院梁誉副主任提供初稿。其余十个专题均由广西大学马克思主义学院徐秦法院长、广西壮族自治区政策研究室（改革办）陈牧主任、梧州学院马克思主义学院吴昊博士（特聘为广西大学马克思主义学院之中国—东盟共同体研究中心研究员）负责编译初稿、修改校译、审核定稿。

　　本书专题一从大学生人生观教育方面进行编译。专题二到专题六从人生价值教育、理想信念教育、理想与现实教育、中国梦与中国精神教育、爱国主义情怀教育等方面进行编译。专题七从改革创新是中华民族最深厚的民族禀赋角度对大学生做改革开放生力军的路径进行编译。专题八和专题九从大学生社会主义核心价值观教育、大学生中国传统美德教育、大学生中国革命道德教育方面进行编译。专题十对大学生公共生活的道德教育进行编译。专题十一和专题十二对大学生的择业观、恋爱观、家庭观和个人品德修养教育进行编译。本书的编译出版可以为有志于从事高校双语思政课教学、中小学双语思想品德课教学的教师提供参考，也可以为大学生、研究生以及广大政治、英语爱好者进行双语思想政治理论的学习提供资料参考。

由于双语思政课教学研究是一个新事物，对其理论和现实问题的探索不可能一蹴而就，加上编译者的水平有限以及出版时间仓促，书中难免有不足之处，诚望广大同人与读者不吝赐教。

编　者
2022 年 4 月 28 日于南宁

目　录

Lecture One
The Questions on the Youth of Life

I. The Connotation of the Outlook on Life

1.The Scientific Understanding of the Essence of Human

In the spring of 1845, Marx came up with the scientific thesis of human nature in *Theses on Feuerbach*: "The essence of human is not the inherent abstraction of a single individual, but the summation of all social relations in its reality."

First, the essence of human is not abstract but realistic, concrete.

Human beings are real and specific social existence. It is not right to do a simple and static analysis of the essence of human. It is necessary to put human back into concrete and real life.

Second, the essence of human is determined by social relations.

Human production activities are social. In order to survive, people produce material goods, thus forming the relation of possession, the relation of exchange, the relation of distribution and the relation of consumption of the means of production——production relations (the most basic social relations).

Human life has social characteristics. Human

专题一
人生的青春之问

一、人生观的内涵

1. 科学认识人的本质

1845 年春，马克思在《关于费尔巴哈的提纲》中提出了人的本质的科学论断："人的本质不是单个人所固有的抽象物。在其现实性上，它是一切社会关系的总和。"

第一，人的本质是现实的、具体的，不是抽象的。

人是现实、具体的社会存在。对人的本质仅仅做一般的简单的静态分析是不对的，必须把人放回到具体的现实生活中去。

第二，人的本质是由社会关系决定的。

人的生产活动具有社会性。人们为了生存进行物质资料的生产因而形成生产，资料的占有关系、交换关系、分配关系、消费关系——生产关系（最基本的社会关系）。

人的生活具有社会性。人

is in a certain social relationship from his birth. For example, a person is in a family relationship when he is born, has a teacher-student relationship and schoolmate relationship when he goes to school, has relationships with colleagues and friends when he works, has new family relationships when he gets married, and so on.

Third, the essence of human, in terms of reality, is the summation of all social relations. It is the organic unity of many social relations based on production relations, including husband and wife relations, friends relations, colleagues relations, family relations and so on.

Fourth, the essence of human develops with the history development. With the development of history, human's social relations are constantly evolving.

Fifth, social attribute is the essential attribute of human.

The natural attributes of human are physiological structures and natural instincts, which are mainly the appetite, sexual desire and self-preservation (defense instinct) three basic functions based on the instinctual needs.

The natural attributes of human are human instinct, the precondition for human survival and continuation, and the material bearer of social attributes. Social attributes are the nature of human showing in a certain social environment, which are mainly represented by labor, language, thinking and so on. Labor endows and enriches the social attributes of human, making human's natural attributes deeply branded with social attributes, and making human's social attributes become the es-

从一出生就处于一定的社会关系中，如刚出生处在家庭关系中，上学了有师生关系、同学关系，就业了有同事关系、朋友关系，结婚了有新的家庭关系，等等。

第三，人的本质在其现实性上是一切社会关系的总和，是以生产关系为基础的包括夫妻、朋友、同事、家庭等诸多社会关系的有机统一。

第四，人的本质随着历史的发展而发展。随着历史的发展，人的社会关系也是不断发展变化的。

第五，社会属性是人的本质属性。

人的自然属性是人的生理结构和自然本能，主要是以本能需要为基础的食欲、性欲和自身保存（防卫本能）三种基本机能。

人的自然属性是人的本能，是人类生存和延续的前提条件，是社会属性的物质承担者。社会属性是人在一定的社会环境中表现出来的性质，主要表现为劳动、语言、思维等。劳动赋予并不断丰富了人的社会属性，使人的自然属性深深打上了社会属性的烙印，使社会属性成为人的本质属性。

sential attributes of human beings.

2.The Connotation of the Outlook on Life

First, the outlook on life is the general viewpoint and opinion on the purpose of life, attitudes towards life, and values of life that people have formed in practice. It is an important part of the world view and a manifestation of certain world view on life issues.

Second, the world view is the overall opinion and fundamental view on the world where people live and the relationship between people and the world. It is formed by people in production and practice.

Third, the relationship between the world view and outlook on life. The world view and outlook on life are closely linked. On the one hand, the world view determines the outlook on life. There is what kind of world outlook, there is what kind of outlook on life. According to dialectical materialism, human and human society are the products of long-term development of nature. All the cognition of human comes from practice and continues to develop in practice. A correct understanding of the meaning of life needs to be based on a correct understanding of the laws of development of the objective world. On the other hand, the outlook on life plays an important role in the consolidation, development and change of the world view.

II. The Content of the Outlook on Life

1.The Purpose of Life

First, the connotation of the purpose of life.

2. 人生观的内涵

第一，人生观是人们在实践中形成的关于人生目的、人生态度、人生价值等问题的总观点和总看法。它是世界观的重要组成部分，是一定的世界观在人生问题上的表现。

第二，世界观是人们对生活在其中的世界以及人与世界的关系的总体看法和根本观点。它是人在生产和实践中形成的。

第三，世界观与人生观的关系。世界观和人生观是紧密联系在一起的。一方面，世界观决定人生观，有什么样的世界观就有什么样的人生观。辩证唯物主义认为，人和人类社会是自然界长期发展的产物，人的一切认识都来自实践，并在实践中不断发展。对人生意义的正确理解，需要建立在对客观世界发展规律正确认识的基础之上。另一方面，人生观又对世界观的巩固、发展和变化起着重要的作用。

二、人生观的内容

1. 人生目的

第一，人生目的的内涵。

The purpose of life is the understanding and answer of people about what people live for. It is the fundamental direction and pursuit on people's behavior in life practice. The purpose of life is the core of the outlook on life, and plays an important role in the practice of life.

Second, the role of life purpose in life is mainly reflected in the following three aspects.

① The purpose of life determines what kind of life path to take.

On the one hand, the purpose of life stipulates the general direction of life activities and specific activities of people. On the other hand, the purpose of life is the source of motivation for life. In order to achieve a certain purpose of life, people will pay attention to cultivate their abilities, temper their will, and struggle aggressively and work hard without stopping. Many ancient and modern Chinese and foreign people with lofty ideals who have created brilliant and magnificent life established correct life goals in their youth. Therefore, when solving a series of major issues in life, they will make correct choices and always move toward the correct direction of life development. Premier Zhou Enlai was determined to study for the rise of China in elementary school. At the beginning of the founding of People's Republic of China, a large number of students who had studied abroad, such as "Chinese pride" Qian Xuesen, "the father of two bombs" Deng Jiaxian, resolutely gave up the excellent conditions of working, studying and living abroad, and returned to their motherland, embarked on a road of national defense modernization by working hard.

人生目的是人们对"人为什么活着"的认识和回答，是人在人生实践中关于自身行为的根本指向和追求。人生目的是人生观的核心，在人生实践中具有重要作用。

第二，人生目的对人生的作用主要表现在以下三个方面。

①人生目的决定走什么样的人生道路。

一方面，人生目的规定了人们人生活动的大方向，对人们所从事的具体活动起着定向的作用。另一方面，人生目的又是人生行为的动力源泉。为达到一定的人生目的，人们会注重培养能力、磨炼意志，做奋发进取的拼搏和持之以恒的努力。古今中外众多创造了辉煌壮丽人生的志士仁人，多在青年时期就确立了正确的人生目的，从而在解决人生的一系列重大问题时，做出了正确的选择，始终朝着正确的人生发展方向前进。周恩来总理在小学时就立志为中华之崛起而读书；中华人民共和国成立之初，一大批留洋学子，如"中国人的骄傲"钱学森，"两弹元勋"邓稼先等人，为了实现振兴中华的人生目的，毅然放弃国外优厚的工作、学习和生活条件，回到祖国，走上了艰苦创业，实现国防现代化之路。

② The purpose of life determines the attitudes towards life.

The road of life is rugged. People will face various contradictions and struggles, and different purposes of life will lead them to adopt different attitudes towards life. The right purpose of life can make people fearless, tenacious, enterprising and optimistic; the wrong purpose of life will make people speculate, take risks and break the law and commit crime, or lead a wasted and indulgent life, or form a cynical, world-weary attitude. In history and real life, many successful people treated the ups and downs of life with an optimistic attitude towards life under the guide of their correct purposes of life. Mrs. Curie encountered countless failures in the study of purification of radium, but with her love for truth, unremitting pursuit of justice, and deep concern for human society, she was unyielding and overcame the unimaginable difficulty, finally she succeeded.

③ The purpose of life determines the choice of life value standard.

The correct purpose of life will make people understand that the value of life lies in the contribution, so that they can put their heart and soul into their work, try their best and perform their duties in social labor; the wrong purpose of life will make people think that the value of life is asking from society or others, and thus in social life they will regard the life pursuing personal self-interest as a valuable and meaningful life, and the life fulfilling

②人生目的决定持什么样的人生态度。

人生道路崎岖不平。面对各种各样的矛盾和斗争，不同的人生目的会使人采取不同的人生态度。正确的人生目的可以使人无所畏惧、顽强不屈、积极进取、乐观向上；错误的人生目的则会使人或是投机钻营、铤而走险、违法犯罪，或是虚度人生、游戏人生、放纵人生，或是悲观消沉、厌世轻生。在历史上和现实生活中，许多事业有成者，无不是在其正确的人生目的的引导下，以昂扬乐观的人生态度正确对待人生的坎坷。居里夫人在镭的提纯过程中有过无数次的失败，但她凭着对真理的热爱、对正义的不懈追求和对人类社会的深切关怀，不屈不挠，战胜了常人难以想象的困难，最终取得了成功。

③人生目的决定选择什么样的人生价值标准。

正确的人生目的会使人懂得人生的价值在于奉献，从而在社会劳动中尽心、尽力、尽责；错误的人生目的则会使人把人生价值理解为向社会或他人进行索取，从而在社会生活中以追逐个人私利的人生为有价值、有意义的人生，以对国家、社会、集体和他人尽义务的人生为无价值、

the obligations of the state, society, collectivity and others as a worthless and meaningless life.

It's obvious that the purpose of life is the navigation mark of life, which guides the course of life. Different life goals will lead to different life choices and thus different life choices will lead to different life pursuits, and different life pursuits determine different life values. Therefore, we must pursue a noble purpose of life.

2. The Attitude towards Life

Discussing the purpose of life is to understand the meaning of life, to define the goals and directions that life should pursue; discussing the attitude towards life can help people think about what kind of life they should own and how to treat it.

First, the connotation of the attitude towards life.

The attitude towards life refers to a stable psychological tendency and basic intention of life problems formed through life practice. To put it simply, the attitude towards life is the way people treat life, is the answer to "how to live".

The attitude towards life not only restricts one's understanding and grasp of life's contradictions and problems, but also affects his mental state and life direction.

Everyone in life practice will encounter contradictions of life, such as justice or profit, honor or disgrace, good or evil, bitterness or happiness, gains or losses, success or failure, fortune or misfortune, life or death. If you treat and deal with these problems with a correct attitude towards life,

无意义的人生。

可见，人生目的是人生的航标，它指引着人生的航向。不同的人生目的会有不同的人生选择，不同的人生选择决定着不同的人生追求，不同的人生追求决定着不同的人生价值。因此，我们要追求高尚的人生目的。

2. 人生态度

讨论人生目的是为了认识生活应有的意义，明确人生应追求的目标和方向；讨论人生态度能帮助人们思考人的一生应该有怎样的生活，从而知道应该如何对待生活。

第一，人生态度的内涵。

人生态度，是指人们通过生活实践所形成的对人生问题的一种稳定的心理倾向和基本意图。简单地说，人生态度是人们对待生活的方式，是对"应该怎样活着"的回答。

人生态度既制约着一个人对人生矛盾和问题的认识与把握，又影响着一个人的精神状态和人生走向。

每个人在人生实践中都会遇到义利、荣辱、善恶、苦乐、得失、成败、祸福、生死等人生矛盾，如果以正确的人生态度对待和处理这些问题，就可以正确地把握人生，取得人生的成功。人

you can correctly grasp life and achieve success in life. The attitude towards life has a significant impact on one's life: ① It will affect one's understanding of issues and conflicts of life ② It will affect one's life direction and mental state; ③ It will affect one's behavioral efficiency: Should we seize every day and treasure every minute, or should we just be lazy, and waste time and life while living a mediocre life?

Second，the relationship between the attitudes towards life and outlook on life.

① The attitude towards life is an important part of the outlook on life. One's outlook on life leads to his attitude towards life. When a person makes a certain choice about his outlook on life, he actually decides how he will treat his life in main aspects and deal with various life issues in practice. Conversely, one's attitude towards life often directly affects his opinion of the whole world and life, thus it also has important influences on his world view and outlook on life.

② The attitude towards life is the expression and reflection of the outlook on life. One's outlook on life is manifested through his attitude towards life. If a person owns an indifferent attitude towards life, his outlook on life must be very mediocre; on the contrary, if a person is full of hope and passion for his life, his outlook on life must be scientific and correct .

3.The Value of Life

Generally speaking, value refers to the relationship that the object attribute satisfies the needs of the subject. The outlook on value are the fundamental ideas about what is value, how to judge

生态度对人的一生有重大影响：①影响着一个人对人生课题和人生矛盾的认识；②影响着一个人的人生走向和精神状态；③影响着一个人的行为效率：是只争朝夕，珍惜分分秒秒呢，还是心灰意懒，于碌碌无为中浪费光阴和生命呢？

第二，人生态度与人生观的关系。

①人生态度是人生观的重要内容。一个人有什么样的人生观就会有什么样的人生态度，当一个人对人生观做出了某种明确的选择，实际上就在主要的方面决定了他将如何对待生活，决定了他在实践中将以怎样的方式处理各种人生问题。反过来，一个人的人生态度往往直接影响他对整个世界和人生的看法，从而对其世界观、人生观也具有重要的影响。

②人生态度是人生观的表现和反映。一个人的人生观是通过他的人生态度体现出来的，一个对生活抱无所谓态度的人，他的人生观一定是庸碌无为的人生观；相反，一个对生活充满希望和激情的人，他的人生观一定是科学正确的人生观。

3.人生价值

一般来说，价值是指客体属性满足主体需要的关系。价值观是关于什么是价值、怎样评判价值、如何创造价值等问题的根本

value, how to create value.

First, the self-value and the social value of life. The value of life inherently contains two aspects: self-value and social value of life.

① The self-value of life is the value of the individual life activities to his own survival and development, which is mainly manifested in the satisfactory degree with his material and spiritual needs.

② The social value of life is the value of the individual life activities to society and others. A normal person, since he is a member of society, must work for the society based on his own duties, which shows that he is meaningful to society. At the same time, most members of the society will give them correct evaluation on his existence.

③ The relationship between self-valve and social value of life. The self-valve and social value of life are not only different from each other, but also closely related and interdependent, which constitutes the contradictory unity of life value together. In human social life, as Marx and Engels said, "everyone is a means and an end at the same time, and only by being a means of others can one achieve one's own end, and only by reaching one's own end can one become a means of others, — this correlation is a necessary fact". Individuals are neither simply the means of society and others, nor simply the end. This "necessary fact" is the basis for our understanding of the dialectical relationship between self-valve and social value of life.

观点。

第一，人生的自我价值与社会价值。人生价值内在地包含了人生的自我价值和社会价值两个方面。

①人生的自我价值，是个体的人生活动对自己的生存和发展所具有的价值，主要表现为对自身物质和精神需要的满足程度。

②人生的社会价值，是个体的人生活动对社会、他人所具有的价值。一个正常的人，既然是社会的一员，就要立足于本职为社会工作，这才能表明他对社会有意义。同时，社会大多数成员对于他的存在也会给予正确的评价。

③人生的自我价值和社会价值的关系。人生的自我价值和社会价值既相互区别又密切联系、相互依存，共同构成人生价值的矛盾统一体。在人的社会生活中，正如马克思、恩格斯所说，"每个人是手段同时又是目的，而且只有成为他人的手段才能达到自己的目的，并且只有达到自己的目的才能成为他人的手段——这种相互关联是一个必然的事实"。个人既不单纯是社会和他人的手段，也不单纯是目的，这个"必然的事实"是我们认识人生的自我价值与社会价值

On the one hand, the self-valve of life is a necessary condition for individual survival and development. The process of individual self-valve improvement is the process of achieving comprehensive development through self-improvement. The realization of self-valve of life constitutes the premise that individuals create greater value for society.

On the other hand, the social value of life is the basis for realizing the self-valve of life. Without social value, the self-valve of life cannot exist. People always live in society, and individuals cannot exist and develop if being separated from society. Individual life activities not only have value attributes that satisfy self-needs, but also inevitably contain value attributes that meet social needs. Man is a person of society, which not only means that the material and spiritual needs of the individual must be satisfied in society, but also means that the way and degree they are satisfied are determined by society. Whether one's needs can be satisfied from society and to what extent it can be satisfied depends on the contribution of his life activities to others and society, i. e. his social value.

Second, the relationship between the value of life and the outlook on life.

The value of life is a special value, and is the role and significance of life practice of human for society and individuals. The value of life is the basis for people to consider life issues from the perspective of value.

的辩证关系的基础。

一方面，人生的自我价值是个体生存和发展的必要条件。个体提高自我价值的过程，就是通过努力自我完善以实现全面发展的过程。人生自我价值的实现构成了个体为社会创造更大价值的前提。

另一方面，人生的社会价值是实现人生自我价值的基础，没有社会价值，人生的自我价值就无法存在。人总是生活在社会当中，无法脱离社会而存在和发展。个体的人生活动不仅具有满足自我需要的价值属性，还必然地包含着满足社会需要的价值属性。人是社会的人，这不仅意味着个体物质和精神的需要必须在社会中才能得到满足，还意味着个体以怎样的方式和在多大程度上得到满足是由社会决定的。一个人的需要能不能从社会中得到满足以及在多大程度上得到满足，取决于他的人生活动对他人和社会的贡献，即他的社会价值。

第二，人生价值与人生观的关系。

人生价值是一种特殊的价值，是人的生活实践对于社会和个人所具有的作用及意义。人生价值就是人们从价值角度考虑人生问题的根据。

The value of life plays an important role in the whole system of the outlook on life, providing a basis for people's choice of life purpose and attitude. If one person pursues the purpose of his life identified by himself,he must think that this kind of life has or can create value, and if one person treats life in some way, that's because he believes that such a way of life makes sense.

In short, one's outlook on life is mainly reflected in three aspects: life purpose, life attitude and life value. The purpose of life is the answer to why people live, and the attitude of life shows how people should treat life,and the value of life distinguishes that what kind of life makes sense. These three aspects complement each other, the purpose of life is the core of the outlook on life, the life purpose leads to life attitude, and thus further leads to the life value one will pursue.

III. The Scientific and Lofty Pursuit of Life

Different life purposes determine different life paths. With wrong purpose of life,people will lose their freedom and happiness. Therefore, we must pursue scientific and noble life goals. The outlook on life involves many specific issues, but the most basic one is the relationship between the individual and the society.

1.The Dialectical Relationship between the Individual and the Society

Individuals and society are the unity of opposite.They are interdependent, mutually restrictive and mutually promoting. Society is made up of specific people. Without people, there is no society. Similarly, people cannot survive once leaving the society. The relationship between the individual and the society is fundamentally the relationship

人生价值在人生观体系中具有重要地位，为人们的人生目的和人生态度的选择提供依据。一个人追求自己认定的人生目的是因为他认为这样的生活具有或者能够创造价值，一个人以某种方式对待生活是因为他认为这种生活方式是有意义的。

总之，一个人的人生观主要是通过人生目的、人生态度和人生价值三个方面体现出来的。人生目的回答人为什么活着，人生态度表明人应当怎样对待生活，人生价值判别什么样的人生才有意义。这三个方面相辅相成，其中人生目的是人生观的核心，有什么样的人生目的就会有什么样的人生态度，就会追求什么样的人生价值。

三、科学高尚的人生追求

不同的人生目的决定不同的人生轨迹，错误的人生目的会使人失去自由和幸福，因而我们要追求科学高尚的人生目的。人生观涉及许多具体问题，但最基本的是个人与社会的关系问题。

1. 个人与社会的辩证关系

个人与社会是对立统一关系，两者相互依存、相互制约、相互促进。社会由具体的人组成，离开了人也就没有了社会。同样，人离开了社会也无法生存。个人与社会的关系根本上是

between personal interests and social interests. Social interests are the unity of all personal interests and the premise and basis for the realization of personal interests. The satisfaction of personal interests can only be achieved through specific social methods under certain social conditions. In a socialist society, personal interests and social interests are unified.

2.The Scientific and Lofty Pursuit of Life

First, "serving the people and contributing to the society" is just the scientific and lofty life pursuit.

Despite the emergence of various life pursuits in the longevity of human society, "serving the people and contributing to the society" is just the scientific and lofty life pursuit. This kind of life pursuit is worthy for us to follow and practice. The decisive role of the human's creating world history also indicates that "serving the people and contributing to the society" is by far the most advanced pursuit of life.

In the history of the development of Marxism, Marx and Engels clearly put forward the idea of "serving the interests of the vast majority" in *The Communist Manifesto*, Lenin put forward the idea of "serving the millions of working people" in *The Party Organization and Party Literature*, and Mao zedong succinctly summarized the viewpoints of Marx and Lenin as "serving the people". Their views reflect the process of the formation and development of the thought and proposition of "serving the people", and reflect the process of the formation, development and perfection of the proletarian outlook on life and moral. In different

个人利益与社会利益的关系。社会利益是所有个人利益的统一，是个人利益得以实现的前提与基础。个人利益的满足只能在一定的社会条件下通过一定的社会方式来实现。在社会主义社会中，个人利益与社会利益是统一的。

2. 科学高尚的人生追求

第一，"服务人民、奉献社会"才是科学高尚的人生追求。

尽管在人类社会漫长的历史中涌现过形形色色的人生追求，但只有"服务人民、奉献社会"才是科学高尚的人生追求，才值得同学们遵奉和践行。人类创造世界历史的决定性作用也指明"服务人民、奉献社会"是迄今最先进的人生追求。

在马克思主义发展史上，从马克思和恩格斯在《共产党宣言》中明确提出的"为绝大多数人谋利益"到列宁在《党的组织和党的文学》中提出的"为千千万万劳动人民服务"，再到毛泽东精辟概括的"为人民服务"，都反映了为人民服务思想和命题的形成及发展的过程，也反映了无产阶级人生观、道德观的形成、发展和完善的过程。在不同的历史时期，中国共产党的几代领导人都结合革命、建设和改革的实

historical periods, the leaders of the Communist Party of China, in combination with the practice of revolution, construction and reform, expounded the profound truth of the outlook on life of "serving the people and contributing to the society".

Second, why is "serving the people and contributing to the society" a scientific and lofty pursuit of life?

Only when a person has established the life pursuit of "serving the people and contributing to the society", can he have a real understanding of the meaning of life, can he clearly grasp the life course and life goal, and deeply understand why people live and what kind of life road they should take.

Only when a person has established the life pursuit of "serving the people and contributing to the society", can he treat life with a correct attitude and give priority to the interests of the people, can he always have a high sense of responsibility to his motherland and the people, and realize his life value in serving the people and contributing to the society.

Only when a person has established the life pursuit of "serving the people and contributing to the society", can he master the correct standard of life value, understand that the value of life lies in dedication first, can he consciously use the truth, kindness and beauty to shape himself, and strive to make himself a noble man.

IV. The Establishment of the Right Attitude towards Life

There are two attitudes towards life: one is

践，阐述了"服务人民、奉献社会"的人生观的深刻道理。

第二，为什么"服务人民、奉献社会"是科学高尚的人生追求？

一个人只有确立了"服务人民、奉献社会"的人生追求，才能对人生的意义有真切的理解，才能清楚地把握人的生命历程和奋斗目标，深刻理解人为什么而活、应走什么样的人生之路等道理。

一个人只有确立了"服务人民、奉献社会"的人生追求，才能以正确的人生态度对待人生，以人民利益为重，始终对祖国和人民具有高度的责任感，在服务人民、奉献社会中实现自己的人生价值。

一个人只有确立了"服务人民、奉献社会"的人生追求，才能掌握正确的人生价值标准，懂得人生的价值首先在于奉献，自觉用真善美来塑造自己，努力使自己成为一个高尚的人。

四、树立正确的人生态度

人生态度分为两种：一种是

optimistic and aggressive, and the other is negative and inactive. Negative and inactive attitudes will hinder success, and only with a optimistic and aggressive attitude can one succeed.

1. The Specific Manifestations of Negative Life Attitude

First, seeing through the world. It is characterized as follows.

① In terms of life, they think that life is meaningless, feeling disappointed about life and society, muddling along and pursuing for nothing.

② In terms of academy, they think little about progress.

③ In terms of life, they are lazy, tired and sluggish, let things drift, and have neither a sense of time nor a sense of discipline.

④ In terms of interpersonal relationship, they prefer to be a loner, sighing the indifference among people while being ironhearted to others.

Second, the pursuit of the enjoyment of pleasure.

Among college students, this attitude of life has considerable impacts, some people have made such a picture of this kind of university students as wearing the brand name, using products of famous brands, eating the steak (western food), pay too much attention to their faces and hanging 'Red card' in study. The criteria for judging things of those who hold this attitude of life is whether these things can bring pleasure and benefits to them, if one thing can bring these they will rush to do it, and if not they'll try to avoid.

Third, the arrogant attitude towards life.

乐观向上、积极进取的，一种是消极无为的。消极无为的态度阻碍成功，只有持乐观向上、积极进取的态度，才能取得成功。

1. 消极的人生态度的具体表现

第一，看破红尘。其具有如下特点。

①在生活方面，认为生活没有意义，对人生和社会悲观失望，得过且过，无所追求。

②在学业上，不思进取。

③生活上松散疲沓，放任自流，既无时间观念又无纪律观念。

④在人际关系上喜欢独来独往，既感叹人情淡漠又对别人很冷漠。

第二，追求享乐。

在大学生中，这种人生态度也有相当影响，有人给这样的大学生作了形象的描绘："穿的是名牌．用的是品牌，吃的是牛排（西餐），看的是脸盘儿，学习挂'红牌'"。他们评判事情的标准是能否给自己带来享乐和实惠，有则趋之，无则避之。

第三，狂妄自大。

For those who hold this attitude of life, their self-consciousness expands, vanity is extremely strong. They only care about themselves, they are arrogant and conceited, they bother to interact with others, and even disdain to combine theory with practice.

Fourth, the critique of everything.

Those who hold this attitude of life are dissatisfied with anyone, and believe that others owe them, and the society is unfair to themselves. They always pick the "thorn" of others and attack the "squats" of the society, complaining all day long. This is a life attitude which denies people's activeness, which is self-centered and irresponsible for others and society. It is not conducive to the growth and success of college students.

2. The Establishment of a Positive and Enterprising Attitude towards Life

First, a serious-minded attitude towards life must be established.

The title of college students is not only a manifestation of a cultural level, but also a symbol of sacred responsibility. College students should be responsible for themselves, for the family, for the country and society, and consciously assume their own responsibilities. Only by treating life with a serious attitude can a person do everything well in life steadily, contribute to the development of mankind and make an achievement for the individual's life. Some people regard "game life" as the fashion, but this irresponsible attitude towards life is incompatible with our social development,

持这种人生态度的人，自我意识膨胀，虚荣心极强，唯我独尊，狂妄自大，不屑与他人相交往，更不屑把理论与实践相结合。

第四，批判一切。

持这种人生态度的人对谁都不满意，自认为别人亏欠自己、社会对自己不公，总是挑别人的"刺"，攻击社会的"瑕疵"，终日牢骚满腹，怨天尤人。这是一种否定人的积极能动性、以个人为中心、对他人和社会不负责任的人生态度，非常不利于大学生成长、成才。

2. 树立积极进取的人生态度

第一，人生须认真。

大学生的称号不仅是一种文化层次的体现，更是一种神圣责任的象征。大学生要对自己负责、对家庭负责、对国家和社会负责，自觉承担起自己应尽的责任。以认真的态度对待人生，才能踏踏实实地做好人生中的每一件事，为人类的发展奉献一份力量，为个人的一生建立一份功业。有些人以"游戏人生"为时尚，这种不负责任的人生态度与社会发展格格不入，会误导人生，使人最

which will mislead life and make people end up being "a white-haired juvenile who mourns in vain".

Second, a pragmatic attitude towards life must be established.

People are always annoyed with the past and worry about the future. In fact, the present thing is just the thing what we should do well. We should live in the present, and transform the lofty ideals into the present concrete actions. We should not have grand plans but little skills and only talk about ideas. Otherwise we will be divorced from reality and achieve nothing.

Third, an optimistic attitude towards life must be established.

Life is rich and colorful, and full of various contradictions and problems. Doom, adversity, failure and suffering are inevitable in everyone's life, the key is how to deal with. Optimistic attitude towards life is an outlook on life which has positive evaluation of life, full of good wishes for life, with no sadness, no lament, and full of passion. In short, it is optimistic, positive and proactive. Being optimistic, loving life, and being confident in life reflects a positive attitude towards oneself, society, and life. This attitude is the psychological basis for people to withstand difficulties and setbacks. The optimistic attitude towards life can be showed as follows.

① The spirit of struggle for aggressive development. This is the concentrated expression of the optimistic attitude of life in the spirit of the

终落得"白了少年头，空悲切"结果。

第二，人生当务实。

人们总是为过去的事懊恼，为未来的事忧愁，其实现在的事才是最应该做好的事。要活在当下，要把远大的理想寓于现在具体的行动中，不可眼高手低、空谈理想，否则就会脱离实际，一事无成。

第三，人生应乐观。

人生是丰富多彩的，也充满了各种矛盾和问题。厄运、逆境、失败和痛苦是不可避免的，关键在于以什么样的态度来面对。乐观主义人生态度是一种对人生做出积极评价，对人生充满美好祝福，不哀伤、不悲叹，并饱含激情的人生观，简而言之就是乐观向上、积极有为。乐观向上、热爱生活，对人生充满自信，体现了对自己、对社会、对生活的积极态度，这种态度是人们承受困难和挫折的心理基础。乐观主义人生态度的表现有以下几个方面。

①积极进取的奋斗精神。这是乐观主义人生态度在时代精神上的集中体现。

times.

② Unremitting will to fight. This is the inner strength of the optimistic attitude towards life.

③ The noble characters of adhering to and pursuing the truth. This is the source of strength to maintain the optimistic attitude towards life.

④ The optimism of loving life. This is an external manifestation of the optimistic life towards life.

Fourth, an enterprising attitude towards life must be established.

Life is like a river, and it is inevitable to enter into a corner, and even encounter rapids and whirlpools. The poet Ai Qing once said: "time flows downstream, life flows upstream." Only by adapting to the trend of historical development and taking a pioneering and enterprising attitude to meet various challenges of life, can we continuously comprehend the true meaning of a better life and experience the joy and happiness of life. We should be proactive and constantly enrich the meaning of life. We should not seek comfort, contentment, conformism and mediocrity.Otherwise, life will lose its due luster. Therefore, we must carry forward the spirit of self-improvement, daring to be first, and indomitability and perseverance.

②坚韧不拔的战斗意志。这是乐观主义人生态度的内在力量。

③坚持和追求真理的高尚品格。这是保持乐观主义人生态度的力量源泉。

④热爱生活的乐观情绪。这是乐观主义人生态度的外在表现。

第四，人生要进取。

人生就像一条河流，免不了进入弯道，甚至会遇到险滩和旋涡。诗人艾青曾说："时间顺流而下，生活逆水行舟。"只有适应历史发展的趋势，以开拓进取的态度迎接人生的各种挑战，才能不断领悟美好人生的真谛，体验生活的快乐和幸福。要积极进取，不断丰富人生的意义，不能贪图安逸、满足现状、因循守旧、碌碌无为。否则，人生就会失去应有的光彩。因此，我们必须发扬自强不息、敢为人先、百折不挠、坚韧不拔的精神。

Lecture Two
The Realization of the Brilliant Life

What are the criteria and methods for evaluating life value? How to achieve the goal of life value? These are unavoidable problems in our life practice and are of great significance on everyone's life path.

I.The Evaluation Criteria of Life Value

1.The Fundamental Scale of the Life Value Evaluation

The fundamental scale of the life value evaluation is to see whether a person's practical activities are consistent with the objective laws of social development and whether they have promoted the historical progress.

2.The Basic Scale of the Life Value Evaluation

Labor and the contribution made to the society and others through labor is the basic scale for society to evaluate a person's life value. Einstein once said: "The value of a person should be based on what he contributes, not what he gets."

The greater the individual contribution to the survival and development of the society and others, the greater the social value of his life is; on the

专题二
成就出彩人生

人生价值的评价标准和方法是什么？如何实现人生价值目标？这些问题都是我们在人生实践中不可回避的问题，在每一个人的人生道路上都具有非常重要的意义。

一、人生价值的评价标准

1. 人生价值评价的根本尺度

人生价值评价的根本尺度是看一个人的实践活动是否符合社会发展的客观规律，是否促进了历史的进步。

2. 人生价值评价的基本尺度

劳动以及通过劳动对社会和他人做出的贡献，是社会评价一个人人生价值的基本尺度。爱因斯坦曾说："一个人的价值，应当看他贡献什么，而不是看他取得什么。"

个体对社会和他人的生存和发展贡献越大，其人生的社会价值也就越大；反之，人生的社会

contrary, the smaller the social value of his life is. If the individual life activities do not contribute to the survival and development of the society and others, but have side effects, then the social value of this kind of life is expressed as negative value.

In the socialist society, The most important standard to measure the value of one's life is to see whether a person is sincerely dedicated to the country and society with his own labor and intelligence, and whether he serves the people wholeheartedly.

In addition to the fundamental scale and basic scale, there are other evaluation criteria such as money and wealth, knowledge and technology, and power status.

II. The Evaluation Methods of Life Value

To evaluate the life value of social members objectively, impartially and accurately, in addition to mastering scientific evaluation criteria, appropriate evaluation methods should be adopted from the following three aspects.

1.The Adherence to the Combination of the Ability with the Contribution

Everyone's occupation is different and their abilities are also different, so they will have different absolute amount of contribution to society. We should never be so naive to think that people with great abilities can realize the life value, and those with weak abilities can not realize the life value. Anyone who works diligently and conscientiously in his own position should be given positive evaluation to his life value.

价值就越小。如果个体的人生活动对社会和他人的生存和发展不仅没有贡献，反而起到某种反作用，那么这种人生的社会价值就表现为负价值。

在社会主义社会，衡量人生价值最重要的标准就在于看一个人是否以自己的劳动和聪明才智为国家和社会真诚奉献，尽心尽力为人民群众服务。

除了根本尺度和基本尺度外，人生价值评价还有诸如金钱财富、知识技术和权力地位等其他评价标准。

二、人生价值的评价方法

要比较客观、公正、准确地评价社会成员人生价值的大小，除了要掌握科学的评价标准外，还要采用恰当的评价方法，具体需要做到以下三个坚持。

1. 坚持能力有强弱与贡献须尽力相统一

每个人的职业不同、能力强弱不同，对社会贡献的绝对量也不同，不能简单地认为能力强的人就能实现人生价值，能力弱的人就不能实现人生价值。任何人，只要在自己的岗位上尽职尽责，兢兢业业，就应该对其人生价值给予积极肯定的评价。

2. The Adherence to the Combination of the Material Contribution with the Spiritual Contribution

In real life, it is easy for people to think that individual contribution to society is only material contribution and ignore the spiritual contribution. In fact, the development and progress of society is the common development and progress of material and spiritual civilization. The value of a person's life should be measured not only by his contribution to society in material aspects, such as creation and invention and the scientific and technological products, but also by his contribution to society in spiritual and ideological aspects, such as theoretical articles and literary works. In the history of human civilization, some have made contributions to the creation of material wealth; some have made contributions to the creation of spiritual wealth; some have not only created material wealth obviously, but also created spiritual wealth prominently. These people, no matter what part of them they are, all have valuable lives.

3.The Adherence to the Combination of One's Own Improvement with One's Own Contribution to Society

The evaluation of the life value mainly depends on the contribution of one's life activities to society, but this does not mean denying the self-worth of life. Society is created by human beings and composed of individuals. The self-improvement and comprehensive development of human beings and the realization of self-worth in life will lay a solid foundation for individuals to create

2. 坚持物质贡献与精神贡献相统一

在现实生活中，人们容易把个人对社会的贡献局限于物质贡献，而忽视其精神贡献。其实，社会的发展与进步是物质文明和精神文明的共同发展与进步。衡量一个人的人生价值，既要看他在物质方面对社会的贡献，如创造发明、科技产品等，又要看他在精神、思想道德方面对社会的贡献，如理论文章、文艺作品等。在人类文明史上，一部分人主要在物质财富的创造方面做出了贡献；另一部分人主要在精神财富的创造方面做出了贡献；还有许多人既明显地创造了物质财富，又突出地创造了精神财富。无论哪一部分人，他们的人生都是有价值的。

3. 坚持完善自身与贡献社会相统一

评价人生价值的大小主要看一个人的人生活动对社会所做的贡献，但这并不意味着否认人生的自我价值。社会是人创造并由个体组成的，人的自我完善和全面发展、人生自我价值的实现将为个体创造更大的社会价值奠定坚实基础。离开自身素质的提

greater social values. Without the improvement of our own quality, contribution to society is an empty talk. Only by constantly improving ourselves can we contribute to society better.

Contemporary college students attach great importance to the realization of the life value. Then, what kind of life value is meaningful to choose and persue? How can we realize our own life value?

III. The Conditions for the Realization of the Life Value

1.Social Objective Conditions for the Realization of the Life Value

The life value is realized in social practice and the formation, exertion and development of human creativity depend on certain social objective conditions. Everyone lives in a social system that is not transferred by personal will, including social institutions, social structures, social relations, and social norms. In this sense, individuals can not choose society. Generally speaking, with the progress of society, the social objective conditions for the realization of the life value can be constantly improved. Since the reform and opening up, China's great achievements in economic and social development and the self-improvement and development of the socialist system with Chinese characteristics have provided favorable conditions and opportunities for people to realize their life values. We must cherish the rare historical opportunities and build our own goal of the life value on the basis of the correct grasp of the actual development conditions of China's society today, and

高，贡献社会就是一句空话。只有不断完善自我，才能更好地为社会做贡献。

当代大学生都很重视实现人生价值，那么，究竟选择和追求怎样的人生价值才是有意义的？如何才能实现自己的人生价值呢？

三、实现人生价值的条件

1.实现人生价值的社会客观条件

人生价值是在社会实践中实现的，人的创造力的形成、发挥和发展都要依赖一定的社会客观条件。每个人都是生活在一个不以个人意志为转移的，包括社会制度、社会结构、社会关系和社会规范等在内的社会系统中的。从这个意义上说，个人是不能选择社会的。一般来说，随着社会的进步，人生价值实现的社会客观条件也在不断地改善。改革开放以来，我国经济社会发展取得了巨大成就，中国特色社会主义制度的自我完善和发展，为人们实现人生价值提供了有利条件和机遇。我们要珍惜难得的历史机遇，把自己的人生价值目标建立在正确把握当今中国社会发展实际的基础上，努力、充分地实现自己的人生价值。

strive to fully realize our own life value.

2.Individual Conditions for the Realization of the Life Value

The individual conditions mainly include ideological and moral quality, scientific and cultural quality, and physiological and psychological quality and so on. Everyone has different conditions from other people's, and we should determine our life value goals realistically according to our own conditions. Knowing ourselves objectively is an important prerequisite for the determination of the life value goal. The pursuit of the life value is not an empty and pure conceptual action, it must be reflected through concrete life activities and the effects of its forms and practices. However, everyone has different conditions. In terms of a specific value goal, although it is appropriate and relatively easy to achieve for one person, it is not necessarily so for another person. Therefore, we should determine our own life value goals according to our own conditions, and can't "do whatever we want".

3. The Constant Enhancement of the Ability to Realize the Life Value

We should constantly improve our own abilities to better achieve the life value. To a considerably large extent, the realization of the life value depends on individual subjective efforts. People can improve their abilities by learning and exercising. College students have strong plasticity and are in a critical period of increasing their knowledge and abilitoes. They can improve their com-

2. 实现人生价值的个体自身条件

个体自身条件主要包括一个人的思想道德素质、科学文化素质、生理心理素质等方面的要素。每个人的自身条件都会与其他人有一定的差异，应当实事求是地根据自身条件来确定自己的人生价值目标。客观地认识自己是确定人生价值目标的重要前提。人生价值的追求不是空洞的纯粹的观念运动，它必然要通过具体的人生活动及其形式和实践的成效来体现。而每个人的自身条件都会与其他人有一定的差异，某一个具体的价值目标，对这个人来说是恰当的、比较容易实现的，而对另一个人来说却未必如此。因此，应当实事求是地根据自身条件来确定自己的人生价值目标，而不可能"随心所欲"。

3. 不断增强实现人生价值的能力和本领

我们要不断提高自身能力，增强实现人生价值的本领。一个人的人生价值的实现程度在很大程度上取决于个人主观努力。人可以通过学习和锻炼提高自己的能力。大学生可塑性强，正处于增长知识和才干的关键时期，可以通过各种方式和途径，全面提

prehensive qualities and abilities comprehensively through various ways and means, and strive to create good conditions for the realization of the life value.

IV. The Establishment of the Correct Contradictory View of Life

In the process of establishing a correct outlook on life, there are many contradictions in life that require us to think and many wrong outlooks on life that blur our direction. Whether we can be confronted with these contradictions in life and establish correct contradictory view of life will directly affect the realization of our life value goals.

1.The Establishment of the Correct View of Happiness

First，what is the correct view of happiness?

At present, the general view of happiness is: happiness is a general category, means that people generally live a good life; family harmony, career success, proper behavior, and perfect personality and so on, are all important factors for happiness. Happiness is a sense of gain, content and satisfaction of the life value.

Happiness is relative and hierarchical. Each person's happiness is different, different people have different standards of happiness. Happiness also has epochal character and is influenced by social development and progress.

Second，how to pursue happiness in life?

① Happiness does not the fall from the sky, happiness comes from struggle. Strivers are not only the people with the richest spiritual wealth, but also the people who understand happiness

高自身的综合素质和能力，努力创造实现人生价值的良好条件。

四、树立正确的人生矛盾观

在树立正确的人生观过程中，有诸多的人生矛盾需要我们去思考，也有不少错误的人生观使我们迷失方向。能否正视这些人生矛盾，能否树立正确的人生矛盾观，都将直接影响我们人生价值目标的实现。

1. 树立正确的幸福观

第一，正确的幸福观什么？

当前，一般意义上的幸福观是：幸福是一个总体性范畴，意味着人总体上生活得美好；家庭和睦、事业成功、行为正当、人格完善等都是幸福的重要因素。幸福感是一种人生价值获得感、知足感和满意感。

幸福感是相对的、有层次性的。每一个人的幸福感都是有差异的，不同的人有不同的幸福标准。幸福感也是有时代性的，受社会发展进步的影响。

第二，如何追求人生幸福？

①幸福不会从天而降，幸福都是奋斗出来的。奋斗者既是精神最为富足的人，也是最懂得幸

most. The process of the pursuit of happiness is the one of not being satisfied with the status quo, constantly pursuing and creating a better life.

② We should constantly accumulate the material and spiritual conditions for the realization of happiness in life. The needs of the realization of happiness in life are in material and spiritual aspects. Achieving happiness is inseparable from certain material conditions. The satisfaction of material needs and the abundance of material life are important aspects of happiness. The satisfaction of spiritual needs and the enrichment of spiritual life are also important aspects. It is also an important aspect of happiness. While pursuing the improvement of material living standards, we must pay more attention to the pursuit of the lofty virtue and personality, and focus on the pursuit of a healthy and upward spiritual life.

③ In the process of the pursuit of happiness, we must correctly handle the relationship between self−interest, intergrated social interest and the interests of others. The realization of personal happiness cannot be at the expense of the intergrated social interest and the interests of others. Only by contributing to the society and serving others can we obtain the environment and conditions needed by happiness, generate greater gain of happiness, and realize the mutual promotion of personal happiness and social progress.

2.The Establishment of the Correct View of Gain and Loss

First, the relationship between gain and loss must be dialetically treated.

福的人。追求幸福的过程就是不满足于现状、不断追求和创造更美好生活的过程。

②我们需不断积累实现人生幸福的物质条件和精神条件。人生幸福的实现有物质和精神两个层面的需求。实现幸福离不开一定的物质条件，物质需要的满足、物质生活的富足是幸福的重要方面，精神需要的满足、精神生活的充实也是幸福的重要方面。在追求物质生活水平提高的同时，我们要更加注重追求德行和人格的高尚，注重追求健康向上的精神生活。

③在追求幸福的过程中，我们需正确处理自身利益与社会整体利益和他人利益的关系。实现个人幸福不能以牺牲社会整体利益和他人利益为代价。只有在为社会做贡献、为他人服务的过程中，我们才能获得幸福所需要的环境和条件，产生更大的幸福感，实现个人幸福与社会进步的相互促进。

2. 树立正确的得失观

第一，辩证地看待得与失的关系。

In the course of life, there are always choices of gain and loss faced by us. We must learn to correctly look at the gain and loss in life, which has an important impact on one's life path and the realization of life value. College students should face the gain and loss in life with a positive and enterprising attitude, make the temporary gains and losses become the wealth of life rather than the burden of life.

Second, how to establish a correct view of gain and loss?

① Don't get caught up in personal gain and loss. There are many things worth having and pursuing in life and the gains and losses of personal interests are only part of the pursuit of life value. A great man should keep the world in mind. It's hard for one to make some achievements if he haggles over every ounce in life and is swayed by considerations of gain and loss at work.

The gain and loss of personal interests can only partially measure the life value. Only by making contributions to the society can one achieve greater life value. Only by pursuing noble morality and getting rid of haggling over the narrow interests can a person win the respect of others and society.

② Don't be content with the temporary "gain". Although the temporary success and harvest may let a person rejoice and be elated, but relative to the whole social development, it is just a wave in the sea. Young people can't just live in the moment, in their own world, but take a long-term view.

在人生道路上，我们总是面临着各种得与失的选择。我们要学会正确看待人生的得与失，这对一个人走好人生之路、实现人生价值有重要影响。大学生要以积极进取的态度去面对生活中的成败得失，使一时的成败得失成为人生的财富，而不是人生的包袱。

第二，如何树立正确的得失观？

①不要拘泥于个人利益的得失。人生值得拥有和追求的东西有很多，个人利益的得失只是人生价值追求的一部分。成大事者，当胸怀天下，如果生活中斤斤计较，工作中患得患失，是很难成就一番事业的。

个人利益的得失只能部分地衡量人生价值的大小，只有在奉献社会中才能实现更大的人生价值；只有追求高尚的道义，摒弃对狭隘利益的计较，才能赢得他人和社会的尊重。

②不要满足于一时的"得"。一时的成功、一时的收获，固然让人欢欣、让人得意，但对于整个社会发展而言，它只是大海中泛起的一朵浪花。青年人不能只活在当下，活在自我世界中，要将眼光放长远一些。

If a person is always satisfied with temporary "gain", he will stop at small successes and achievements, and will not continue his efforts, which leads to the final failure. Countless successes or failures and gains or losses in history have explained this truth in life. Life gives more opportunities to those who are good at and bold in innovation and creation. Life neither favors those who are conservative and satisfied with the status quo, nor waits for those who are lazy and enjoy their achievements.

③ Don't be afraid of the temporary "loss". There are gains and losses in life, which is the basic law in the life path. For some reason, we may have to lose some benefits and miss some opportunities. It is a loss in the present, but in some sense, it is an experience of life.It enriches the content of life, is the precious wealth of life. Therefore, a life with some gains and some losses is more meaningful.

"A fall into the pit, a gain in your wit" "Misfortune might be a blessing in disguise". Gain is not necessarily a good thing, and loss is not necessarily a bad thing.

3. The Establishment of the Correct View on Bitterness and Optimism

Both bitterness and optimism are the common life experiences. Bitterness and optimism are both opposite and unified, and can transform mutually under certain conditions. For college students, they should establish the correct view on bitterness and optimism, consciously develop the spirit of endur-

一个人如果总是满足于一时的"得"，往往会停步在小小的成功和已有的成绩上，放弃继续努力，导致最后的失败。历史上无数成败、得失的事例都诠释了这条人生道理。生活从不眷顾因循守旧、满足现状者，从不等待不思进取、坐享其成者，而是将更多机遇留给善于和勇于创新创造的人们。

③不要惧怕一时的"失"。人生有得就有失，这是人生道路中的基本规律。因为某些因素我们可能不得不失去某些利益，错失某些机遇。这就当下来说是一种损失，但从某种意义上来说，这种失去是人生的一种经历，丰富了人生的内容，是人生的宝贵财富。因此，有得又有失的人生才更有意义。

"吃一堑，长一智" "塞翁失马，焉知非福"。得到了不一定是好事，失去了也不一定是坏事。

3. 树立正确的苦乐观

苦与乐都是常见的人生体验。两者既对立又统一，在一定条件下又可以相互转化。对于大学生来说，树立正确的苦乐观，就是要自觉养成吃苦精神，切忌"坐等天上掉馅饼"。

ing hardship, and can not "sit and wait for pie to fall from the sky".

"The sharpness of the sword comes from grinding, and the fragrance of plum blossom comes from the bitter cold." True happiness can only be transformed from the hardship of struggle. In the process of growing up, college students must accurately grasp the dialectical relationship between bitterness and optimism, and strive to be a pioneer who overcomes difficulties and struggles hard.

4. The Establishment of the Correct view on Prosperity and Adversity

Prosperity and adversity are two different situations in the course of life. Different attitudes towards prosperity and adversity reflect different life values.

Moving forward in prosperity is like sailing with the current. Favorable factors such as nature climate conditions, geographical environment and popular support make it easier for people to approach and achieve their goals. However, in the favorable atmosphere, under the superior conditions, a person easily become proud and pampered, complacent, leading to his will decline.

Struggling in adversity is like rowing against the current. If you don't advance, you will fall back. Only in the struggle of adversity, can we have a sense of gain and a sense of achievement that is hard to get in prosperity. For challengers, adverse circumstances can temper their will, cultivate their character, accumulate experience in overcoming difficulties and enrich their life experience.

"宝剑锋从磨砺出,梅花香自苦寒来。"真正的快乐只能由奋斗的艰苦转化而来。大学生在成长过程中,要准确把握苦与乐的辩证关系,努力做迎难而上、艰苦奋斗的开拓者。

4. 树立正确的顺逆观

顺境和逆境是人生历程中两种不同的境遇。对待顺境和逆境的不同态度,体现了不同的人生价值观。

顺境中前进,如同顺水行舟,天时、地利、人和等有利因素使人们更容易接近和实现目标。但是,顺境中的宽松气氛、优越条件又容易使人滋生骄娇二气,自满自足,意志衰退。

在逆境中奋斗,犹如逆水行舟,不进则退,需要付出更大的努力和更多的艰辛才可能成功。在逆境中奋斗,会有顺境中难以得到的获得感和成就感。对于挑战者而言,逆境的恶劣环境可以磨炼意志、陶冶品格、积累战胜困难的经验、丰富人生阅历。

We must take advantage of the opportunity and be quick, brave to advance, which is the learning in favourable circumstance, and the pathway being good at seizing the opportunity to constantly enrich and improve ourselves. Although we are in the trough of life, we must study hard and work hard in the tribulation, and keep moving forward, which is the knowledge in adversity, and the pathway turning pressure into driving force.

Whether our circumstances are good or bad, the effect on life is twofold. The key is how to recognize and treat them. Only by being good at using prosperity and bravely facing up to adversity and overcoming adversity, can the life value be realized.

5.The Establishment of the Correct View on Life and Death

Life and death is a pair of basic contradiction throughout life. The course of life is an unchanging natural phenomenon and natural process from birth to death. In a sense, just because everyone has only one short life, life is precious. How to understand and treat life and death, not only directly affects one's actual life, but also reflects the level of his life realm.

College students should firmly establish the awareness of precious life, treat life well and cherish it, rationally face up to the natural laws of birth, aging, illness and death, and try their best to make their life blossom out of the brilliance of life should be.

顺势而快上，乘风而勇进，这是身处顺境的学问，是善于抓住机遇不断丰富与完善自己的途径；处低谷而力争，受磨难而奋进，这是身处逆境的学问，是将压力变成动力之所为。

无论是顺境还是逆境，对人生的作用都是双重的，关键是怎样去认识和对待它们。只有善于利用顺境，勇于正视逆境和战胜逆境，人生价值才能得以实现。

5. 树立正确的生死观

生与死是贯穿人生始终的一对基本矛盾。生命的历程是一个从生到死的过程，有生必有死，这是恒常不变的自然现象。从一定意义上说，正是因为生命短暂，每个人只有一次生命，才更显示了人生的弥足珍贵。如何认识、对待生与死，不仅直接影响一个人的实际生活，更体现了其人生境界的高低。

大学生要牢固树立生命可贵的意识，善待生命，珍惜生命，理性面对生老病死的自然规律，努力使自己的生命绽放应有的光彩。

Although human life is limited, the life value is unlimited. It is the correct view on life and death for college students to create infinite life value in their limited life, devote their limited life to serve the people and the great cause of national rejuvenation.

6. The Establishment of the Correct View on Honor and Disgrace

Honor and disgrace is a pair of basic moral category. "Rong" is honor, which refers to the praise and approval given by the society for the fulfillment of social obligations, and the positive psychological experience of individuals. "Ru" means disgrace, which refers to the condemnation given by the society for the failure of fulfilling social obligations, and the negative psychological experience of individuals. The view on honor and disgrace is the fundamental view and attitude of people towards the issue of honor and disgrace, and it is the embodiment and expression of certain social ideological and moral principles and norms. The yearning for and pursuit of honor is the embodiment of people's realization of higher life value. On the contrary, disgrace is regarded as a blot on the way of life, which directly affects the positive evaluation of their own life.

In the socialist society, college students should establish the view concept on honor and disgrace of "eight honors and eight disgraces". Its specific content includes : take ardently loving the motherland to be an honor and jeopardizing the motherland to be a disgrace, take serving the people to be an honor and deviating from the people to

人的生命是有限的，而生命的价值却是无限的。在有限的生命中创造出无限的人生价值，将有限的生命投入无限的为人民服务和民族复兴的伟大事业中，是大学生应有的正确的生死观。

6. 树立正确的荣辱观

荣辱是一对基本道德范畴。"荣"即荣誉，是指社会对个人履行社会义务所给予的褒扬与赞许，以及个人所产生的自我肯定性心理体验；"辱"即耻辱，是指社会对个人不履行社会义务所给予的贬斥与谴责，以及个人所产生的自我否定性心理体验。荣辱观是人们对荣辱问题的根本看法和态度，是一定社会思想道德原则和规范的体现和表达。对荣誉的向往和追求是人们实现较高的人生价值的体现；反之，耻辱被视为人生道路上的污点，直接影响对自己人生的肯定性评价。

在社会主义社会，大学生应树立的正确的荣辱观是社会主义荣辱观。其具体内容包括：以热爱祖国为荣、以危害祖国为耻，以服务人民为荣、以背离人民为耻，以崇尚科学为荣、以愚昧无知为耻，以辛勤劳动为荣、以好

be a disgrace, take the pursuit of science to be an honor and the unwisdom and ignorance to be disgrace, take the industrious labor to be an honor and the indolence to be a disgrace, take the unification and mutual aid to be an honor and the self-seeking at the expense of others to be a disgrace, take the honesty and trustworthiness to be an honor and forgetting morality and justice at the sight of benefit to be a disgrace, take observing discipline and obeying law to be an honor and violating laws and disciplines to be a disgrace, and take the hard struggle to be an honor and the extravagance and dissipation to be a disgrace.

逸恶劳为耻，以团结互助为荣、以损人利己为耻，以诚实守信为荣、以见利忘义为耻，以遵纪守法为荣、以违法乱纪为耻，以艰苦奋斗为荣、以骄奢淫逸为耻。

V. The Opposition of Wrong Outlook on Life

五、反对错误的人生观

1. The Manifestation of Wrong Outlook on Life

1. 错误人生观的体现形式

To establish the life pursuit of serving the people and contributing to the society and realize the greatest life value, we must resolutely resist all kinds of wrong outlook on life.

要确立服务人民、奉献社会的人生追求，实现最大的人生价值，就要坚决抵制各种错误的人生观。

First, the money-oriented outlook on life should be opposed.

第一，反对拜金主义人生观。

The money worship outlook on life is the outlook on life that believes money can dominate everything and regards pursuing money as the ultimate goal in life. Money worship, as a social trend of thought, is formed along with the development of capitalism. The money-oriented outlook on life mystifies and sanctifies money, regards money as a halidom, takes pursuing and acquiring money as the purpose of life and the whole meaning of life, and takes money as the sole standard to measure the value of life. The harm of using money wor-

拜金主义人生观是一种认为金钱可以主宰一切，把追求金钱作为人生至高目的的人生观。拜金主义作为一种社会思潮是伴随着资本主义的发展而形成的。拜金主义人生观将金钱神秘化、神圣化，视金钱为圣物，以追逐和获取金钱作为人生的目的和生活的全部意义，把金钱作为衡量人生价值的唯一标准。用拜金主义指导生活实践，并由此确立人生

ship to guide life practice and establish the purpose of life is obvious: if money becomes the purpose of human existence and all practical activities, life will be meaningless; there is no relationship between people except the naked interest and the ruthless exchange of money, and human dignity and emotion will be drowned. The money worship is an important ideological source that causes such ugly phenomena as the power-for-money trade, bribery, and venality.

Second, the hedonistic outlook on life should be opposed.

The hedonistic outlook on life is a kind of outlook on life that regards pleasure as the purpose of life, and advocates that the sole purpose and whole content of life lies in satisfying the needs and pleasures of the senses. It is a legitimate need for people to enjoy life after hard work, which is also beneficial to economic and social development. However, if pleasure, especially the pleasure of the senses, is treated as the sole purpose, and as an "ism" to interpret the whole meaning of life, it is an narrow-minded understanding of people's needs, and the purpose of life thus established is not correct. For example, some college students use their hard-earned money earned by their parents to keep up with the rich and ostentatious, spend more than they can afford, chase after famous brands and luxuries, and some even go deep into debt. These wrong ideas and behaviors harm not only the healthy growth of college students, but also the social atmosphere. Therefore, college students must have a deep understanding of China's national conditions and correctly understand

目的，其危害显而易见：如果金钱成为人的存在和全部实践活动的目的，生命就会失去意义；人与人之间除了赤裸裸的利害关系、冷酷无情的金钱交易关系，再没有其他的关系，人的尊严和情感将被淹没。拜金主义是引发权钱交易、行贿受贿、贪赃枉法等丑恶现象的重要思想根源。

第二，反对享乐主义人生观。

享乐主义人生观是一种把享乐作为人生目的的人生观，主张人生的唯一目的和全部内容在于满足感官的需求与快乐。人们在辛勤劳作之后享受生活是正当的需要，是有利于经济社会发展的。然而，如果把享乐尤其是感官的享乐变成唯一目的，作为一种"主义"去诠释人生的全部意义，则是对人的需要的一种褊狭理解，由此确立的人生目的是不正确的。比如，一些大学生用父母辛苦劳作挣来的血汗钱比阔气、摆排场，在消费上超出自己的承受能力，追逐名牌和奢侈品，有的甚至负债累累。这些错误的观念和行为，不仅危害大学生的健康成长，而且危害社会风气。因此，大学生一定要摆脱享乐主义的陷阱，正确理解消费与节约的关系，树立健康文明的消费观念。

the relationship between consumption and saving, get rid of the hedonism trap, establish a healthy and civilized consumption concept.

Third, the extremely individualistic outlook on life should be opposed.

Individualism is an ideological system and moral principle with personal interests as the starting point and destination. It advocates that the individual is the end with the highest value, and society and others are only the means to achieve the end of the individual. Individualism is the product of private ownership of the means of production and the core of the bourgeois outlook on life. In the early stage of the bourgeois revolution, individualism was of positive significance in fighting for individual rights and freedoms and opposing feudal autocracy. However, since the 19th century, some acute bourgeois thinkers have realized that it also has a destructive side to society. Since the 20th century, western thinkers have criticized individualism more frequently. As a bourgeois outlook on life, individualism and the socialist outlook on life of serving the people are fundamentally opposite. Extreme individualism is a form of individualism, which emphasizes the focus on the individual, denies the value of the society and others, and even pursues its own life goals at the expense of others. Extreme individualism manifests itself in the relationship between individuals and others and society as extreme egoism and narrow utilitarianism. We should take a clear stand against the individualistic outlook on life, especially the extreme one.

第三，反对极端个人主义人生观。

个人主义是以个人利益为出发点和归宿的一种思想体系和道德原则，主张个人本身就是目的，具有最高价值，社会和他人只是达到个人目的的手段。个人主义是生产资料私有制的产物，是资产阶级人生观的核心。在资产阶级革命的早期，在争取个人权利和自由、反封建专制方面，个人主义具有积极意义，但是从19世纪开始，一些敏锐的资产阶级思想家就已经意识到它还具有销蚀社会的一面。20世纪以来，西方思想家对个人主义的批判更是不绝于耳。个人主义作为资产阶级的人生观，与社会主义为人民服务的人生观是根本对立的。极端个人主义是个人主义的一种表现形式，它突出强调以个人为中心，否认社会和他人的价值，甚至不惜采用损人利己的方式来追求自己的人生目标。极端个人主义在个人与他人、与社会的关系上表现为极端利己主义和狭隘功利主义。我们应旗帜鲜明地反对个人主义人生观，特别是极端个人主义人生观。

2.The Common Features of the Wrong Outlooks on Life

Although all of the above-mentioned erroneous outlooks on life are different in form and content, they share common characteristics.

First, they are the outlooks on life of the exploiting classes and reflect narrow class interests. They cannot have the broad mind and lofty aspirations of the proletariat, still less can they represent the interests of the masses.

Second, they fail to grasp the correct relationship between individuals and society, ignore or deny that sociality is the essential attribute of human existence and activities, and their starting point and foothold of discussing life issues are their own selfish interests.

Third, their understanding of human needs is one-sided, exaggerating the needs of some aspects of life, while ignoring the comprehensiveness of human and the comprehensive needs of life.

VI.The Achievement of the Life Value Goal

The realization of the value of life is not something that comes from thinking, but from struggling. A good goal of life value can be turned into reality by social practice. The realization of the goal of life value is a process of practice. Although a person has set the right value goal, if he just blindly self-appreciate, self-praise, he will be difficult to achieve his life value goal. Without the practice of creating life value, no value goal can be realized.

2. 错误人生观的共同特征

上述种种错误的人生观尽管在形式上五花八门、在内容上不尽一致，但它们却有着共同的特征。

第一，它们都是剥削阶级的人生观，反映的都是狭隘的阶级利益，不可能具有无产阶级的宽广胸怀和远大志向，更不能代表人民群众的利益。

第二，它们都没有把握个人与社会的正确关系，忽视或否认社会性是人的存在和活动的本质属性，讨论人生问题的出发点和落脚点都是一己私利。

第三，它们对人的需要的理解是片面的，夸大了人生的某方面需要，而无视人的全面性和人生的全面需要。

六、实现人生价值目标

人生价值的实现不是想出来的，而是奋斗出来的。美好的人生价值目标要靠社会实践才能转化为现实。人生价值目标的实现是一个实践的过程。虽然一个人确立了正确的价值目标，但是如果他只是一味地自我欣赏、自我赞叹，他也难以实现他的人生价值目标。离开了创造人生价值的实践活动，任何价值目标都不可能实现。

Contemporary college students should consciously put their own life value goals in line with the historical direction, let it walk with the motherland, and be with the people, and create meaningful life in the practice of serving the people and contributing to society.

1.The Life Value Goal in Line with the Historical Direction

History is moving forward and society is constantly improving, we can't just be onlookers, but be active participants. It is the basic requirement for us to realize the value of life in practice and complete the gorgeous turn of life to follow the trend of social development, conform to the law of social development, and advance social development and progress.

Contemporary college students must correctly understand the world and China's development trend, respect and comply with the choices of the history and the people, accurately grasp the important strategic opportunities for China's development, promote the national self-confidence, enhance the sense of responsibility of the times, keep pace with the history direction, and share the destiny with the times.

2.The Life Value Goal Combining with the Motherland Development

Contemporary college students must develop with the motherland, make their due contributions to the prosperity of our country and the rejuvenation of our nation so as to realize their own life value.

Only by consciously linking the goals of life

当代大学生应自觉地将自己的人生价值目标与历史同向、与祖国同行、与人民同在，在服务人民、奉献社会的实践中创造有意义的人生。

1. 与历史同向的人生价值目标

历史在不断向前，社会在不断进步，我们不能只做旁观者，而要做积极的参与者。顺应历史潮流，顺应社会发展趋势，符合社会发展规律，推动社会发展进步，是我们在实践中实现人生价值，完成人生华丽转身的基本要求。

当代大学生要正确认识世界和中国发展大势，尊重、顺应历史的选择和人民的选择，准确把握中国发展的重要战略机遇期，提升民族自信心，增强时代责任感，与历史同步伐，与时代共命运。

2. 与祖国同行的人生价值目标

当代大学生要与祖国同发展，为实现国家富强、民族振兴做出自己应有的贡献，实现自己的人生价值。

青年人只有自觉将人生目标

with the future and destiny of the country and the nation, can the greatest realization of the life value be achieved. Contemporary China is in the critical period of the great rejuvenation of the Chinese nation, and there is still a long way to go for it to build a strong socialist modernized country. Contemporary college students must correctly understand the historical responsibilities and missions endowed by the state and the nation, and consciously strive and develop together with the state and the nation.

3.The Life Value Goal Combining with the Masses

It is a rich and meaningful life to live with the people, to share the destiny with them, to always think about the people, and to consciously devote oneself to the cause of serving the people.

The masses are the creators of history and the masters of the country. College students must realize the value of life in the process of serving the people and realizing the interests of the people. Only by taking the road of combining with the people, learning from the people, absorbing the nutrition from the people, and resolutely safeguarding the fundamental interests of the overwhelming majority of the people, can they accomplish much in the course of their lives. A person can only enjoy youth for one time in his life. When a person connects his life with the cause of the people when he is young, his youth will be colorful.

同国家和民族的前途命运紧紧联系在一起，才能最大限度地实现人生价值。当代中国正处于实现中华民族伟大复兴的关键时期，建设社会主义现代化强国任重道远。当代大学生要正确认识国家和民族赋予的历史责任和使命，自觉与国家和民族共奋进、同发展。

3. 与人民同在的人生价值目标

与人民同呼吸、共命运，时刻想着人民，处处为了人民，自觉投身于为人民服务的事业中，这样的人生才是丰富的、有意义的。

人民群众是历史的创造者，是国家的主人。大学生要在为人民群众服务、实现人民群众利益的过程中实现人生价值。只有走与人民群众相结合的道路，向人民群众学习，从人民群众中汲取营养，做中国最广大人民根本利益的维护者，才能使自己的人生大有作为。人的青春只有一次。如果一个人在青年时期就把自己的人生与人民的事业紧密相连，那么他的青春就是多彩的。

Lecture Three
The Firm Adherence to the Ideal and Faith

I. The Connotation and Features of Ideal

1. The Connotation of Ideal

The word "ideal" is originated from the Greek word "ideal", which means the goal of life. In ancient China, the ideal was called "Zhi", i.e. ambition. Confucius said that "the most important commander in the army may be changed, but the ambition of an ordinary man cannot be changed".

Ideal, which is formed in practice, and which has the possibility of realization, is people's yearning and pursuit for the future society and goals of self-development, and it is the concentrated embodiment of people's world view, outlook on life and values in the goal of struggle.

2. The Types of Ideal

Ideal can be classified into different types according to different criteria. From the perspective of subject, ideal can be divided into individual ideal and social ideal. From the perspective of periodicity, ideal can be divided into short-term ideal and long-term ideal. From the perspective of content, ideal can be divided into life ideal, professional ideal, moral ideal and so on.

3. The Features of Ideal

First, ideal has the nature of transcendence.

专题三
坚定理想信念

一、理想的内涵与特征

1. 理想的内涵

"理想"一词最初来源于希腊语"ideal",意思是人生的奋斗目标。在中国古代,理想叫作"志",即志向。孔子讲"三军可夺帅也,匹夫不可夺志也"。

理想是人们在实践中形成的、有实现可能性的、对未来社会和自身发展目标的向往与追求,是人们的世界观、人生观和价值观在奋斗目标上的集中体现。

2. 理想的类型

根据不同的标准,可以将理想划分为不同的类型。从主体来看,理想可以分为个人理想和社会理想;从周期来看,理想可以分为近期理想和远期理想;从内容来看,理想可以分为生活理想、职业理想、道德理想等。

3. 理想的特征

第一,理想具有超越性。

The reason why ideal can become a great force to promote people to create a better life is that it not only originates from reality, but also transcends reality. The ideal is produced in reality, but it is not a simple depiction of the status quo, but a future reality connected with the goal of struggle, and it is the vision and expectation of people for a better life in the future. Ideal is beyond reality and higher than reality. The ideal is about the vision of "how should the future be", and is the value goal that points to the future, but the reality is "how the actuality is now". There is always a certain gap between ideal and reality. People not only live at present, but also in the pursuit of the future, and continue to transform the reality according to their own blueprint for the future. For example, more than 2,000 years ago, mankind had the assumption of "clairvoyance" and "clairaudience". Many people were tireless for this. However, the social productivity and scientific technology at that time were backward, and human beings could not realize these dreams. Today, the uses of mobile phones, radar and information technology have made these ideals become reality. There will be more new technologies and new inventions emerge in the future, this is how human society develops.

Second, ideal has the nature of practicality.

As a product of certain social practice, ideal is the crystallization of people's rational understanding of social practical activities under certain historical conditions. Without practice, the creation of any ideal is impossible. The realization of the

理想之所以能够成为一种推动人们创造美好生活的巨大力量，就在于它不仅源于现实，而且超越现实。理想在现实中产生，但它不是对现状的简单描绘，而是与奋斗目标相联系的未来的现实，是人们对未来美好生活的憧憬和期待。理想是对现实的超越，它高于现实。理想是关于未来"应怎样"的设想，是指向未来的价值目标，而现实是现在实际"是怎样"，它们之间总是有一定的差距。人不仅生活在现在，而且生活在对未来的追求之中，并根据自己对未来的设计蓝图不断地改造着现实。比如，两千多年前，人类就有了"顺风耳""千里眼"的设想，许多人为此孜孜不倦，但当时的社会生产力和科学技术落后，人类无法实现这些设想，而今天手机、雷达和信息技术的使用使其成为现实。以后还会有更多新技术新发明出现，人类社会就是这样发展的。

第二，理想具有实践性。

作为一定社会实践的产物，理想是处在特定历史条件下的人们对社会实践活动理性认识的结晶。离开了实践，任何理想都不可能产生。理想的实现，同样离

ideals is also inseparable from practice. Only in the process of transforming the objective and subjective world can people take practice as a bridge and turn ideal into reality. Ideal comes into being in practice, develops in practice, and can only be realized in practice. Mr. Lu Xun once said that people can't be separated from society, just as a man cannot be away from the earth by pulling his hair. Without reality, people's ideal will become daydream and fantasy. In the pursuit of our ideals, we must have a clear sense of reality.

Third, ideal has the nature of epoch.

Ideal is the product of a certain age, so it bears the brand of a certain historical age. Due to the differences in the development level of productive forces, the social and historical conditions and the political and economic relations, people have different breadth and depth of the understanding of social reality, social practical activities and their development law, so the ideal will be different. The epochal character of ideal is reflected not only in its constraints on the conditions of the times, but also in its development with the development of the times. With social development and progress and the gradual deepening of the understanding of the law of social development and the law of human development, people will constantly adjust, enrich and develop their own ideals.

At different stages of life, a person will have different ideals. For example, one's personal ideal in childhood may be to be a singer, in youth to be a writer, and in adulthood to be a successful busi-

不开实践。人们只有在改造客观世界和主观世界的过程中才能以实践为桥梁，化理想为现实。理想在实践中产生，在实践中发展，而且只有在实践中才能实现。鲁迅先生曾说过，一个人想要离开社会而生存，那正像人拔着自己的头发想离开地球一样的不可能。脱离了现实，人的理想就变成了空想和幻想。我们在追求理想的过程中，必须有清醒的现实意识。

第三，理想具有时代性。

理想是一定时代的产物，带着特定历史时代的烙印。由于生产力发展水平、社会历史条件和政治经济关系的不同，人们对社会现实状况、社会实践活动及其发展规律认识的广度和深度也不同，因而理想会有所不同。理想的时代性不仅体现为它受时代条件的制约，而且体现为它随着时代的发展而发展。随着社会的发展进步，随着对社会发展规律和人的发展规律的认识逐步深化，人们也会不断地调整、丰富和发展自己的理想。

在人生的不同阶段，一个人会产生不同的理想。比如，一个人在童年、青年、成年时期的理想可能分别是歌唱家、文学家、

nessman.

II. The Connotation and Features of Faith

1. The Connotation of Faith

Like ideal, faith is also a spiritual phenom—enon peculiar to human beings. Established on the basis of certain cognition, faith is the spiritual state of people's firm belief in and practice of certain thoughts or things. Faith is an organic unity of cognition, emotion and will, which provides a powerful spiritual drive for people to pursue their ideal goals indefatigably.

2. The Features of Faith

First, faith has the nature of persistence.

Once faith is formed, it will not be easily changed. When a person has a firm faith, he will devote himself to the cause of the achievement of his goal, his mind is highly concentrated, his attitude is full of enthusiasm, and his behavior is firm. The firm faith makes people have a strong mental willpower, not be moved by interests, not be disturbed by temptation, not be afraid of difficulties.

Xia Minghan, a revolutionary martyr, wrote the following poem: "as long as a person firmly believes in the truth of Communism, it doesn't matter if his head is cut off. Even if Xia Minghan was killed by the enemy, there were still successors fighting for the truth of Communism." This poem is exactly a reflection of a generation of revolutionaries' unwavering faith in communism.

Edison, a great modern inventor, was a man with firm faith. In the course of inventing the

成功商人。

二、信念的内涵与特征

1. 信念的内涵

同理想一样，信念也是人类特有的精神现象。信念是人们在一定的认识基础上确立的对某种思想或事物坚信不疑并身体力行的精神状态。信念是认知、情感和意志的有机统一体，为人们矢志不渝、百折不挠地追求理想目标提供了强大的精神动力。

2. 信念的特征

第一，信念具有执着性。

信念一旦形成，就不会轻易改变。当一个人抱有坚定信念时，他就会全身心投入为实现目标而努力奋斗的事业中去，精神上高度集中，态度上充满热情，行为上坚定不移。坚定的信念使得人们具有强大的精神定力，不为利益所动，不为诱惑所扰，不为困难所惧。

革命烈士夏明翰的就义诗"砍头不要紧，只要主义真。杀了夏明翰，还有后来人"，就反映了一代革命者对共产主义信仰的坚贞不移。

现代大发明家爱迪生就是一个有着坚定信念的人。在发明电

electric light, he tested 9,000 substances without success. Some people concluded that he would not succeed. "I just found 9,000 species of substances that can't be used as filament," he said with a smile. He finally succeeded after more than 10,000 experiments. What's the force that supports him to experiment so doggedly? It is his firm faith that he must be able to find a material that can be used as filament. If, like others, he had suspected that the substance was impossible to exist, he would have given it up.

Second, faith has the nature of diversity.

On the one hand, different people will form different faiths due to their differences in social environment, ideology, interests, life experience and personality characteristics. On the other hand, the same person may also form different types and levels of faiths and thus form their faith systems.

In the faith system, high-level faiths determine low-level faiths, and low-level faiths obey high-level faiths. Belief is the highest level of belief, with the greatest force of unity. Belief can be divided into blind faith and scientific belief. Blind faith is the superstition and fanatical worship of the illusory world, unrealistic ideas, absurd theories, etc, and scientific faith comes from people's correct cognition of the development law of nature and human society.

The ancients said: "If a man has enough ambition, no matter how far he wants to reach, he can eventually reach. There is no limit between the

灯的过程中，他试验了9000种物质也没成功，有人断定他不会成功，他却笑着说："我只是发现了9000种物质不能做灯丝。"在试验了10，000余次之后他终于获得了成功。支持他如此顽强地试验下去的力量是什么？就是他认为自己必能找到一种物质可做灯丝的坚定信念。如果他也像其他人一样怀疑这种物质根本就不可能存在的话，那么他还会恐怕早就放弃了。

第二，信念具有多样性。

一方面，不同的人由于社会环境、思想观念、利益需要、人生经历和性格特征等方面的差异，会形成不同的信念；另一方面，同一个人也会形成不同类型和层次的信念，并由此构成其信念体系。

在信念体系中，高层次的信念决定低层次的信念，低层次的信念服从高层次的信念。信仰是最高层次的信念，具有最大的统摄力。信仰有盲目和科学之分。盲目的信仰就是对虚幻的世界、不切实际的观念、荒谬的理论等的迷信和狂热崇拜，而科学的信仰则来自人们对自然界和人类社会发展规律的正确认识。

古人云："志之所趋，无远勿届，穷山距海，不能限也。志之所向，无坚不入，锐兵精甲，不

mountains and the sea. If a man has enough ambition, no matter how strong the defense of the place he wants to reach is it can not stop him." People with high aspirations can reach any distant place and break through any solid thing.

III. The Inner Relationship between Ideal and Faith

Ideal and faith are always interdependent. Ideal is the object of faith, and faith is the guarantee of the realization of ideal. Without ideal, which people believe and pursue, faith cannot be produced; without faith, which is the kind of persistent yearning for and pursuit of the goal, ideal is difficult to realize. In this sense, ideal and faith are inextricably linked. Because of this, people often combine ideal and faith as "the ideal and faith".

Ideal and faith are the core of the human spiritual world and the "calcium" of the human spirit. No ideal belief, or no firm ideal belief, will cause the spirit "lack of calcium", and thus will get "chondropathy". Without spiritual "calcium", a person will be prone to spiritual emptiness or even fall into a spiritual desert. It is impossible to feel the fullness of spiritual life, let alone undertake the historical responsibilities entrusted by the times.

1. Ideal Guides the Direction and Faith Determines Success or Failure

If society is the sea and life is a small boat, then the ideal and faith is the lighthouse for piloting and the sail for voyage. Life without ideal and faith is like a boat without direction and pow-

能御也。"志存高远的人，再遥远的地方也能达到，再坚固的东西也能突破。

三、理想和信念的内在关系

理想和信念总是相互依存。理想是信念所指的对象，信念则是理想实现的保障。离开理想这个人们确信和追求的目标，信念就无从产生；离开信念这种对奋斗目标的执着向往和追求，理想就无法实现。从这个意义上说，理想和信念是紧密联系在一起的。也正因如此，人们常将理想与信念合称为"理想信念"。

理想信念是人的精神世界的核心，是人精神上的"钙"。没有理想信念或理想信念不坚定，精神上就会"缺钙"，就会得"软骨病"。一个人精神上"缺钙"，就容易精神空虚甚至陷入精神荒漠，既不可能感受精神生活的丰满充实，更不可能承担时代所赋予的历史重任。

1. 理想指引方向，信念决定成败

如果说社会是大海，人生是小船，那么理想信念就是引航的灯塔和远航的风帆。没有理想信念的人生，就像失去了方向和

er, drifting everywhere in the waves of life, even sinking in the rapids. Ideal and faith is the intrinsic driving force of life development. Therefore in college, college students should not only improve their knowledge level, enhance their practical ability, but also firm up their lofty ideals and faiths.

2. Ideal and Faith Shows the Goal of Struggle

Life is a process of struggle in practice. To make life meaningful, we must follow the right path of life under the guidance of scientific ideals and faiths. Ideals and faiths are the orientators of human thoughts and behaviors. Once established, ideals and faiths can make people clear direction and inspire spirits. Even if the road ahead is tortuous and the life situation is complex, people can see the hope and dawn of the future, and never lose the direction of progress. Only those who have firm ideals and faiths can be unswerving and indomitable. They will steadfastly strive to achieve their stated goals regardless of difficulties and dangers. People's ideals and faith reflect the expectations of society and people's own development. Therefore, what kind of ideals and faith means what kind of expectations and ways to transform nature and society, shape and achieve people themselves. Only by setting up lofty ideals and faith can we solve the important life problems such as the meaning of life, the value of struggle and what kind of person we should be.

Through the ages, all people who have made achievements pay attention to the establishment of life ideal, i.e. life goal and ambition. once es-

动力的小船，在生活的波浪中随处漂泊，甚至会沉没于急流之中。理想信念是人生发展的内在动力。因此，在大学期间，大学生不仅要提高知识水平，增强实践才干，更要坚定崇高的理想信念。

2. 理想信念昭示奋斗目标

人生是一个在实践中奋斗的过程。要使生命富有意义，就必须在科学的理想信念的指引下，沿着正确的人生道路前进。理想信念是人的思想和行为的定向器，一旦确立就可以使人方向明确、精神振奋，即使前进的道路曲折、人生的境遇复杂，也能使人看到未来的希望和曙光，永不迷失前进的方向。只有理想信念坚定的人，才能始终不渝、百折不挠，不论风吹雨打，不怕千难万险，坚定不移地为实现既定目标而奋斗。人的理想信念反映的是对社会和人自身发展的期望。因此，有什么样的理想信念，就意味着以什么样的期望和方式去改造自然和社会，塑造和成就自身。只有树立崇高的理想信念，才能够解答好人生的意义、奋斗的价值以及做什么样的人等重要的人生课题。

古往今来，凡是有作为的人无不注重人生理想即人生目标和志向的确立。理想一经确立，就

tablished, ideal can make people have a clear direction, as far as possible to avoid detours, so as to avoid blindness, confusion and emptiness.

3.Ideal and Faith Provides the Motive Force for Progress

The higher the ambition, the greater the driving force. A person with lofty and firm ideals and faiths, will have amazing perseverance and unremitting efforts to achieve career. On the contrary, if a person does not have lofty and firm ideals and faiths, he may idle away his life, and even become corrupt and degenerate and go astray. One of the important reasons why numerous outstanding figures can make extraordinary achievements in ordinary posts and create miracles under extremely difficult conditions is that they have lofty and firm ideals and faiths, and the driving force of perseverance generated by them. A person's ideals and faiths established in college will have a great impact on his future life.

A great life comes from great goals, great goals will produce great driving force. A psychologist once put forward a famous formula, namely, driving force = target value × expectation probability, which vividly reveals the directly proportional relationship between the driving force of personal struggle and the ideal. When one strives for an ideal with great target value, there will be a strong internal driving force. On the contrary, if the target value is small or the expectation probability is low, there will be a lack of driving force due to the loss of confidence. In history, those who have made contributions to the cause of human progress are all those who have lofty ideals and be inspired and stimulated by lofty ideals.

可以使人方向明确，少走弯路，不致盲目、迷惘和空虚。

3. 理想信念提供前进动力

志向高远，便力量无穷。一个人有了崇高坚定的理想信念，才会以惊人的毅力和不懈的努力成就事业。与此相反，一个人如果没有崇高坚定的理想信念，就有可能浑浑噩噩、庸庸碌碌、虚度一生，甚至腐化堕落、走上邪路。无数杰出人物之所以能在平凡的岗位上做出不平凡的业绩，在极其困难的条件下创造奇迹，一个重要的原因就在于他们具有崇高坚定的理想信念，从而具有披荆斩棘、锲而不舍的动力。一个人大学时期确立的理想信念，对其今后的人生之路将产生重大影响。

伟大的人生源于伟大的目标，伟大的目标产生伟大的动力。有位心理学家曾提出过一个著名的公式，即动力＝目标价值×期望概率，形象地揭示了个人拼搏的动力与理想之间的正比例关系。当一个人为了具有巨大目标价值的理想而奋斗时，就会产生强大的内在动力。反之，如果目标价值不大或期望概率较低，就会因丧失信心而缺乏动力。历史上，凡是为人类进步事业做出贡献的人，无一不具有崇高的理想，并受崇高理想所鼓舞、所激励。

4. Ideal and Faith Improves the Spiritual Realm

Ideal and faith is an important measure of a person's spiritual realm. As the core of people's spiritual world, on the one hand, ideal and faith can unify all aspects of people's spiritual life and make the spiritual world become a healthy and orderly system to avoid spiritual emptiness and confusion. On the other hand, it can guide people to continuously pursue higher life goals, and during the process of the pursuit and realization of ideal goals,improve the spiritual realm and shape noble personality. During the process of the pursuit of the ideal and the realization of the ideal,people should constantly face various challenges, resist various temptations, break through various limitations and overcome various difficulties. This process is not only the process of people's spiritual world from narrow to lofty, from empty to full, from hesitation to persistence, but also the process of a person climbing along the ladder of self-growth and perfection and gradually improving the spiritual realm.

5. Ideal and Faith is the Key Element for College Students to Grow into Talents

Contemporary college students shoulder the hope of the motherland and the nation, bearing the entrustments of their families and relatives and being full of the yearning for a better life in the future. Therefore, College students should not only improve their knowledge level, enhance their practical ability, but also strengthen their scientific and lofty ideals and faiths, and understand the fundamental of life, which is of great significance

4. 理想信念提高精神境界

理想信念是衡量一个人精神境界高低的重要标尺。理想信念作为人的精神世界的核心，一方面能使人的精神生活的各个方面统一起来，使人的精神世界成为一个健康有序的系统，避免精神空虚和迷茫；另一方面能引导人们不断地追求更高的人生目标，并在追求和实现理想目标的过程中提升精神境界、塑造高尚人格。在追求理想和实现理想的过程中，人们要不断面对各种挑战、抵御各种诱惑、突破各种局限、克服各种困难。这个过程既是人的精神世界从狭隘走向高远、从空虚走向充实、从犹疑走向执着的过程，也是一个人沿着自我成长和完善的阶梯不断攀登、逐步提升精神境界的过程。

5. 理想信念是大学生成才的关键要素

当代大学生肩负着祖国和民族的希望，承载着家庭和亲人的嘱托，满怀着对未来美好生活的向往。因此，大学生不仅要提高知识水平，增强实践才干，更要坚定科学、崇高的理想信念，明确做人的根本，这对于其成长成才具有重要意义。

to their growth.

First, ideal and faith guides college students to be what kind of people.

"Having ideal" has a more prominent position among the goals of new person of "four haves" of having ideal, having morality, having culture and having discipline, which indicates that ideal and faith has a great relationship with "becoming what kind of people". "Becoming what kind of people" is a life lesson that college students face all the time. Only by setting up noble ideals and faiths can college students solve this important life lesson.

Second, ideal and faith guides college students to take what kind of path.

College students are faced with a series of life issues, such as the establishment of life goals, the formation of life attitude, the enrichment of knowledge and talent, the setting of development direction, the choice of job, and how to choose friends, how to fall in love, how to face setbacks, how to overcome difficulties and so on. The solution of these issues requires a general principle and goal, which needs college students to establish scientific and lofty ideal and faith, so that they can make their future life path more and more broad, and make their precious life full of value, achievements and pride.

Third, ideal and faith inspires college students to study for what.

For contemporary college students, the question of "why to learn" is closely linked to the question of "what path to take" and "what kind of person to be". The arduous task of building a moderately prosperous society in all respects and a

第一，理想信念引导大学生做什么人。

在有理想、有道德、有文化、有纪律的"四有"新人的目标中，"有理想"占据更加突出的位置，这表明理想信念与"做什么人"关系重大。"做什么人"是大学生在学习生活中时时面对的人生课题。大学生只有树立高尚的理想信念，才能够很好地解答这一重要的人生课题。

第二，理想信念指引大学生走什么路。

大学生普遍面临着一系列人生课题，如人生目标的确立、生活态度的形成、知识才能的丰富、发展方向的设定、工作岗位的选择以及如何择友、如何恋爱、如何面对挫折、如何克服困难等。这些问题的解决需要有一个总的原则和目标，这就需要大学生确立科学、崇高的理想信念，使将来的人生道路越走越宽广，使宝贵的一生富有价值，卓有成就，充满自豪。

第三，理想信念激励大学生为什么学。

对当代大学生而言，"为什么学"的问题，是与"走什么路""做什么人"的问题紧密联系在一起的。全面建成小康社会和建设社会主义现代化强国的艰

strong modernized socialist country, the historical mission of the great rejuvenation of the Chinese nation, and personal growth success all require college students to study hard. Only by setting up lofty ideals and faiths, can college students clarify the purpose and significance of study, stimulate a strong sense of responsibility and mission to study for the prosperity of the country, the rejuvenation of the nation and their own success, and strive to master the ability to build the motherland and serve the people. No matter what occupation college students are engaged in in the future, they should closely associate their personal ambition with the future and destiny of the country and the nation, and closely associate their personal learning prog-ress with the prosperity of the motherland in the future, so that the flowers of ideals and faiths will bear rich fruits of growth.

IV. What Kind of Ideal and Faith Should be Held Firm to

The enhancement of ideological cultivation and the improvement of spiritual realm require us to firmly grasp the core of the ideal and faith. The realization of the country's prosperity, the great rejuvenation of the nation and the people's pursuit for a better life cannot be achieved without the strong support of lofty ideals and faiths. College students in the new era should establish the scien-tific belief of Marxism, and set up the lofty ideal of Communism and the common ideal of socialism with Chinese characteristics.

1. The Establishment of Scientific Belief of Marxism

Firm ideals and faiths must be based on a

巨任务、中华民族伟大复兴的历史使命个人的成长成才都需要大学生努力学习。大学生只有树立崇高的理想信念,才能明确学习的目的和意义,激发为国家富强、民族振兴和自身成才而发愤学习的强烈责任感与使命感,努力掌握建设祖国、服务人民的本领。大学生不论今后从事什么职业,都要把个人的奋斗志向同国家和民族的前途命运紧紧联系在一起,把个人今天的学习进步同祖国明天的繁荣昌盛紧紧联系在一起,使理想信念之花结出丰硕的成长之果。

四、坚定什么样的理想信念

要加强思想修养、提高精神境界,就必须牢牢把握理想信念这个核心。实现国家的繁荣富强、民族的伟大复兴、人民的美好生活,离不开崇高理想信念的有力支撑。新时代大学生应当确立马克思主义科学信仰,树立共产主义远大理想和中国特色社会主义共同理想。

1.确立马克思主义科学信仰

坚定的理想信念必须建立在

profound understanding of Marxism and a deep grasp of the laws of history. Marxism, as the fundamental guiding ideology of our party and country, is not only an inevitable result of the development of Chinese history since modern times, but also a historical choice long explored by the Chinese people. The choice of Marxism is determined by its strict scientific system, distinct class position and great practical guiding role. Only by establishing scientific belief of marxism can college students truly establish lofty ideals and faiths, see the essence and direction clearly in the complex social phenomena, serve the people and make greater contributions to the society.

Marxism embodies the unity of scientificity and revolutionary character. Marxism profoundly reveals the universal laws of nature, human society and the development of human thinking, and points out the direction for the development and progress of human society. Marxism adheres to the position of safeguarding the interests, and takes realizing the free and comprehensive development of the people and the liberation of the whole mankind as its duty, thus reflecting the beautiful vision of mankind for the ideal society. Marxism reveals the essence, internal relations and development rules of things, and is a "great cognitive tool", as well as a powerful ideological weapon for people to observe the world and analyze problems. Times are changing and society is developing, but the basic principles of Marxicm are still scientific truth. Although great and profound changes have taken place in our era compared with that of Marx,

对马克思主义的深刻理解上，建立在对历史规律的深刻把握上。马克思主义作为我们立党立国的根本指导思想，是近代以来中国历史发展的必然结果，是中国人民长期探索的历史选择，也是由马克思主义严密的科学体系、鲜明的阶级立场和巨大的实践指导作用决定的。大学生只有确立马克思主义科学信仰，才能真正树立崇高的理想信念，在错综复杂的社会现象中看清本质、明确方向，为服务人民、奉献社会，做出更大的贡献。

马克思主义体现了科学性和革命性的统一。马克思主义深刻揭示了自然界、人类社会、人类思维发展的普遍规律，为人类社会发展进步指明了方向。马克思主义坚持维护人民利益的立场，以实现人的自由而全面的发展和全人类解放为己任，反映了人类对理想社会的美好憧憬。马克思主义揭示了事物的本质、内在联系及发展规律，是"伟大的认识工具"，是人们观察世界、分析问题的有力思想武器。时代在变化，社会在发展，但马克思主义基本原理依然是科学真理。尽管我们所处的时代同马克思所处的时代相比发生了巨大而深刻的变化，但从世界社会主义五百年的大视野来看，我们依然处在马克

from the perspective of world socialism for the five hundred years, we are still in the historical era indicated by Marxism. This is the scientific basis for the maintainence of the firm confidence in Marxism and the triumphalism in socialism.

Marxism has a distinctive practical character. It is not only committed to scientifically explaining the world, but also committed to actively transforming it. On the tombstone of Marx in the Highgate Cemetery in London, a famous quote from Marx is engraved: "philosophers have only explained the world in different ways, but the problem lies in transforming the world." This sentence clearly shows the fundamental feature that Marxism attaches great importance to practice and takes the transformation of the world as its own responsibility. It is just under the guidance of Marxism that socialism changes from utopia to science, and from scientific theory to social practice. The emergence of socialist countries and the establishment of socialist system have profoundly changed the direction of human history. Although the upheaval in Eastern Europe and the disintegration of the Soviet Union have caused serious setbacks to the world socialist movement, the general trend of historical development has not changed. The successful practice of socialism with Chinese characteristics, in particular, has irrefutably proved that Marxism is a powerful ideological weapon to understand and transform the world, and that socialism has a bright future. In the history of human thought, no other theory except Marxism has exerted such a wide and profound influence on the

思主义所指明的历史时代。这是对马克思主义保持坚定信心、对社会主义保持必胜信念的科学根据。

马克思主义具有鲜明的实践品格。它不仅致力于科学解释世界，而且致力于积极改变世界。在伦敦海格特公墓的马克思墓碑上，镌刻着马克思的一句名言："哲学家们只是用不同的方式解释世界，而问题在于改变世界。"这鲜明地表明了马克思主义重视实践、以改造世界为己任的基本特征。正是在马克思主义的指导下，社会主义由空想变成科学，由科学理论转变为社会实践。社会主义国家的出现和社会主义制度的建立深刻改变了人类历史的走向。虽然东欧剧变和苏联解体使世界社会主义运动遭受了严重挫折，但是历史发展的总趋势并没有改变。特别是中国特色社会主义的成功实践，无可辩驳地证明了马克思主义是认识世界和改造世界的强大思想武器，社会主义拥有光明的未来。在人类思想史上，还没有一种理论像马克思主义那样对人类文明进步产生如此广泛而巨大的影响。

progress of human civilization.

Marxism has the theoretical character of keeping pace with the times and the enduring vitality. Marxism was born in the mid-19th century, but did not stop in the 19th century. As an open theoretical system, Marxism does not exclude all scientific knowledge and achievements of civilization created by human beings, but absorbs and extracts them and applies them to promote the progress of social history. The entry of Marxism into China not only triggered the profound transformation of Chinese civilization, but also went through a process of gradual sinicization. In various historical periods of revolution, construction and reform, the Communist Party of China has adhered to the integration of the basic principles of Marxism with China's concrete realities, used Marxist standpoints, viewpoints and methods to study and solve various major theoretical and practical problems, continuously promoted the sinicization, modernization and popularization of Marxism, and guided the Party and people to make great achievements in the new-democratic revolution, socialist revolution, socialist construction and reform and opening up. Practice has proved that Marxism can display its strong vitality, creativity and charisma as long as it is combined with national conditions, progresses with the times, and shares the destiny with the people. Deng Xiaoping pointed out: "I firmly believe that more and more people will support Marxism in the world, because Marxism is a science.It uses historical materialism to reveal the laws of the development of human society." No matter how the times change and how

马克思主义具有与时俱进的理论品格和持久的生命力。马克思主义诞生于 19 世纪中叶，但并没有停留在 19 世纪。作为一个开放的理论体系，马克思主义不但不排斥而且吸收、提炼人类创造的一切科学知识和文明成果，并将其运用于推动社会历史的进步。马克思主义进入中国，既引发了中华文明的深刻变革，也走过了一个逐步中国化的过程。在革命、建设、改革的各个历史时期，中国共产党坚持马克思主义基本原理同中国具体实际相结合，运用马克思主义立场、观点、方法研究解决各种重大理论和实践问题，不断推进马克思主义中国化、时代化、大众化，指导党和人民取得了新民主主义革命、社会主义革命和社会主义建设、改革开放的伟大成就。实践证明，马克思主义只要与本国国情相结合、与时代发展同进步、与人民群众共命运，就能焕发出强大的生命力、创造力和感召力。邓小平指出："我坚信，世界上赞成马克思主义的人会多起来的，因为马克思主义是科学。它运用历史唯物主义揭示了人类社会发展的规律。"无论时代如何变迁、科学如何进步，马克思主义始终占据着真理和道义的制高点，具有强大持久的生命活力。

science progresses, Marxism still stands on the commanding heights of truth and morality, and has strong and enduring vitality.

Marxism is the fundamentality of the continuous development of the cause of the Party and the people, and the source of power of continuous advance of the Party and the people. "The belief in Marxism, socialism and communism is the political soul of the Communists and the spiritual pillar of the Communists to withstand any tests." If we deviate from or give up Marxism, we will lose our soul and lose our way. The most important thing for college students to hold firmly up to their Marxist beliefs is to learn and master the standpoints, viewpoints and methods of Marxism,establish correct world view and historical view, accurately grasp the development trend of the times and guide the way and direction of life with scientific ideals and faiths.

2.The Establishment of the Lofty ideal of Communism

Marxism scientifically predicts the ideal state of the future society and points out the development direction of human society. The Communist society is a society in which the material wealth is greatly enriched, the distribution is realized according to needs, the spiritual state of people is greatly improved, and everyone's free and comprehensive development is realized. Communism can be realized only on the basis of full and highly developed socialist society. Since its foundation, the Communist Party of China has established the lofty ideal of Communism, and has always united

马克思主义是党和人民事业不断发展的根本，是党和人民不断奋进的力量源泉。"对马克思主义的信仰，对社会主义和共产主义的信念，是共产党人的政治灵魂，是共产党人经受住任何考验的精神支柱。"背离或放弃马克思主义，就会失去灵魂、迷失方向。大学生坚定马克思主义信仰，最重要的是学习和掌握马克思主义的立场、观点、方法，确立正确的世界观和历史观，准确把握时代发展潮流，以科学的理想信念指引人生前进的道路和方向。

2. 胸怀共产主义远大理想

马克思主义科学预测了未来社会的理想状态，指明了人类社会的发展方向。共产主义社会是物质财富极大丰富、实现按需分配、人的精神境界极大提高、每个人自由而全面发展的社会。共产主义只有在社会主义社会充分发展和高度发达的基础上才能实现。中国共产党从成立之日起就确立了共产主义的远大理想，始终团结带领中国人民朝着这个远大理想前行。

and led the Chinese people to move forward towards this great ideal.

Communism is a process of unification of realistic movement and long-term goal. Communism is a lofty social ideal, a doctrine about proletarian liberation and a realistic movement. The great ideal of Communism is both future-oriented and realistic. It not only reflects people's yearning for the future society, but also is a historical process and realistic movement that starts from the reality to constantly meet people's realistic interest needs, promote people's all-round development, and promote social development and progress. Some people believe that the Communist ideal is too far away from the reality to be realized, which actually separates the dialectical unity relationship between the Communist ideal and the reality. As a matter of fact, the thought and practice of Communism have long existed in our real life, and the view that "Communism is a vague fantasy" and "Communism has not been tested in practice" is totally wrong.

The ultimate realization of the lofty ideal of Communism is a long and arduous historical process, which requires painstaking efforts from generation to generation. Review the historical process of the communist movement. From the publication of *The Communist Manifesto* in 1848 to the establishment of the first socialist country in 1917, from the development of many socialist countries after the Second World War to the upheaval in Eastern Europe and the disintegration of the Soviet Union. in late 1980s and early 1990s,

共产主义是现实运动和长远目标相统一的过程。共产主义是崇高的社会理想，是关于无产阶级解放的学说，也是一种现实运动。共产主义远大理想既是面向未来的，又是指向现实的，不仅反映了人们对未来社会的美好向往，更是一个从现实的人出发，不断满足人的现实利益需求、推进人的全面发展、推动社会发展进步的历史过程与现实运动。有人认为，共产主义理想离现实太遥远，是无法实现的，这实际上割裂了共产主义远大理想与现实的辩证统一关系。事实上，共产主义的思想和实践早已存在于我们的现实生活中，那种"共产主义是渺茫的幻想""共产主义没有经过实践检验"的观点是完全错误的。

共产主义远大理想的最终实现是一个漫长、艰辛的历史过程，需要一代又一代人付出艰苦的努力。回顾共产主义运动的历史进程，从1848年《共产党宣言》问世到1917年第一个社会主义国家建立，从第二次世界大战后一大批社会主义国家勃然兴起到20世纪80年代末90年代初东欧剧变、苏联解体，再到新时代中国特色社会主义焕发出前所

and then to the vigorous vitality of socialism with Chinese characteristics for a new era, the ideals and practices of socialism and Communism have neither stopped because of setbacks, nor entered the history museum as predicted by some people in the west, but showed a brighter future in the hard exploration. The road to the realization of the ideal is difficult and tortuous, the realization of the great ideal of Communism is even more in need of generation after generation of unremitting struggle and continuous efforts.

As contemporary college students, we must correctly understand the relationship between the great ideal of Communism and the common ideal of socialism with Chinese characteristics. The realization of Communism is our great ideal, and the persistence and development of socialism with Chinese characteristics is a real effort towards that ideal. As long as we are full of firm faith, we will be full of power when we practice. On "the long march way" of the new era, college students should constantly enhance their confidence in the path, theory, system and culture of socialism with Chinese characteristics, consciously become firm believers and faithful practitioners of the lofty ideal of Communism and the common ideal of socialism with Chinese characteristics, and strive for the lofty ideal and faith.

3. The Establishment of the Common Ideal of Socialism with Chinese Characteristics

Only when we share common ideals can we move forward in step. Under the leadership of the Communist Party of China, the persistence and

未有的生机和活力，社会主义和共产主义的理想与实践不仅没有戛然而止，没有像西方某些人所预言的那样进入历史博物馆，反而在长期的艰辛探索中展现出更加光明的前景。理想实现的路途是艰难曲折的，共产主义远大理想的实现更需要一代又一代人的不懈奋斗和接续努力。

作为当代大学生，我们要正确认识共产主义远大理想和中国特色社会主义共同理想之间的关系。实现共产主义是我们的远大理想，坚持和发展中国特色社会主义就是为实现远大理想所进行的实实在在的努力。要走好新时代的"长征路"，大学生就要不断增强中国特色社会主义道路自信、理论自信、制度自信、文化自信，自觉做共产主义远大理想和中国特色社会主义共同理想的坚定信仰者、忠实实践者，为崇高理想信念而矢志奋斗。

3. 树立中国特色社会主义共同理想

有共同理想，才能有共同步调。在中国共产党领导下，坚持和发展中国特色社会主义，实现

development of socialism with Chinese character-istics and the realization of the great rejuvenation of the Chinese nation require us to set up the com-mon ideal of socialism with Chinese characteris-tics. This common ideal, which has broad social consensus, convincing inevitability, universality and inclusiveness, not only closely links the inter-ests of the state and the nation with those of indi-viduals, but also organically combines the common aspirations of all social strata and groups, as well as intensively represents the interests and aspi-rations of China's workers, farmers, intellectuals and other workers, builders and patriots. College students should firmly establish the common ideal and firm belief of taking the path of socialism with Chinese characteristics and striving for the great rejuvenation of the Chinese nation under the lead-ership of the Communist Party of China.

Both history and reality tell us that only so-cialism can save China and only socialism with Chinese characteristics can develop China. Social-ism with Chinese characteristics has been not only the theme of all the Party's theories and practic-es, but also the fundamental achievement made by the Party and the people through untold hardships and at a great price. The fundamental reason for all the achievements and progress we have made since reform and opening up can be summed up as follows: we have opened up a path of socialism with Chinese characteristics, formed a theoretical system of socialism with Chinese characteristics, established a system of socialism with Chinese characteristics, and developed a socialist culture

中华民族伟大复兴，必须树立中国特色社会主义共同理想。这个共同理想 把国家、民族与个人紧紧地联系在一起，把各个阶层、各个群体的共同愿望有机结合在一起，集中代表了我国工人、农民、知识分子和其他劳动者、建设者、爱国者的利益和愿望，有着广泛的社会共识，具有令人信服的必然性、广泛性和包容性。大学生要牢固确立在中国共产党领导下走中国特色社会主义道路、为实现中华民族伟大复兴而奋斗的共同理想和坚定信念。

历史和现实都告诉我们，只有社会主义才能救中国，只有中国特色社会主义才能发展中国。中国特色社会主义是改革开放以来党的全部理论和实践的主题，是党和人民历尽千辛万苦、付出巨大代价取得的根本成就。改革开放以来我们取得一切成绩和进步的根本原因，归结起来就是：开辟了中国特色社会主义道路，形成了中国特色社会主义理论体系，确立了中国特色社会主义制度，发展了中国特色社会主义文化。中国特色社会主义道路是实现社会主义现代化、指引中

with Chinese characteristics. The road of social-ism with Chinese characteristics is the only way to realize socialist modernization and guide the Chinese people to create a better life of their own. The system of theories of socialism with Chinese characteristics is not only a correct theory that guides the Party and the people to realize the great rejuvenation of the Chinese nation along the path of socialism with Chinese characteristics, but also a scientific theory that keeps pace with the times. The system of socialism with Chinese characteris-tics, an advanced system with distinctive Chinese characteristics, obvious institutional advantages and strong self-improvement capability, provides a fundamental institutional guarantee for the de-velopment and progress of contemporary China. The culture of socialism with Chinese character-istics, which is a powerful spiritual force for the Chinese people to advance triumphantly, is rooted in the fine traditional Chinese culture nurtured by the 5,000 years civilization of the Chinese nation and the great practice of socialism with Chinese characteristics, and is forged on the basis of the revolutionary culture and advanced socialist cul-ture created by the Chinese people in revolution, construction and reform under the leadership of the Communist Party of China. Socialism with Chi-nese characteristics is both a great cause we must continue to advance and a fundamental guaran-tee for opening up our future. In the new ear, the overall task of the adherence to and development of socialism with Chinese characteristics is to re-alize socialist modernization and the great reju-

国人民创造自己美好生活的必由之路。中国特色社会主义理论体系是指导党和人民沿着中国特色社会主义道路实现中华民族伟大复兴的正确理论，是立于时代前沿、与时俱进的科学理论。中国特色社会主义制度是当代中国发展进步的根本制度保障，是具有鲜明中国特色、明显制度优势、强大自我完善能力的先进制度。中国特色社会主义文化源自中华民族 5000 多年文明历史所孕育的中华优秀传统文化，熔铸于党领导人民在革命、建设、改革中创造的革命文化和社会主义先进文化，植根于中国特色社会主义伟大实践，是中国人民胜利前行的强大精神力量。中国特色社会主义，既是我们必须不断推进的伟大事业，又是我们开辟未来的根本保证。新时代坚持和发展中国特色社会主义的总任务是实现社会主义现代化和中华民族伟大复兴，在全面建成小康社会的基础上，分两步走在本世纪中叶建成富强民主文明和谐美丽的社会主义现代化强国。

venation of the Chinese nation, and take two steps to turn China into a strong modernized socialist country that is prosperous, strong, democratic, culturally advanced, harmonious and beautiful by the middle of this century on the basis of finishing building a moderately prosperous society in all respects.

The leadership of the Communist Party of China is the most essential feature of socialism with Chinese characteristics. The communist party of China is the vanguard of the Chinese working class, the Chinese people and the Chinese nation, and the core of leadership for the cause of socialism with Chinese characteristics. Since its birth, the Communist Party of China has taken it as its original aspiration and mission to seek happiness for the Chinese people and rejuvenation for the Chinese nation, and united and led the people of all ethnic groups in unremitting efforts to overcome all kinds of difficulties and obstacles and achieve great victories in revolution, construction and reform. The great victory achieved by Chinese people under the leadership of the Communist Party of China has enabled the Chinese nation, with more than 5,000 years of civilization history, to move forward towards modernization in an all-round way, and given Chinese civilization new vigor and vitality in the process of modernization; enabled the socialist proposition with a history of more than 500 years to successfully open up a path with a high degree of feasibility in the world's most populous country; brought remarkable achievements to the People's Republic of China with a history of

中国共产党的领导是中国特色社会主义最本质的特征。中国共产党是中国工人阶级的先锋队，同时是中国人民和中华民族的先锋队，是中国特色社会主义事业的领导核心。中国共产党自诞生之日起，就把为中国人民谋幸福、为中华民族谋复兴作为自己的初心和使命，并团结带领全国各族人民不懈奋斗，战胜各种艰难险阻，不断取得革命、建设、改革的伟大胜利。中国共产党领导中国人民取得的伟大胜利使具有5000多年文明历史的中华民族全面迈向现代化，让中华文明在现代化进程中焕发出新的蓬勃生机；使具有500年历史的社会主义主张在世界上人口最多的国家成功开辟出具有高度现实性和可行性的正确道路；使具有70多年历史的新中国建设取得举世瞩目的成就，让中国这个世界上最大的发展中国家在短短30多年里摆脱贫困并跃升为世界第二大经济体，创造了人类社会发展史上惊天动地的发展奇迹。在当

70 years, lifted China, the world's largest developing country, out of poverty and into the world's second largest economy in just over 30 years, and enabled China to create an earth-shattering miracle of development in the history of human society. In today's China, only the Communist Party of China can lead the Chinese people to uphold and develop socialism with Chinese characteristics, and can lead the Chinese people to create a happy life and realize the great rejuvenation of the Chinese nation.

今中国，只有中国共产党，才能领导中国人民坚持和发展中国特色社会主义，才能担当起带领中国人民创造幸福生活、实现中华民族伟大复兴的历史使命。

Lecture Four
The Pursuit of Youth Dream Based on the Realization of Chinese Dream

Ideal and faith is not only a problem of ideology but also a problem of practice. In the pursuit of ideal, people often feel the contradiction between ideal and reality. Since college students tend to be confused by the contradiction between ideal and reality, it is necessary for them to correctly understand the relationship between them.

I. Dialectically Treating the Contradiction between Ideal and Reality

1.The Contradiction Between Ideal and Reality

In daily life, when we deal with the relationship between ideal and reality, we often only see the opposite side of the both, but cannot see the unity of the both.

From the opposite side of ideal and reality, there are often two kinds of cognitive biases: one bias is to use ideal to deny reality, and when it is found that reality does not meet ideal expectations, one may be disappointed with the reality, and even adopt a total negative attitude towards reality; another bias is to use reality to deny ideal. In the process of pursuing ideals, when encounter difficulties, one will produce fearful feelings, feeling that the ideal is out of reach, losing the confidence

专题四
在实现中国梦的实践中放飞青春梦想

理想信念是一个思想认识问题，更是一个实践问题。在追求理想的过程中，人们常常会感受到理想与现实的矛盾。思想活跃的青年大学生，容易对理想与现实的矛盾产生困惑，这就需要正确认识理想与现实的关系。

一、辩证看待理想与现实的矛盾

1. 理想与现实的矛盾

在日常生活中，我们在处理理想与现实的关系时，往往只看到二者对立的一面，而看不到二者统一的一面。

理想与现实对立的一面往往会产生两种认识偏向：一种偏向是用理想来否定现实，当发现现实不符合理想预期的时候，就对现实大失所望，甚至对现实采取全盘否定的态度；另一种偏向是用现实来否定理想，在追求理想的过程中一遇到困难就产生畏难情绪，觉得理想遥不可及，丧失为理想而奋斗的信心和勇气，直

and courage to struggle for the ideal, and finally give up the ideal.

Ideal is controlled by reality and developed on the basis of realistic understanding and thinking. On the one hand, reality contains ideal factors and fosters ideal development; on the other hand, ideal contains reality, and under certain conditions, ideal can be transformed into future reality. When you talk about ideal out of reality, ideal will become idle dream.

2. The Chronicity, Arduousness and Tortuosity to Realize Ideal

Realizing ideal is a process. Throughout the history of the development of human society, the realization of any kind of ideals is not easy, and it will encounter all kinds of difficulties and twists and turns, full of hardships and bumps.

Generally speaking, the lower an ideal goal is, the less time and effort it takes to realize; the higher an ideal goal is, the moretime and effort it takes to realize. The chronicity nature of ideal realization is a test of people's patience and confidence, and must be fully prepared for.

It is not easy to realize ideals, and the road to ideals is full of twists and turns. Just due to twists and turns, the road to pursuing ideals is longer. Sometimes, certain road seems to be very direct and closest to the target, but when it comes to the end, there is a gap between the road and the ideal goal, and it is hopeless. This should be considered in relation with the general goals, and be seen as the necessary stage to realize the terminal ideal.

至放弃理想。

理想受现实的制约，是在现实认识的基础上发展起来的。一方面，现实中包含着理想的因素，孕育着理想的发展；另一方面，理想中包含着现实，在一定的条件下，理想可以转化为现实。脱离现实而谈理想，理想就会成为空想。

2. 实现理想的长期性、艰巨性、曲折性

理想的实现是一个过程。纵观人类社会发展史，任何一种理想的实现都不是轻而易举的，必然会遇到各种各样的困难和波折，充满艰险和坎坷。

一般来说，理想目标越低，实现它所需要的时间和努力就越少；理想目标越高，实现它所需要的时间和努力就越多。理想实现的长期性是对人们的耐心和信心的考验，对此必须做好充分的思想准备。

通向理想的道路不是笔直的，而是充满曲折的。正由于曲折，追求理想的道路才更加漫长。有时候，某条道路似乎很直接，离目标最近，但走到最后却发现它与理想目标隔着一道鸿沟，可望而不可即。这需要联系总体目标来考虑，将其看作实现最终理想的必经阶段。只有这

Only in this way can we be full of the enthusiasm of ideals for what we are doing.

3. Hard Struggle is an Important Condition for Realizing Ideal

General Secretary Xi Jinping said: "It is impossible for human beings to achieve their beautiful ideals without hard struggle."

A convention to commemorate the 80th anniversary of the victory of the Long March was held in the Great Hall of the People on October 21, 2016. Xi Jinping, General Secretary of the Central Committee of the Communist Party of China, President of the State and Chairman of the Central Military Commission, delivered important speeches at the General Assembly.

"During the Long March, the heroic Red Army fought bitterly at the Xiangjiang River, made four crossings at the Chishui River, ingeniously crossed the Jinsha River, and fought their way across the Dadu River. They seized the Luding Bridge, fought ferociously at Dushu Town, captured Baozuo, and trekked through the Wumeng Mountains. They repel millions of vicicus pursuers They conquered the air-sparse icebergs and snow ridges, crossed the uninhabited swamps and grasslands, and drove 25,000 miles across more than ten provinces. As the Red Army's main force carried out the Long March, the Red Army and guerilla units that stayed behind in base areas endured the most grueling conditions to wage a guerilla fight with the support of local people. In the northwest, Red Army forces founded the

样，我们才能对正在做的事情充满理想的热忱。

3. 艰苦奋斗是实现理想的重要条件

习近平总书记说："人类的美好理想，都不可能唾手可得，都离不开筚路蓝缕、手胼足胝的艰苦奋斗。"

2016年10月21日，纪念红军长征胜利80周年大会在人民大会堂隆重举行。中共中央总书记、国家主席、中央军委主席习近平在大会上发表重要讲话。

"长征途中，英雄的红军，血战湘江，四渡赤水，巧渡金沙江，强渡大渡河，飞夺泸定桥，鏖战独树镇，勇克包座，转战乌蒙山，击退上百万穷凶极恶的追兵阻敌，征服空气稀薄的冰山雪岭，穿越渺无人烟的沼泽草地，纵横十余省，长驱二万五千里。主力红军长征后，留在根据地的红军队伍和游击队，在极端困难的条件下，紧紧依靠人民群众，坚持游击战争。西北地区红军创建陕甘革命根据地，同先期到达陕北的红二十五军一起打破了敌人的重兵'围剿'，为党中央把中国革命的大本营安置在西北创造了条件。东北抗日联军、坚持

Shaanxi-Gansu Revolutionary Base Area, together with the Red 25th Army, which arrived in northern Shaanxi earlier, broke the enemy's heavy 'encirclement and suppression' campaign and created conditions for the Party Central Committee to place the headquarters of the Chinese revolution in the northwest. Meanwhile, the Northeast Anti-Japanese United Army, the organizations of the Communist Party of China that continued to operate in Kuomintang-controlled areas, and various other forces under the leadership of the Communist Party of China also carried out their own bitter struggles, making an unforgettable contribution to the success of the Long March."

The Long March was a triumph for the ideals and the beliefs of Chinese Communists. As the poem reads, "their bones hardened by the wind and rain that penetrated their clothes, their will tempered by the wild greens that eased their hunger; officers and soldiers endured the bitterness together, whose revolutionary ideals rising above all else."

the spirit of the Long March tells us the importance of hard struggle for the success of our cause.

First, hard struggle is a kind of spiritual outlook and moral quality that can meet difficulties, be diligent and frugal, persevere in struggle, not fear hardships and not stop till achieving goals.

Second, hard struggle is of great significance. It is the foundation and source of all cultural achievements in human society. Hard struggle is the fundamental way and guarantee for realizing

在国民党统治区工作的党组织以及党领导的各方面力量都进行了艰苦卓绝的斗争，都为长征胜利作出了不可磨灭的贡献。"

长征的胜利，是中国共产党人理想的胜利，是中国共产党人信念的胜利。正如"风雨浸衣骨更硬，野菜充饥志越坚；官兵一致同甘苦，革命理想高于天。"

长征精神告诉我们艰苦奋斗对事业成功的重要性。

第一，艰苦奋斗是一种迎难而上、坚韧不拔、克勤克俭、顽强拼搏、不畏艰险、不达目的誓不罢休的精神风貌和道德品质。

第二，艰苦奋斗具有重要意义，是人类社会一切文化成果的基础和源泉，是实现全国各族人民共同理想的根本途径和保证。

the common ideals of the whole nations in the country. We must achieve our own personal ideals through struggle hard.

Third, it is decided by the basic national conditions of China at this stage to continue to carry forward the spirit of hard struggle. At this stage, China's economic and social development is still unbalanced, and the Per Capita Gross National Product is still very low. Compared with developed countries, there is still a big gap. In rural areas, especially in some mountainous and remote areas, the lives of the masses are still not rich, and they are still relatively backward in infrastructure, culture, education and health. To change this situation, we need to carry forward the entrepreneurial spirit of hard struggle. Only by carrying forward the entrepreneurial spirit of hard struggle can we gather the spirit and strength of the whole nation and inspire people to overcome various difficulties and realize the grand goal of socialist modernization.

II.The Unity of Individual Ideal and Social Ideal

1.The Connotation of Individual Ideal and Social Ideal

First, the connotation of individual ideal.

Individual ideal refers to the yearning for and pursuit of individual's future material and spiritual life under certain historical conditions and social relations. It contains life ideal, moral ideal, professional ideal, and political ideal and so on.

Second, the connotation of social ideal.

我们要实现自己的个人理想，也要艰苦奋斗。

第三，现阶段要继续发扬艰苦奋斗的精神，这是由我国现阶段的基本国情决定的。现阶段，我国经济和社会的发展还很不平衡，人均国民生产总值仍然较低，同发达国家相比，还有很大差距。在农村，尤其是在一些山区和边远地区，群众的生活还不富裕，不论是基础设施还是文教卫生事业，都还比较落后。要改变这种状况，就需要我们发扬艰苦奋斗的创业精神。只有发扬艰苦奋斗的创业精神，才能凝聚全民族的精神和力量，鼓舞人们战胜各种困难，实现社会主义现代化的宏伟目标。

二、个人理想与社会理想的统一

1.个人理想和社会理想的内涵

第一，个人理想的内涵。

个人理想是指处于一定历史条件和社会关系中的个体对自己未来的物质生活、精神生活所产生的种种向往和追求，包括生活理想、道德理想、职业理想和政治理想等。

第二，社会理想的内涵。

Social ideal refers to the common ideal of the social collective and even all members of society, i.e. the common goal of dominant position in the whole society.

Upholding and developing socialism with Chinese characteristics, and realizing the great rejuvenation of the Chinese nation is the greatest reality of modern China and the common social ideal of all Chinese people.

2.The Dialectical Relationship between Individual Ideal and Social Ideal

On the one hand, individual ideal is guided by social ideal, and social ideal determines and restricts individual ideal.

On the other hand, social ideal is the concise and sublimation of individual ideal. Social ideal is based on individual ideal, and individual ideal embodies social ideal.

III.The Realization of the Life Ideal

The future of everyone cannot be separated from the future of the country. Without the future of the country, there is no future for everyone.

1. College Students Should Aim High

There are double meanings of "ambition" here: one is the dreaming for the future goal, and the other is the determined will to achieve the goal. Having a high ambition, we can conform to the historical development trend and achieve success in our career.

2.College Students Should Aspire to Do Great Thing

On May 3, 2017, Xi Jinping expressed his

社会理想是指社会集体乃至社会全体成员的共同理想,即在全社会占主导地位的共同奋斗目标。

坚持和发展中国特色社会主义、实现中华民族伟大复兴是当代中国最大的现实,也是全体中国人民的共同社会理想。

2. 个人理想与社会理想的辩证关系

一方面,个人理想以社会理想为指引,社会理想决定和制约着个人理想。

另一方面,社会理想是对个人理想的凝练和升华,社会理想以个人理想为基础,个人理想体现着社会理想。

三、人生理想的实现

每个人的前途都离不开国家的前途,没有国家的前途就没有个人的前途。

1. 立志当高远

这里的"志"具有双重含义:一是对未来目标的向往,二是实现目标的顽强意志。

志存高远,才能顺应历史发展趋势,在事业上取得成就。

2. 立志做大事

2017 年 5 月 3 日,习近平在

affirmation to the students for setting up great aspirations at the theme group day of the second-grade team branch of the second year of the School of Civil and Commercial Economic Law of China University of Political Science and Law. He pointed out that ambition is the premise of all beginnings, and young people should have an ambition to do great causes but not to be a senior official. Today, "doing great causes" is to dedicate ourselves to the great cause of socialism with Chinese characteristics in the new era. No matter what specific and ordinary jobs, they are worth doing as long as they are connected with this great cause and serves the motherland and the people.

3.College Students Should Realize Their Lofty Aspirations with Their Practical Actions

Start from now on, and start from the things around you. The ancients said: "the huge tree that fills one's arms grows from a ting seedling; the platform of nine layers starts from the earth; the journey of a thousand miles starts from the foot."

The youth are full of energy like the sun rising in the morning. They are interested in and very sensitive to new things. "Youth is the most active and energetic force in the whole society. They are most willing to learn and least conservative, especially in the era of socialism." This is the advantage and the brightest highlight of young people.

Xi Jinping pointed out at the 19th National Congress of the Communist Party of China: a country will be full of hope and have a great tomorrow only when its younger generations have

中国政法大学民商经济法学院本科二年级2班团支部主题团日活动上，对大家树立远大的志向表示肯定。他指出，立志是一切开始的前提，青年要立志做大事，不要立志做大官。在今天，"做大事"就是献身于新时代中国特色社会主义伟大事业。无论是什么具体、平凡的工作，只要是与这一伟大事业相联系、服务于祖国和人民的，就值得我们去做。

3. 立志须躬行

古人云："合抱之木，生于毫末；九层之台，起于累土；千里之行，始于足下。"

青年人朝气蓬勃，就像早晨八九点钟的太阳。青年喜新、喜奇、喜变，对新鲜事物甚为敏感。"青年是整个社会力量中的一部分最积极最有生气的力量。他们最肯学习，最少保守思想，在社会主义时代尤其是这样。"这是青年人的优势和最鲜明的亮点。

习近平同志在党的十九大报告中指出："青年一代有理想、有本领、有担当，国家就有前途，民族就有希望。"青年要有

ideals, ability, and a strong sense of responsibility. Young people must have ideals, carry forward the scientific spirit, uphold the excellent traditional culture of the Chinese nation, consciously practice the core values of socialism, and be the promoters, propagators, and practitioners of Xi Jinping Thought on Socialism with Chinese Characteristics for a New Era, Struggle to achieve "the two centenary" goals.

Contemporary college students should establish the ideals that the country needs and suit themselves; practice their own abilities to be responsible for important tasks; have an indomitable and brave heart.

College students in the new era should link the destiny of the individual with the destiny of the country and the people, establish the ambition of dedication for the country and serving the people, consciously integrate the personal ideal pursuit into the struggle to realize the Chinese Dream of national rejuvenation.

理想，要弘扬科学精神，秉承中华民族优秀传统文化，自觉践行社会主义核心价值观，做习近平新时代中国特色社会主义思想的推动者、宣传者、践行者，为实现"两个一百年"奋斗目标贡献力量。

当代大学生应该做到：树立国家需要、适合自己的理想；练就可堪大用、能担重任的本领；胸怀百折不挠、勇往直前的担当。

新时代的大学生应当把个人的命运与国家和人民的命运联系在一起，立为国奉献、为民服务之志，自觉把个人的理想追求融入为实现中华民族伟大复兴的中国梦的奋斗当中。

Lecture Five
The Chinese Spirit is the Soul of the National Rejuvenation and Prosperity

Today, to complete the goal of building a socialist modernization with Chinese characteristics and achieve the Chinese dream of national rejuvenation nation, we must use the Chinese spirit to converge Chinese power. So, what exactly is the Chinese spirit? What is the relationship between the Chinese spirit and the Chinese dream? This is the logical approach and main content of this chapter.

Xi Jinping pointed out: "The Chinese culture has a long history and accumulates the deepest spiritual pursuit of the Chinese nation. It represents the unique spiritual identity of the Chinese nation and provides rich nourishment for the Chinese nation to survive and develop."

I. The Chinese Nation's Possession of the Excellent Tradition of Attaching Importance to Its Own Spirit Cultivation

The 5, 000-year livilization of the Chinese nation has not only bred a splendid and world-famous Chinese civilization, but also created a unique spiritual temperament and spiritual character, forming an excellent tradition of advocating the spirit. This tradition runs through the process of the struggle of the Chinese nation, and promotes

专题五
中国精神是兴国强国之魂

今天，我们要完成中国特色社会主义现代化强国的建设目标，要实现中华民族伟大复兴的中国梦，就必须用中国精神汇聚起中国力量。那么，究竟什么是中国精神？中国精神和中国梦的关系是什么？这是本章的逻辑进路和主要内容。

习近平指出："中华文化源远流长，积淀着中华民族最深层的精神追求，代表着中华民族独特的精神标识，为中华民族生生不息、发展壮大提供了丰厚滋养。"

一、中华民族拥有重精神的优秀传统

中华民族五5000多年的文明不仅孕育出了光辉灿烂、享誉世界的中华文明，还塑造出了独特的精神气质和精神品格，形成了崇尚精神的优秀传统。这一传统贯穿在中华民族筚路蓝缕的奋斗历程中，推动着中华民族的发

the Chinese nation's development and growth. It is an important spiritual identity of the Chinese nation. So what is the spirit and how to understand the Chinese nation's tradition of advocating spirit?

1. The Mainstream View of Ancient Chinese Thinkers

It has always been the mainstream view of ancient Chinese thinkers to attach importance to and advocate spiritual life rather than material life.

First, the cultivation of simple life was emphasized.

In *The Analects of Confucius·Shuer*, there is such a passage: " Eat coarse grains, drink cold water, bend your arms as a pillow, and fun is in it. The wealth that is obtained by improper means is like a cloud in the sky for me."

Du Fu also said in his poem *Danqing Introduces Cao General's Hegemony* that You've been pninting your whole life and you don't know when you're getting old, but you know when you're getting rich.

In *The Analects of Confucius·Yongye*, there is a Confucius's comment on Yan Hui: "One food, one drink, in the poor lane, people can not worry about it, and return to their pleasure. Sacred return！" Later, people simplified the phrase "one food, one drink" to "one food and one drink"， which was used to describe the simple life and the happy way to live in poverty.

Second, the ancient Chinese people especially emphasized the guidance and control of desire with moral reason and spiritual character, and always kept alert to the private desire and greed.

展壮大，是中华民族重要的精神标志。那么到底什么是精神，又如何理解中华民族重精神的传统呢？

1. 中国古代思想家们的主流观点

轻物质生活，重精神生活，一直是中国古代思想家们的主流观点。

第一，主张简朴的生活。

《论语·述而》中有这样一段话："饭疏食，饮水，曲肱而枕之，乐亦在其中矣。不义而富且贵，于我如浮云。"

杜甫的《丹青引赠曹将军霸》中也有这样一句："丹青不知老将至，富贵于我如浮云。"

《论语·雍也》中有一句孔子评价颜回的话："一箪食，一瓢饮，在陋巷，人不堪其忧，回也不改其乐。贤哉，回也！"后来人们将"一箪食，一瓢饮"简化成"箪食瓢饮"这个成语，用来形容生活简朴，安贫乐道。

第二，中国古人特别强调用道德理性和精神品格对欲望进行引导和控制，时刻对私欲、贪欲保持警惕。

In the ancient literary work Guanzi Taboo, there is such a sentence: "Only with a lofty moral, a person will not be confused by exteral things." It means that if you are morally noble, you will not be confused by things that are not right. It is believed that only by upholding noble spiritual pursuits can we resist and fight corruption.

Mencius believed that "there is no better way of cultivating the heart than reducing the desire."

Xuncius advocates "if a man controls his desires with moral caltivation, he will be happy and not disordered; a man who has forgotten the morality by satifying his own desires will be confused and unhappy."

2.The Unremitting Pursuit of Moral Ideals

The adherence to idealism is a typical embodiment of the spirit advocation of the ancient Chinese people.

Chinese scholar-bureaucrats pursue the moral principles, for example, Confucian pursues the moral principles of "benevolence, love and harmony", Mohism pursues the mutual beneficial ideal of "mutual love, mutual benefit".

3.The Emphasis on the Moral Cultivation and Moral Indoctrination

First, the self-cultivation and moral education are emphasized.

Confucius said: "What worries me is that I do not cultivate my character, that I do not practice my learning, that I do not do what I hear and that I do not correct my shortcomings." Confucius's main concern is to cultivate himself with moral standards, without which all good deeds will be

古文学作品《管子·戒》中有这样一句话："道德当身，故不以物惑。"意思是，如果自己道德高尚，就不会被外界不正的东西所迷惑，认为只有坚持高尚的精神追求，才能拒腐反贪。

孟子认为"养心莫善于寡欲"。

荀子主张"以道制欲"，认为"君子乐得其道，小人乐得其欲"，"以道制欲，则乐而不乱；以欲忘道，则惑而不乐。"

2. 对道德理想的不懈追求

对理想主义情怀的坚守，是中国古人崇尚精神的典型体现。

中国士大夫追求道义理想，如儒家追求"仁爱和谐"的道德理想，墨家追求"兼相爱，交相利"的互利理想。

3. 对道德修养和道德教化的重视

第一，强调修身和德教。

孔子说："德之不修，学之不讲，闻义不能徙，不善不能改，是吾忧也。"孔子所忧思的首要问题就是要用道德规范进行修身，否则，一切善事将无从做起。孟子说："人有恒言，皆曰

impossible to start. Mencius said: "People have an oral saying that the foundation of the world is the countries, the foundation of a country is homes, and the foundation of a home is individuals." Personal moral self-cultivation is the cornerstone of a home, a country and the world. Without personal moral self-cultivation, there will be no stability of a home and a country and the governance of the world. This is why we say that "the integrity of a gentleman begins with self-cultivation and then makes the world peaceful". Xuncius also expressed the same principle with the saying: "A gentleman devotes himself to his inner ideological accomplishment. He should be modest in his behavior and devote himself to the accumulation of his own virtues and follow the correct principles to deal with things."

Self-cultivation is not only a moral goal of Confucianism, but also a basic skill of Taoism and Buddhism. The benevolence of Confucianism, the quietness of Taoism, and the empty space of Buddhism are not only the realm of personality cultivation, but also the way to cultivate perfect personality.

Just because self-cultivation is the foundation of managing a home, governing a country and the world, in education, special attention should be paid to cultivating people with morality, to cultivating gentlemen for society, and to educating villains.

Zhu Xi, an educator in the Southern Song Dynasty, insisted on putting moral education at the top of school education. He believed that only

'天下国家'。天下之本在国，国之本在家，家之本在身。"个人的道德修身是家、国、天下的基石，没有个人的道德修身，便无家、国的安定和天下的治理，所谓"君子之守，修其身而天下平"就是这个道理。荀子也表述了同样的道理："君子务修其内而让之于外，务积德于身而处之以遵道。"

修身既是儒家的一种道德目标，也是道家和佛家的基本功。儒家的仁、道家的静、佛家的空，既是人格修养的境界，也是完善人格的修养方法。

正是因为修身是齐家、治国、平天下的基础，所以在教育中应特别重视培养有道德的人，要为社会培养君子，教化小人。

南宋的教育家朱熹坚持把道德教育放在学校教育的首位，认为学生有了较高的道德修养，学

when students had higher moral cultivation, could the cultural knowledge they learned play a proper role. He said "Saints teach people with certain principles. Shun 'dispatched Qi to serve as a disciple to teach the people moral relations: there is kinship between father and son' there is etiquette between monarch and minister 'there is internal and external differences between husband and wife' there is order of dignity and inferiority between old and young 'there is virtue of integrity between friends' ... All the above are the principles. He believed that "essence of the study of the previous emperors is to understand human relations". Therefore, he founded the school with the aim of "developing the teaching of the former king as a measure of governing the state", started with the cultivation of mind and body, carried it out between "five human relations", and treated "understanding human relations" as the educational purpose.

In modern times, especially during the May 4th Movement, the pioneers of the New Culture Movement and the bourgeois democratic revolutionaries sharply criticized and reformed the traditional Confucian culture, especially the content of traditional moral education, but they inherited the traditional spirit of attaching importance to moral education critically. For example, Mr. Cai Yuanpei strongly opposed the educational purposes of "loyalty to the emperor" and "respect for Confucius" of the Qing Dynasty, but advocated "cultivating a healthy personality and developing the spirit of republicanism", and put forward the

到的文化知识才能发挥正当的作用。他说，"圣人教人有定本，舜'使契为司徒，教以人伦：父子有亲，君臣有义，夫妇有别，长幼有序，朋友有信'……皆是定本"。他认为"先王之学以明人伦为本"。因此，他"明先王之教学所以为道"，由明心修身入手，而推行于"五伦"之间，把"明人伦"作为教育的目的。

到了近代，特别是五四时期，新文化运动的先驱者和资产阶级民主革命派尽管都对儒家的传统文化，特别是对传统道德教育的内容进行了猛烈的抨击和改造，但是对重视品德教育的传统精神还是进行了批判的继承。例如，蔡元培先生极力反对清王朝"忠君""尊孔"的教育宗旨，提倡"养成健全人格，发展共和精神"，提出了"五育并举"的教育方针，即军国民教育、实利主义教育、公民道德教育、世界观

educational policy of "Educating Five Domains Simultaneously", which referred to military and national education, utilitarian education, civic moral education, world view education and aesthetic education. He also put forward that citizen's morality is the core of "Educating Five Domain".

Second, the early, staged and hierarchical moral education have been attached importance to.

China's moral education tradition not only pays attention to educating people and putting moral education first, but also pays attention to the early, staged and hierarchical moral education. The hierarchy of Chinese traditional moral education is firstly manifested in the order of family first, and then society, and then country; secondly manifested as enlightenment, cultivation and talent education. This gradual process from form to content forms a complete moral education system. Chinese traditional family education enlightens children's ethics and behavioral norms by means of simple and understandable language, from the aspects of self-cultivation, willingness to learn and grow up, dealing with people and things properly, making and connecting friends well, respecting parents, respecting old people and caring for children, family harmony, etc.

For example, *Family Management Maxim* is a famous "family education" textbook, which was written by the famous educator Zhu Bolu in the late Ming and early Qing Dynasties. It is famous for advocating industriousness and thrift, and teaching children the right way to be a good man.

Third, the social role of customs is emphasized.

教育和美感教育，并提出"五者以公民道德为中坚"。

第二，注重道德教育的早期性、阶段性和层次性。

中国的道德教育传统不仅注重育人为本、德育为先，而且注重道德教育的早期性、阶段性和层次性。中国传统道德教育的层次性，首先表现在先家庭，后社会，再国家；其次表现为启蒙、养成与成才教育。这种从形式到内容的循序渐进形成了一套完整的道德教育体系。中国传统的家庭教育通过浅显易懂的语言，从修身做人、勉学成才、待人接物、交友处世、孝敬父母、敬老爱幼、家庭和睦等各个方面对子女进行伦理道德和行为规范的启蒙教育。

例如，明末清初著名教育家朱柏庐的《朱子家训》（又名《朱子治家格言》），就是一部著名的"家训"教材。它以提倡勤劳节俭、教子做人的正道而著名。

第三，重视习俗的社会作用。

Moral education is also manifested in the indoctrination of the people and the formation of moral customs, i.e. emphasizing the social role of customs.

For example, Su Shi of the Song Dynasty regarded the social atmosphere as the "vitality" of the country. He believed the reason why a country survived or died was not the strength or weakness, but the depth or shallowness of the moral orientation impact; the reason why the duration of a country was long or short was also not the strength or weakness, but the good or bad of the social customs. Therefore, he urged those in power to pay attention to the cultivation of social morality in order to preserve the "vitality" of the country.

Gu Yanwu in the late Ming and early Qing Dynasties also had a profound understanding of the social role of moral customs. He believed that "witnessing the trend of the world and knowing the key to governing chaos must be in people's minds and customs. Therefore, it is indispensable to transfer people's minds and rectify customs." When he saw the decline of the world, he realized that the key to governing the country's disorder was custom. If he wanted to change customs, he had to advocate moral education. He also believed: "Custom, the world's great event." He not only realized the influence of social customs on the state's governance of disorder, and called the custom "the world's great event" but also realized that the improvement of social customs lies in moral education.

4.The respect for the Ideal Personality

The pursuit of lofty ideal personality is con-

道德教育还表现在化民成俗上，即重视习俗的社会作用。

例如，宋代的苏轼就把社会风气看作国家的"元气"。他认为，国家的生死存亡不在于实力的强弱，而在于道德风气影响的深浅；国家寿命的长短也不在于国家实力的强弱，而在于社会风气的好坏。因此，他劝说当权者重视社会道德风气的培养，以保存国家的"元气"。

明末清初的顾炎武对道德风俗的社会作用的认识也很深刻，他认为："目击世趋，方知治乱之关必在人心风俗，而所以转移人心，整顿风俗，则教化纪纲为不可缺矣。"他看到世事的败落，才知道国家治乱的关键在于风俗，而要做到移风易俗，就必须提倡道德教化。他还认为："风俗者，天下之大事也。"他不但认识到了社会风俗对国家治乱的影响，把风俗称为"天下之大事"，而且认识到社会风气的改善在于道德教化。

4. 对理想人格的推崇

追求崇高的理想品格，集中

centratedly embodied in "being a man". Tao-ism believes that we should obey nature and be "real person" and "perfect person" who are free in the world. Confucianism advocates self-re-straint and reverence, respecting ourselves and doing things, and benefiting the people, so that the people can become "the sage of human re-lations". In the hearts of the Chinese people, the basic understanding of the way to be a man is judged by personality and morality, such as "se-niority and morality" "moral integrity" "integ-rity" "open-minded" "high morality" and so on, which are all praises of the realm of being a man. From the small details of life, the way to be a man is to "conduct oneself properly" "act rightly, stand upright" "act in accordance with one's words and deeds" "be kind to others, be kind to oneself" "be open-minded". That is to say, everything must be done to maintain personal dignity, maintain one's own moral integrity, and maintain one's own pride. As a person's complete personality pursuit or as a life ideal, the general goal of the way to be a man is to benefit one's native place and accumu-late virtue and do good deeds, that is, not only to maintain or cultivate one's own good moral char-acter, but also to be a person beneficial to the so-ciety and the people. What really reflects the value of being a person and shows a person's personal integrity is the performance at the critical point of life choice. For example, the national heroes Wen Tianxiang, Yue Fei and Shi Kefa would rather sac-rifice their lives than surrender to the enemy. They are not only "loyal ministers" in the general sense

体现在"做人"上。道家认为应该顺乎自然,做逍遥于天地之间的"真人""至人",而儒家主张克己复礼,做"其行己也恭,其事上也敬,其养民也惠,其使民也义"的君子,成为"人伦之至"的圣人。在中国民众心中,对做人之道的基本理解都是以人格道德为判断尺度的,如"年高德劭""品行端正""为人正直""胸襟坦荡""高风亮节"等都是对做人的境界的赞誉。从生活中的细节来说,做人之道就是"品行端方""行得正,立得直""言行一致,表里如一""与人为善,与己为善""光明磊落,襟怀坦荡"等,即做任何事都要保持人格尊严,保持自己的道德节操,保持自己作为一个人的自豪感。从作为一个人的完整的人格追求或作为一种人生理想来说,做人之道的一般目标就是造福桑梓、积德行善,即不仅要保持或培育自己良好的道德品格,而且需要做一个对社会、对人民有益的人。而真正能体现做人的价值,能显示一个人的人格节操的,还是在重大人生抉择关口的表现。例如,文天祥、岳飞、史可法等民族英雄,宁可牺牲自己的生命,也决不降敌变节,他们不仅是一般道德意义上的"忠臣",而且通过忠君、爱国、抗敌、守节等具体

of morality, but also demonstrate their lofty dignity and perfect personality as a person through their specific acts and moral principles such as loyalty to the monarch, patriotism, resistance to the enemy and observance of integrity. The actions of Qu Yuan and Su Wu not only embody the value connotation of patriotism and loyalty to the monarch, but also represent the persistence of their ideals and beliefs and a spirit of devotion to the truth.

5.The Communist Party of China's Inheritance and Promotion of the Chinese Nation's Excellent Tradition of advocating Spirit

The Communist Party of China is a faithful successor and firm promoter of the Chinese nation's excellent tradition of advocating spirit. In the various historical periods of revolution, construction and reform, the Communist Party of China has emphasized the importance of dealing with the relationship between material and spirit, giving full play to the dynamic role of human spirit, and developed the Chinese nation's excellent tradition of advocating spirit.

Since modern times, especially since the Opium War, the Chinese people have suffered from the spiritual oppression of feudal rule and the spiritual aggression of imperialism, which led some people become "mentally bankrupt".

The greatest achievement of the May 4th Movement is the completion the spiritual enlightenment. It let people start to stand up spiritually and move from passivity to initiative. It is precisely this spiritual initiative that has found a correct development path for China. The reason why the

行为和道德原则表明了自己作为一个人的崇高气节和完美人格。屈原、苏武等人的行为，除了寄寓着爱国、忠君的价值内涵外，还代表着对自己理想信念的执着，代表着一种为真理而献身的精神。

5.中国共产党对中华民族重精神的优秀传统的继承和弘扬

中国共产党是中华民族重精神的优秀传统的忠实继承者和坚定弘扬者。在革命、建设、改革的各个历史时期，中国共产党都强调要处理好物质和精神的关系，重视发挥人的精神的能动作用，使中华民族重精神的优秀传统进一步发扬光大。

近代以来，特别是鸦片战争以来，中国人民在遭受了封建统治的精神压迫和帝国主义的精神侵略，致使一些人"精神沦丧"。

五四运动最大的功绩就是完成了精神启蒙，让人开始从精神上立起来，从被动走向主动，也正是这种精神上的主动，为中国找到了一条正确的发展道路。中国共产党之所以能够取得长征的

Communist Party of China has won the victory of the Long March and the War of Resistance Against Japan is the crucial role of its spiritual strength.

At the closing meeting of the Seventh National Congress, Mao Zedong emphasized that we should transform China with the spirit of removing mountains by Yugong. At the second plenary session of the Eighth Central Committee, when discussing maintaining the political nature of arduous struggle, Mao Zedong stressed that "people should have some spirit".

Since the reform and opening up, the Communist Party of China has attached great importance to the construction of spiritual civilization. By strengthening the construction of civic morality, carrying out patriotism education, ideals and faiths education, cultivating and carrying forward national spirit, advocating and practicing Socialist Core Values, the Party has vigorously improved the ideological pursuit and spiritual realm of all the people.

Today, the rejuvenation of our nation is not only to realize the economic take-off, but also to inspire and highlight our unique spiritual outlook and build our national future with Chinese spirit.

II. Chinese Spirit

1. The Connotation of Chinese Spirit

On March 17, 2013, at the first session of the Twelfth National People's Congress, General Secretary Xi Jinping pointed out: "To realize the Chinese dream, we must carry forward Chinese spirit.

胜利、抗日战争的胜利，就是应为精神的力量发挥了至关重要的作用。

毛泽东在中共七大闭幕会上强调要用愚公移山精神来改造中国，在中共八届二中全会上论述保持艰苦奋斗的政治本色时又强调"人是要有一点精神的"。

改革开放以来，中国共产党高度重视精神文明建设，通过加强公民道德建设，开展爱国主义教育、理想信念教育，培育和弘扬民族精神，倡导和践行社会主义核心价值观，大力提高全体人民的思想追求和精神境界。

今天，我们民族的复兴不仅仅是实现经济的腾飞，更重要的是振奋和彰显我们独有的精神风貌，用中国精神打造我们民族的未来。

二、中国精神

1. 中国精神的内涵

2013年3月17日，在十二届全国人大一次会议上，习近平总书记指出："实现中国梦必须弘扬中国精神。这就是以爱国主

This is the national spirit with patriotism as its core and the spirit of the times with reform and innovation as its core. This spirit is the soul of revitalizing the country and strengthening the country with cohesion." It can be seen that the "Chinese Spirit" is put forward to solve the problems in the historical process of realizing the great rejuvenation of the Chinese nation. It is placed under the framework of the realization of the Chinese Dream. It is the need of cohesion and unity in China's reform and opening-up, and the spiritual impetus to encourage the people of the whole country to advance bravely. Since the connotation of "Chinese Spirit" was put forward in March 2013, General Secretary Xi Jinping has put forward "Chinese Spirit" many times on different occasions and for different objects.

The Chinese spirit is the fundamental spiritual pursuit of the Chinese nation in its reflection on its historical experience and reality. It serves as a carrier to form a national spirit that characterizes the blood of its own culture and the mirror of the times.

The national spirit with patriotism as the core and the spirit of the times with reform and innovation as the core constitute the basic connotation of the Chinese spirit. Vigorously carrying forward the Chinese spirit and cultivating the common spiritual home of the Chinese nation requires not only vigorously carrying forward the great national spirit with patriotism as the core, but also vigorously carrying forward the great spirit of the times with reform and innovation as the core.

义为核心的民族精神，以改革创新为核心的时代精神。这种精神是凝心聚力的兴国之魂、强国之魂。"由此可见，"中国精神"是为解决当前实现中华民族伟大复兴的中国梦的历史进程的问题而提出的，是置于中国梦实现的大框架之下的，是中国在改革开放中凝心聚力、团结一致的需要，是激励全国人民奋勇前进的精神动力。自 2013 年 3 月提出"中国精神"的内涵之后，习近平总书记又在不同场合，针对不同的对象，多次提出"中国精神"。

中国精神是中华民族在对自身历史体验和现实状况的反思中沉淀出的根本精神追求，并以此为载体形成表征自己文化血脉与时代镜像的国家精神。

以爱国主义为核心的民族精神和以改革创新为核心的时代精神，构成了中国精神的基本内涵。大力弘扬中国精神，培育中华民族共同的精神家园，既需要大力弘扬以爱国主义为核心的伟大民族精神，也需要大力弘扬以改革创新为核心的伟大时代精神。

2.The Content of the Great Chinese National Spirit

The great national spirit cultivated, inherited and developed by the Chinese people in the long-term struggle has provided a powerful spiritual impetus for China's development and the progress of human civilization. The content of great Chinese national spirit is as follows.

First, the Chinese nation has a great spirit of creativity.

In the long history of thousands of years, the Chinese people have always worked diligently, invented and created. In China, there are Great thought masters like Lao Zi, Confucius, Zhuang Zi, Mencius, Mo Zi, Sun Zi and Han Feizi. The Chinese people invented papermaking, gunpowder, printing, compasses and other great scientific and technological achievements that profoundly affected the progress of human civilization. They created great works of literature, such as *the Book of Songs*, Chu Ci, Han Fu, Tang poetry, Song Ci, Yuan Qu, Novels of Ming and Qing Dynasties. They passed on the great epic that shocked people, such as *King Gesar, Manas, Jangar*, built the great works of the Great Wall, Dujiangyan, Grand Canal, Forbidden City, and Potala Palace. Today, the creative spirit of the Chinese people is promoting the rapid development of our country and striding ahead in the world. As long as more than 1.4 billion Chinese people continue to carry forward this great creative spirit, they will surely be able to create one miracle after another!

Second, the Chinese nation has a great spirit of struggle.

2. 伟大的中华民族精神的内容

中国人民在长期奋斗中培育、继承、发展起来的伟大民族精神，为中国发展和人类文明进步提供了强大的精神动力。伟大的中华民族精神的内容如下。

第一，伟大的创造精神。

在几千年历史长河中，中国人民始终辛勤劳作、发明创造，产生了老子、孔子、庄子、孟子、墨子、孙子、韩非子等闻名于世的伟大思想巨匠，创造了造纸术、火药、印刷术、指南针等深刻影响人类文明进程的伟大科技成果，创作了诗经、楚辞、汉赋、唐诗、宋词、元曲、明清小说等伟大文艺作品，传承了格萨尔王、玛纳斯、江格尔等震撼人心的伟大史诗，建设了万里长城、都江堰、大运河、故宫、布达拉宫等气势恢宏的伟大工程。今天，中国人民的创造精神推动着我国日新月异地向前发展，大踏步走在世界前列。只要14亿多中国人民始终发扬这种伟大的创造精神，就一定能够创造出一个又一个奇迹！

第二，伟大的奋斗精神。

In the long history of thousands of years, the Chinese people have always been rejuvenated and self-improving. They have developed and built the vast and beautiful rivers and mountains of the motherland, opened up vast sea territory with thousands of hectares of waves, opened up vast grainfields with rich resources, governed thousands of rivers, overcame countless natural disasters, built a number of scattered towns and villages, developed a full range of industries, and formed a colorful life. Since ancient times, the Chinese people have understood that happiness comes from struggle. Today, all that the Chinese people possess embodies their own wisdom, hard work and sweat. As long as more than 1.4 billion Chinese people continue to carry forward this great spirit of struggle, they will surely achieve the grand goal of creating a better life!

Third, the Chinese nation has a great spirit of unity.

In the long history of thousands of years, the Chinese people have always united in one heart and the same boat, established a unified multi-ethnic country, and developed 56 ethnic groups that are multi-integrated and harmonious, and formed a family of Chinese nationalities that help each other. Especially after the modern times, under the grim situation of foreign aggression, the people of all ethnic groups in China hand in hand, side by side, bravely fighted to defeat all the evil and aggressors, defending national independence and freedom, co-writing the magnificent epic of the Chinese nation of defending motherland and

在几千年历史长河中，中国人民始终革故鼎新、自强不息，开发和建设了祖国辽阔秀丽的大好河山，开拓了波涛万顷的辽阔海疆，开垦了物产丰富的广袤粮田，治理了千百条大江大河，战胜了数不清的自然灾害，建设了星罗棋布的城镇乡村，发展了门类齐全的产业，形成了多姿多彩的生活。中国人民自古就明白，要幸福就必须奋斗。今天，中国人民所拥有的一切都凝聚着自己的聪明才智，浸透着自己的辛勤汗水。只要14亿多中国人民始终发扬这种伟大的奋斗精神，就一定能够实现创造更加美好的生活的宏伟目标！

第三，伟大的团结精神。

在几千年历史长河中，中国人民始终团结一心、同舟共济，建立了统一的多民族国家，发展了56个民族多元一体、和谐融洽的民族关系，形成了守望相助的中华民族大家庭。特别是近代以后，在外来侵略的严峻形势下，我国各族人民手挽着手、肩并着肩，浴血奋战，打败了一切穷凶极恶的侵略者，捍卫了民族独立和自由，共同书写了中华民族保卫祖国、抵御外侮的壮丽史诗。今天，中国取得的令世人瞩

resisting the foreign aggression. Today, China's achievements in the development of the world's attention are the result of concerted efforts of the people of all nationalities in the country. The Chinese people have profoundly realized from their personal experience that unity is power and unity can move forward, a split country cannot develop and make progress. As long as more than 1.4 billion Chinese people have always carried forward this great spirit of unity, they will surely be able to form a powerful force that is brave and forward-looking and unbreakable!

Fourth, the Chinese nation has a great spirit of dream.

In the long history of thousands of years, the Chinese people have always cherished dreams and pursued unremittingly, not only formed the concept of a well-off life, but also upheld the feelings of working for the public world. Ancient Chinese mythology, such as Pangu opening the world, Nuwa repairing the sky, Fuxi's painting, Shennong tasting grass, Kuafu chasing the sun, Jingwei filling the sea, Yugong moving the mountain, etc., deeply reflect the Chinese people's persistent spirit of pursuing and realizing their dreams. The Chinese people believe that no matter how high the mountains are, if they insist in climbing, they can always reach the top; and no matter how long the road is, if they insist in walking, they will surely reach the destination. Since modern times, the realization of the great rejuvenation of the Chinese nation has become the greatest dream of the Chinese nation. The Chinese people have persevered and continuously struggled for more than 170

目的发展成就，更是全国各族人民同心同德、同心同向努力的结果。中国人民通过亲身经历深刻认识到，团结就是力量，团结才能前进，而一个四分五裂的国家不可能发展进步。只要14亿多中国人民始终发扬这种伟大的团结精神，就一定能够形成勇往直前、无坚不摧的强大力量！

第四，伟大的梦想精神。

在几千年历史长河中，中国人民始终心怀梦想、不懈追求，不仅形成了小康生活的理念，而且秉持天下为公的情怀。盘古开天、女娲补天、伏羲画卦、神农尝草、夸父追日、精卫填海、愚公移山等我国古代神话深刻反映了中国人民勇于追求和实现梦想的执着精神。中国人民相信，山再高，往上攀，总能登顶；路再长，走下去，定能到达。近代以来，实现中华民族伟大复兴成为中华民族最伟大的梦想，中国人民百折不挠、坚韧不拔，以同敌人血战到底的气概、在自力更生的基础上光复旧物的决心、自立于世界民族之林的能力，为实现这个伟大梦想进行了170多年的持续奋斗。今天，中国人民比历史上任何时期都更接近、更有信

years to realize this great dream with the spirit of fighting the enemy to the end, the determination to restore the old things on the basis of self-reliance and the ability to stand among the world's nations. Today, the Chinese people are closer, more confident and capable of realizing the great rejuvenation of the Chinese nation than at any time in history. As long as more than 1.4 billion Chinese people have always carried forward this great spirit of dream, they will surely realize the great rejuvenation of the Chinese nation!

The great national spirit which is nurtured, inherited and developed by the industrious and brave Chinese people with patriotism as the core is the basis to strengthen the self-confidence in the socialist road with Chinese characteristics, to be theoretical confident, institutional confident and cultural confident. It is also the fundamental force for the Chinese nation to move forward without hindrance.

III.The Essence of Chinese Spirit

As an ideology, the Chinese spirit is a special social consciousness, a conscious reflection of a certain social and economic form and the political system determined by the economic form as the ideological superstructure of the society. This is the general essence of Chinese spirit. Therefore, we should analyze the essence of Chinese spirit basing on practice and focusing on ideological concepts. It should be clear that the core of Chinese spirit is the value concept.

心和能力实现中华民族伟大复兴。只要 14 亿多中国人民始终发扬这种伟大的梦想精神，就一定能够实现中华民族伟大复兴！

勤劳勇敢的中国人民培育、继承、发展起来的以爱国主义为核心的伟大民族精神，是坚定中国特色社会主义道路自信、理论自信、制度自信、文化自信的底气，是中华民族风雨无阻、高歌行进的根本力量。

三、中国精神的本质

作为一种意识形态，中国精神是特殊的社会意识，是作为社会的思想上层建筑对一定社会经济形态以及由此决定的政治制度的自觉反映，这是中国精神的一般本质。因此，应立足于实践、着眼于思想观念对中国精神的本质进行分析，明确中国精神的核心是价值理念。

1. Chinese Spirit is the Ideological System and Value Concept Gained from Practice

First, Chinese spirit is a special social consciousness derived from the practice of the people.

As the superstructure of ideology, ideology is a special social consciousness, a special form of development of social consciousness system, and occupies an extremely important position in the various components of social consciousness system. In the overall structure of social consciousness, ideology, as a high-level content, plays a guiding and commanding role to other components. The main body of ideology is the masses, and its primary essence is practicality. Therefore, the main body of Chinese spirit must also be the masses. The masses have created the material wealth of society and created the spiritual wealth of society. They are the main body of practice and the creator of history.

Chinese spirit must have practicality. It originates from the practice of natural and social transformation of Chinese people. It reflects the spiritual style of the Chinese people's, unity and progress, and can be reshaped in the process of the historical task of realizing the great rejuvenation of the Chinese nation. When discussing the essence of Chinese spirit, we should not always emphasize its systematic theory, but see it as a product of practice, which requires the combination of theory and practice.

Second, Chinese spirit is an ideological system with strong cohesion and appeal.

As the ideological superstructure of the society, Chinese spirit is a sociology system con-

1. 中国精神是由实践所得的思想体系和价值理念

第一，中国精神是由人民群众实践所得的特殊社会意识。

作为思想的上层建筑，意识形态是一种特殊的社会意识，是社会意识体系的一个特殊发展形式，在社会意识体系的各组成部分中占有极其重要的位置。在社会意识这个总体结构中，作为高层次内容的意识形态对其他各个组成部分都具有指导和统帅的作用。意识形态的主体是人民群众，它的首要本质是实践性。因此，中国精神的主体也必然是人民群众。人民群众创造了社会的物质财富，也创造了社会的精神财富，是实践的主体，是历史的创造者。

中国精神必然具有实践性，它来源于中华儿女改造自然、改造社会的实践，体现的是中国人民团结奋进的精神风貌，于当代实现中华民族伟大复兴的中国梦的历史任务进程中得以重塑。我们在讨论中国精神的本质时，不能总是强调它的系统理论性，更要看到其作为实践的产物对理论和实践相结合的要求。

第二，中国精神是具有强大凝聚力和号召力的思想体系。

中国精神作为社会的思想上层建筑，从内容上看包括政

sisting of political, legal, philosophical and moral theories. Specifically speaking, Chinese spirit advocates socialist democracy with Chinese characteristics, follows the legal framework of socialism with Chinese characteristics, cultivates socialist core values, and carries out the construction of socialist spiritual civilization. However, as an ideological system, Chinese spirit has great cohesion and appeal. It provides great spiritual driving force for the masses, and permeates concepts, values, theories and beliefs into the masses. Under the influence of Chinese spirit, all members of society will form a unified will, goals and actions, form a further recognition of the society, form a united, progressive and positive atmosphere in the whole society, and prompt all Chinese people to contribute to the Chinese dream of the great rejuvenation of the Chinese nation.

Third, Chinese spirit is the value concept advocated by Chinese society at present.

Ideology has a strong value orientation. In essence, it coheres and attracts all members of society with values, and provides people with certain value ideals and belief choices, also provides people with certain judgment criteria and value criteria for value orientation, so as to achieve certain political goals and serve the country's realistic strategic missions. Chinese spirit reflects the value judgment of the proletariat, reflects the national spirit with patriotism as the core and the spirit of the times with reform and innovation as the core. The 17th National Congress of the Communist

治、法律、哲学、道德等社会学说，是由思想观点组成的系统化的思想观念体系。具体来说，中国精神倡导的是中国特色社会主义民主政治，遵循的是具有中国特色的社会主义法律框架，培育的是社会主义核心价值观，进行的是社会主义精神文明建设。但中国精神作为一种思想体系，极具凝聚力和号召力，为人民群众提供了巨大的精神驱动力，将观念、价值、理论、信念等渗透到人民群众之中。在中国精神的影响下，全体社会成员会形成统一的意志、目标和行动，并形成对社会的进一步认同，在全社会形成团结奋进、积极向上的氛围，促使全体中华儿女为实现中华民族伟大复兴的中国梦而奉献一己之力。

第三，中国精神是当前中国社会所倡导的价值理念。

意识形态具有强烈的价值指向性，在本质上是以价值观念来凝聚和吸引全体社会成员，并为其提供一定的价值理想和信仰选择，还为其价值导向提供一定的判断标准和价值尺度，从而实现一定的政治目标，为国家的现实战略任务服务。中国精神反映的是无产阶级的价值判断，反映的是以爱国主义为核心的民族精神和以改革创新为核心的时代精

Party of China put forward the socialist core value system. The 18th National Congress of the Communist Party of China once again emphasized the construction of the socialist core value system and actively nurtured and practiced the socialist core values. It can be said that the socialist core values are the general consensus of the Chinese people's cohesion, Chinese spirit is based on the socialist core values to cohere China's strength and shape the spiritual outlook of Chinese people.

2. Chinese Spirit Embodies the Overall Will of the Country with Chinese Characteristics

As a national spirit, Chinese spirit is different from the national spirit, and embodies the overall will of the country. It is different from the traditional culture of the Chinese nation, and focuses on the positive achievements of the transformation of the world by the Chinese nation. It is different from the spirits of other nations, and has distinct Chinese characteristics.

First, Chinese spirit embodies the overall will of the country.

Chinese spirit is different from national spirit. First, national spirit is an excellent component that a nation naturally accumulates in the process of its emergence and development, and it develops naturally according to the law of history. However, Chinese spirit is a conscious national act, reflecting the overall will of the country. General Secretary Xi Jinping pointed out that Chinese spirit is the soul of rejuvenating the country and strengthening the country with cohesion. It can be seen from this that its proposal is based on serving the real-

神。党的十七大提出了社会主义核心价值体系，党的十八大再次强调社会主义核心价值体系建设，积极培育和践行社会主义核心价值观。可以说，社会主义核心价值观是当下中国人民凝心聚力的普遍共识，中国精神是以社会主义核心价值观来凝聚中国力量，塑造中国人民的精神风貌的。

2. 中国精神体现具有中国特色的国家整体意志

作为一种国家精神，中国精神不同于民族精神，它体现的是国家的整体意志；不同于中华民族传统文化，它偏重的是中华民族改造世界的积极成果；更不同于其他民族的精神，它具有鲜明的中国特色。

第一，中国精神体现国家整体意志。

中国精神不同于民族精神。首先，民族精神是一个民族在产生及发展过程中自然而然积淀而成的优秀成分，是遵循历史规律自然发展起来的；而中国精神却是有意识的国家行为，体现的是国家的整体意志。习近平总书记指出，中国精神是凝心聚力的兴国之魂、强国之魂。由此可见，它的提出是以服务于中国梦的实现和激励国人实现中华民族伟大

ization of the Chinese dream and motivating the Chinese people to realize the great rejuvenation of the Chinese nation. Second, national spirit focuses on cultural elements, which is an excellent cultural tradition formed by a nation in its long historical development. It has more natural and social attributes. However Chinese spirit adds political elements on the basis of cultural elements and emphasizes its political attributes. So we generally say that cultivating and strengthening Chinese spirit is an integral part of the overall construction and overall development of socialism with Chinese characteristics. Therefore, from a vertical point of view, Chinese spirit is different from national spirit. Chinese spirit should not only look into history, but also be based on reality. Chinese spirit includes not only the national spirit condensed from the long-term historical development of the Chinese nation, but also the spirit of the times based on the situation and development of different times. It is the unity of the two. Only when the national spirit has the characteristics of the times can it have a vivid development force, only when the spirit of the times has the characteristics of the nationalities can it be recognized and promoted. The two are interrelated and interacted, which constitute the core content of Chinese spirit together.

Second, Chinese spirit represents the positive achievements of the Chinese nation in reforming the world.

Chinese traditional culture is formed by Chinese people in thousands of years of practice of transforming nature and society. It reflects the character, psychological will and spiritual outlook

复兴为背景的。其次，民族精神侧重于文化元素，是一个民族在自身漫长的历史发展过程中所形成的优秀文化传统，更多地具有自然属性及社会属性；而中国精神则在文化元素的基础上增加了政治元素，更为强调其政治属性。所以，我们通常说培育和强化中国精神是中国特色社会主义事业整体建设、总体发展的有机组成部分。因此，从纵向的角度看，中国精神不同于民族精神。中国精神既应观照历史，又应立足现实。中国精神既包括中华民族在长期历史发展中凝结而成的民族精神，也包括基于不同时代境遇和发展状况所形成的时代精神，是二者的统一。民族精神具有时代性才能有鲜活的发展力量，时代精神具有民族性才能得到认同和弘扬，二者相互联系、相互作用，共同构成了中国精神的核心内容。

第二，中国精神代表中华民族改造世界的积极成果。

中华民族传统文化是中华儿女在几千年改造自然、改造社会的实践中形成的，体现的是中华儿女的性格气质、心理意志和精

of Chinese people and embodies in all aspects of social life. Chinese traditional culture has fostered national psychology and formed certain ideological concepts, value ideals and standards of conduct. It has a vital impact on the development of the Chinese nation and personal growth. The spiritual life in contemporary Chinese society contains not only excellent ideological resources reflecting the spirit of the Chinese nation and the spirit of the times, but also negative psychology and personality tendencies that are incompatible with the positive and vigorous national spirit. Specifically speaking, the spirits of unity and patriotism are the fine spirits nurtured by the excellent Chinese traditional culture. They have played different historical roles in different historical periods, and have promoted the progress of the country to a certain extent. However, there are still some dregs in Chinese traditional culture, such as feudal ideas of "three principles and five constants" "preserving the law of nature and destroying human desires", which need to be eliminated and discarded on the basis of discrimination. It can be said that Chinese spirit is different from Chinese traditional culture. It inherits and develops the excellent achievements of the ideological and cultural development of the Chinese nation.

Third, Chinese spirit is different from the spirits of other countries or nationalities.

In the modern academic history of China, Chinese spirit is not a new topic. Its direct source is the awakening of national consciousness brought about by the invasion of China by the Western powers in the 19th century. Gu Hongming

神风貌，体现在社会生活的方方面面。中华民族传统文化培育了民族心理，形成了一定的思想观念、价值理想和行为标准，对于中华民族的发展及个人的成长都具有至关重要的影响。当代中国社会的精神生活既包含体现中华民族精神和时代精神的优秀思想资源，也包含与积极向上的民族精神不相适应的消极心理和人格倾向等。具体来说，团结一致的精神、爱国主义精神等都是中华民族优秀传统文化所滋生和培育的优秀精神，它们在不同的历史时期发挥了不同的历史作用，而且都在一定程度上推动了国家的进步。然而，中华民族传统文化中还存在着一些糟粕，如"三纲五常""存天理，灭人欲"等封建思想，这是需要我们在辨别的基础上予以剔除和舍弃的。可以说，中国精神不同于中华民族传统文化，它所继承和发扬的是中华民族思想文化中的优秀成果。

第三，中国精神不同于其他国家或民族的精神。

在中国现代学术史上，中国精神不是一个新问题，它的直接源头是19世纪西方列强入侵中国带来的国家意识的觉醒。关于中国精神与他国精神的不同之处，

first gave his opinions on the differences between Chinese spirit and the spirits of other countries. In the book *Chinese Spirit*, he regards the four outstanding spiritual traits of profundity, simplicity, broad-mindedness and sensitivity as the excellent qualities of Chinese people, and holds that only Chinese people have these four outstanding spiritual traits. However, in the current society, we should not only recognize the commonalities between Chinese spirit and the spirits of other countries, such as love for peace and pursuit of harmony, but also be good at digging, refining and summarizing the differences between Chinese spirit and the spirits of other countries, i.e. the unique characteristics of Chinese spirit.

In the current international and domestic situation, compared with the spirits of other countries and nationalities, Chinese spirit embodies the following three unique spiritual connotations: First, the spirit of taking the people as the main body. People are the important subjects to realize the Chinese dream, so we should fully respect the initiative of the people. The spirit of taking the people as the main body is the spiritual characteristic of our country that is different from other countries. Second, the spirit of reform and innovation. Since the reform and opening up, we have emancipated the mind, sought truth from facts and kept pace with the times, broken the closed and rigid situation, greatly enriched and expanded the connotation of Chinese spirit, injected the elements of the times into Chinese spirit, and made reform and innovation the main theme of Chinese spirit. Continuous reform and innovation is also the charac-

辜鸿铭最早给出了他的见解，他在《中国人的精神》这本书中将深沉、纯朴、博大、灵敏这四种优秀的精神特质作为中国人的优秀品质，并认为只有中国人才具有这四种优秀精神特质。然而，在当前社会，我们不仅要承认中国精神与他国精神所具有的共性，如热爱和平、追求和谐等，还要善于挖掘、提炼、总结中国精神与他国精神的不同之处，即中国精神表现出的中国所独有的特性。

在当今国际国内形势下，中国精神同其他国家或民族相比，体现出以下三点独特的内涵：首先，人民群众为主体的精神。人民群众是实现中国梦的重要主体，因此我们应该充分尊重人民群众的首创精神。以人民群众为主体的精神是我国不同于他国的精神特质。其次，改革创新的精神。改革开放以来，我们解放思想、实事求是、与时俱进，打破了封闭僵化的局面，极大地丰富和扩展了中国精神的内涵，为中国精神注入了时代元素，使改革创新成为中国精神的主旋律。不断地改革创新，也是中国精神不同于他国精神的特点。最后，自信的精神。十一届三中全会以后，我们开辟了建设中国特色社

teristic of Chinese spirit different from the spirits of other countries. Finally, the spirit of self-confidence. After the Third Plenary Session of the Eleventh Central Committee, we have opened up a historical road to build socialism with Chinese characteristics, made China stand among the nations of the world, and strengthened the ideals and faiths of socialism with Chinese characteristics. Unswervingly implementing the party's basic program and basic line at the present stage, having self-confidence for socialism with Chinese characteristics, theoretical self-confidence, institutional self-confidence, cultural self-confidence is the important feature of the current Chinese spirit.

IV.Chinese Spirit must be Carried forward to Realize the Chinese Dream

Chinese spirit is the soul of rejuvenating and strengthening the country. To realize the Chinese Dream, we must carry forward Chinese spirit, take the high spiritual banner as the guide, take the strong spiritual pillar as the support, unite and rally the wisdom and strength of all the people, and strive for the realization of the Chinese Dream.

1. The Chinese Spirit is the Spiritual Bond that Binds China's Strength

To promote the great cause of the times of national rejuvenation, we must have a strong spiritual cohesion of all people with one mind and all aspirations. The masses of the people are the main force for historical development and social progress. To uphold and develop socialism with Chinese characteristics and realize the great rejuvenation of the Chinese nation, the most fundamental

会主义的历史道路，使中国屹立于世界民族之林，坚定了中国特色社会主义的理想信念。坚定不移地贯彻执行党在现阶段的基本纲领和基本路线，具有中国特色社会主义道路自信、理论自信、制度自信、文化自信，更是当前中国精神的重要特点。

四、实现中国梦必须弘扬中国精神

中国精神是兴国强国之魂。实现中国梦，必须弘扬中国精神，以高扬的精神旗帜为指引，以强大的精神支柱为支撑，团结凝聚全体人民的智慧和力量，为实现中国梦而努力奋斗。

1. 凝聚中国力量的精神纽带

要推进民族复兴的时代伟业，我们必须有万众一心、众志成城的强大精神凝聚力。人民群众是历史发展和社会进步的主体力量。坚持和发展中国特色社会主义、实现中华民族伟大复兴最根本的力量是人民，最强大的力量是团结凝聚起来的人民。"大

force is the people, and the most powerful force is the united people. "The movement of Dapeng doesn't depend on only one feather, and the speed of a fine horse doesn't depend on the power of one foot." Xi Jinping pointed out: "China must gather and stimulate the strength of 1.4 billion people to fly high and run fast." Without strong spiritual power, China will repeat the tragedy of fragmentation since modern times. Carrying forward Chinese spirit plays an important cohesive role in maintaining the survival and development of the Chinese nation and safeguarding national unity. In contemporary China, we must use Chinese spirit to lead the people of all ethnic groups to think and strive for one goal. With the wisdom and strength of 1.4 billion people, we must muster an invincible and magnificent force to strive for the realization of the Chinese Dream of the great rejuvenation of the Chinese nation.

2. Chinese Spirit is the Spiritual Driving Force that Stimulates Innovation and Creativity

At present, the cause of socialism with Chinese characteristics that we are engaged in is an unprecedented creative cause. The value and significance of Chinese spirit as the soul of rejuvenating the country and strengthening the country are more prominent. Throughout the history of human development, innovation has always been an important force for the development of a country and a nation, and has always been an important force for the advancement of human society. The motivation of realizing dreams, coping with challenges, and creating the future can only come from

鹏之动，非一羽之轻也；骐骥之速，非一足之力也。"习近平指出："中国要飞得高、跑得快，就得汇集和激发近14亿人民的磅礴力量。"没有强大的精神力量，中国就会重演近代以来四分五裂、一盘散沙的悲剧。弘扬中国精神，对于维系中华民族的生存与发展、维护国家统一和民族团结发挥着重要的凝聚作用。在当代中国，必须用中国精神引领各族人民心往一处想、劲往一处使，用14亿人的智慧和力量汇集起不可战胜的磅礴力量，为实现中华民族伟大复兴的中国梦而努力奋斗。

2. 激发创新创造的精神动力

当前，我们正在从事的中国特色社会主义事业是一项前无古人的创造性事业，中国精神作为兴国强国之魂的价值和意义更为凸显。纵观人类发展史，创新始终是一个国家、一个民族发展的重要力量，也始终是推动人类社会进步的重要力量。实现梦想、应对挑战、创造未来的动力只能从发展中来、从改革中来、从创新中来。中国共产党带领人民通过改革开放这一新的伟大革命开

development, from reform, and from innovation. The Communist Party of China led the people to open up the road of socialism with Chinese characteristics through the new great revolution of reform and opening up, which made China take great strides to catch up with the times. To advance the great cause of the new era, we must have a strong spirit of innovation, creativity and progress, have courage to change and innovate, never be rigid and never stagnate, so that all the people will always maintain an upward spiritual state and inject strong spiritual force into the realization of the Chinese Dream.

3.The Chinese Spirit is the Spirit Willpower for Advancing the Great Cause of National Rejuvenation

No nation in the world can follow the path of others to achieve its own development and revitalization, and no nation will achieve its glory and dreams in the uncertain and moving minds. upholding and developing socialism with Chinese characteristics requires us to correctly understand the contemporary world and China's development trend, correctly understand Chinese characteristics, and strengthen road confidence, theoretical confidence, institutional confidence, and cultural confidence. Only by consciously carrying forward Chinese spirit, enhancing national self-respect and self-confidence, and steadfastly following our own path, can all people have a rock-solid spirit and belief in the journey to realize the great cause of rejuvenation, and push our cause forward to the other side of the glory.

辟了中国特色社会主义道路，使中国大踏步赶上了时代。要推进新时代的伟大事业，就必须有创新创造、向上向前的强大精神奋发力，勇于变革、勇于创新，永不僵化、永不停滞，使全体人民始终保持昂扬向上的精神状态，为实现中国梦注入强大的精神力量。

3. 推进复兴伟业的精神定力

世界上没有一个民族能够亦步亦趋地走别人的道路实现自己的发展和振兴，也没有一个民族会在心神不定、游移彷徨中成就自己的光荣和梦想。坚持和发展中国特色社会主义，需要我们正确认识当前世界和中国的发展大势，正确认识中国特色，坚定道路自信、理论自信、制度自信、文化自信。只有自觉弘扬中国精神，增强民族自尊心和自信心，坚定不移走自己的路，才能使全体人民在实现复兴伟业的征途中拥有坚如磐石的精神和信仰力量，坚定不移把我们的事业不断推向前进，直至光辉的彼岸。

Lu Xun once said, "Only the soul of the people is valuable, and only when he develops, can China make real progress." As the hope of the nation and the future of the motherland, college students must work hard to carry forward the national spirit with patriotism as the core and the spirit of the times with reform and innovation as the core, transform Chinese spirit into a youthful act, and bravely carry forward and practice Chinese spirit, contribute their own wisdom and strength to the country's prosperity, national rejuvenation, and people's happiness.

鲁迅曾说："惟有民魂是值得宝贵的，惟有他发扬起来，中国才有真进步。"作为民族的希望和祖国的未来，大学生要努力弘扬以爱国主义为核心的民族精神和以改革创新为核心的时代精神，将中国精神转化为青春行动，勇做弘扬和践行中国精神的时代先锋，为国家富强、民族振兴、人民幸福贡献自己的智慧和力量。

Lecture Six
The Ways to Become
a Loyal Patriot

I.The Connotation and Requirements of Patriotism

Patriotism embodies the people's deep feelings for their motherland, reflects the individual dependence on the motherland, and is the unity of people's sense of belonging, identity, dignity and honor to their homeland, nation and culture. It is a moral requirement, political principle and legal norm to regulate the relationship between the individual and the motherland, as well as the core of the national spirit.

1.The Connotation of Patriotism

First, patriotism is a deep emotion.

To survive in society, we all need to obtain physical materials for survival and development, and seek spiritual home to comfort our souls. All of this comes first from our motherland. So we call our motherland "mother". If we lose our motherland, we will be homeless vagrants. The prosperity of our motherland requires everyone of us to devote the power of love. But more importantly, we need our motherland, our motherland also needs our love and deserves our love.

专题六
如何成为一个忠诚的
爱国者

一、爱国主义的内涵及要求

爱国主义体现了人民群众对自己祖国的深厚感情，反映了个人对祖国的依存关系，是人们对自己的故土家园、民族和文化的归属感、认同感、尊严感与荣誉感的统一。它是调节个人与祖国之间关系的道德要求、政治原则和法律规范，也是民族精神的核心。

1. 爱国主义的内涵

第一，爱国主义是一种深厚的情感。

我们每个人都要在社会中生存，都要获得生存发展的物质资料，都要寻求慰藉心灵的精神家园，而这一切首先源于祖国。所以，我们把祖国称为"母亲"，失去祖国母亲，人们就是无家可归的流浪儿。祖国母亲的繁荣富强需要我们每一个人倾注爱的力量。但更重要的是，我们需要祖国，祖国也需要我们去爱，值得我们去爱。

Our love for our motherland is selfless, whether our motherland is poor or strong, bullied or proud. During the Opium War and the War of Resistance against Japan, our motherland and people suffered abuse and devastation from foreign powers, and countless patriots and people of lofty ideals sacrificed their precious lives. The poor motherland needs us to change, the rich and powerful motherland needs us to create. As the famous Hungarian poet Petofi said: "Even if the world gives me treasure and honor, I will not leave my motherland. Because even though my motherland is in disgrace, I still like, love and bless my motherland."

Second, patriotism is a moral requirement, political principle and legal norm.

Patriotism is not only people's deep feelings towards their motherland, but also a moral requirement, political principle and legal norm. It is also a moral quality that we as a person and a qualified citizen should possess and a norm of conduct that we should abide by. Napoleon once said: "Patriotism is the first virtue of civilized people" "What is the highest morality of mankind? That is patriotism." Mr. Xu Teli, Mao Zedong's teacher, once said: "The people not only have the right to love their country, but also patriotism is an obligation and a glory." Therefore, patriotism embodies not only the moral level of individuals, but also the responsibilities and obligations that individuals should fulfill. It is an important legal norm of our country, a political foundation to unite the people of all nationalities, and a principle to measure the political attitude of every Chinese.

我们对祖国的爱是无私的，无论祖国是贫弱还是富强，是遭受欺凌还是扬眉吐气。在鸦片战争和抗日战争时期，我们的祖国和人民饱受外国列强的凌辱和蹂躏，无数爱国者和仁人志士献出了他们的宝贵生命。祖国贫弱，需要我们去改变；祖国富强，需要我们去创造。正如匈牙利著名诗人裴多菲所说："纵使世界给我珍宝和荣誉，我也不愿离开我的祖国。因为纵使我的祖国在耻辱之中，我还是喜欢、热爱、祝福我的祖国。"

第二，爱国主义是一种道德要求、政治原则和法律规范。

爱国主义不仅是人们对祖国母亲的深厚情感，更是一种道德要求、政治原则和法律规范，是我们作为一个人、一个合格的公民应该具备的道德品质和应该遵守的行为规范。拿破仑曾说："爱国是文明人的首要美德""人类最高的道德是什么？那就是爱国之心。"毛泽东的老师徐特立先生也曾经说过："人民不仅有权爱国，而且爱国是个义务，是一种光荣。"因此，爱国不仅体现了个人的道德水平，更是个人应当履行的责任和义务，是我国重要的法律规范，还是团结各族人民的政治基础和衡量每个中国人政治态度的重要原则。

Third, the connotation of patriotism in the new era.

Under the background of the new era, the patriotism has not only inherited the outstanding tradition of patriotism in history, but also absorbed the spirit of the new era and enriched its connotation. Building and developing socialism with Chinese characteristics has become the theme of patriotism in the new era. At the present stage, patriotism is mainly manifested in carrying forward the national spirit and the spirit of the times, dedicating oneself to building and defending the cause of socialist modernization, and dedicating oneself to the cause of promoting the reunification of the motherland. Next, we will analyze the connotations of patriotism in the new era from four aspects.

The first one is the consistency of patriotism and love for socialism.

Patriotism is a historical category. It has different contents in different periods and stages of social development. In contemporary China, patriotism is first reflected in the love for socialist China, patriotism and love for socialism are unified. This unification is the inevitable result of China's historical development.

The destiny of modern China since the Opium War of 1840 faces two major contemporary issues: first, overthrowing the rule of imperialism and feudalism and achieving national independence and people's liberation; Second, completely changing the state of poverty and backwardness, and achieving prosperity of the country and common prosperity for the people as masters of the country. These are two major contemporary issues

第三，新时期爱国主义的内涵。

在新的时代背景下，爱国主义既继承了历史上爱国主义的优秀传统，又吸纳了鲜活的时代精神，内涵更加丰富。建设和发展中国特色社会主义成为新时期爱国主义的主题。现阶段，爱国主义主要表现为弘扬民族精神与时代精神，献身于建设和保卫社会主义现代化事业，献身于促进祖国统一的事业。下面从四个方面分析新时期爱国主义的内涵。

一是爱国主义与爱社会主义的一致性。

爱国主义是一个历史范畴，在社会发展的不同时期、不同阶段有着不同的时代内容。在当代中国，爱国主义首先体现在对社会主义中国的热爱上，爱国主义与爱社会主义是统一的。这种统一是中国历史发展的必然结果。

1840年鸦片战争以来的近代中国的命运面临着两大时代课题：一是推翻帝国主义和封建主义的统治，实现民族独立和人民解放；二是彻底改变国家贫穷落后的面貌，实现国家繁荣富强、人民当家作主和共同富裕。这是历史向中国的各个政党、阶级、领袖们提出的两大时代课题，无

raised by history to political parties, classes and leaders in China. Numerous people with lofty ideals have explored and tried to solve these issues, but have never been able to find the right answer. The communist Party of China gave a qualified answer in front of these two conyemporary issues. The Communist Party of China led Chinese people to realize national liberation and people's liberation Socialism is not an empty slogan, but the historical choice of the Chinese people. It embodies the fundamental interests of the country, the nation and the people. Since the founding of the People's Republic of China, especially since the reform and opening up, under the leadership of the Communist Party of China, China has gradually become a prosperous socialist country.

Patriotism is not abstract but linked with a specific country. In real society, patriotism is often translated into support for the political system and government policies that safeguard the interests of the nation. China's modern history tells us that only socialism can save China. Since reform and opening up, China's achievements have proved that only reform and opening up can develop China, and only when the path of socialism with Chinese characteristics is opened up under the leadership of the Communist Party of China, can China achieve its international status and prosperity. History has proved that socialism is the fundamental interest of the Chinese people and the Communist Party of China is the strong leadership core of the cause of socialism with Chinese characteristics. Therefore, patriotismis consistent with love for socialism, the Communist Party of China and the peoples gov-

数仁人志士为此探索、尝试，但始终没能找到正确答案。中国共产党人面对这两大时代课题给出了合格答卷。中国共产党领导中国人民实现了民族独立和人民解放，建立了社会主义国家。社会主义不是一句空洞的口号，而是中国人民的历史选择，体现了国家、民族和人民的根本利益。中华人民共和国成立以来，尤其是改革开放以来，在中国共产党的领导下，中国逐渐成为繁荣昌盛的社会主义国家。

爱国不是抽象的，而是与具体国家联系在一起的。在现实社会，爱国主义常常转化为对维护本国本民族利益的政治制度、政府政策的支持。中国近代史的发展历程告诉我们，只有社会主义才能救中国。改革开放以来我国取得的成就证明，只有改革开放才能发展中国，只有在中国共产党的领导下开创中国特色社会主义道路，才有今天中国的国际地位和繁荣富强。历史证明，社会主义是中国人民的根本利益所在，中国共产党是中国特色社会主义事业的坚强领导核心，始终代表着最广大人民群众的根本利益，因此爱国主义和爱社会主义、爱中国共产党、爱人民政府

ernment. Of course, we cannot ask our compatriots in Hong Kong and Macao to stick to the consistency of patriotism and love for socialism, because although Hong Kong and Macao have returned to China, the principle of "one country, two systems" has not changed. Therefore, different people should have different requirements for the consistency of patriotism and love for socialism. As comrade Deng Xiaoping said: "patriotic compatriots from Hong Kong, Macao, Taiwan and overseas cannot be required to support socialism, but at least they cannot oppose the socialist new China."

Patriotism and love for socialism are consistent. While supporting the socialist system, we must translate this enthusiasm into action, strive to learn scientific and cultural knowledge, devote ourselves to socialist modernization, and make our own contribution to building socialism with Chinese characteristics.

The second one is the consistency of patriotism and the support for the reunification of the motherland.

Maintaining unity and opposing separatism are one of the fine traditions of patriotism. In the new era, support for the reunification of the motherland is still an important connotation of patriotism. Although there are different levels of requirements on "the consistency of patriotism and love for socialism", but "the consistency of patriotism and support for the reunification of the motherland" should be the ideological consensus of all Chinese people.

To support for the reunification of the motherland is not only the responsibility of Chinese

是一致的。当然，对于港澳同胞，还不能要求他们坚持爱国主义与爱社会主义的统一，因为香港、澳门虽然已经回归祖国，但"一国两制"的方针没有改变。因此，对爱国主义与爱社会主义统一的问题，要针对不同的人有不同的要求。正如邓小平同志所说："港澳、台湾、海外的爱国同胞，不能要求他们都拥护社会主义，但是至少也不能反对社会主义的新中国。"

爱国主义与爱社会主义是一致的，我们在拥护社会主义制度的同时，还要把这种热情转化为行动，努力学习科学文化知识，积极投身社会主义现代化建设，为建设中国特色社会主义贡献自己的一份力量。

二是爱国主义与拥护祖国统一的一致性。

维护统一、反对分裂是爱国主义的优良传统之一。在新的时代条件下，拥护祖国统一仍是爱国主义的重要内涵。虽然在"爱国主义与爱社会主义的一致性"上有不同层次的要求，但"爱国主义与拥护祖国统一的一致性"应该是所有中华儿女的思想共识。

拥护祖国统一不仅是生活在内地的中国公民的责任，而且是

citizens living on the mainland, but also the responsibility of all Chinese people, including compatriots in Hong Kong, Macao and Taiwan as well as overseas Chinese. A person only by loving his own motherland, and always maintaining the unity of the motherland, can be respected by others.

It is clear that carrying forward patriotism and carrying forward the national spirit and carrying forward the spirit of the times have the same consistency. Carrying forward the national spirit is the deep foundation of patriotism, and carrying forward the spirit of the times is the practical embodiment of patriotism. They are two aspects of the same problem.

The third one is respecting and inheriting the history and culture of the Chinese nation.

Chinese excellent traditional culture is the lifeblood of the Chinese nation spirit, which contains the ideological nutrition and practical wisdom of Chinese nation formed and accumulated from generation to generation. It is the culture gene of the continuation of Chinese nation and also our foothold in world culture, meanwhile, adds confidence and pride to Chinese people and Chinese nation from deep in heart. The understanding and acceptance of the long history and profound culture of the motherland is an important condition for the cultivation and development of people's feelings of patriotism, so we must respect and inherit the history and culture of the Chinese nation, and activate the vitality of the Chinese excellent traditional culture through the spirit of the times. We should carry forward cultural genes, extract

包括港澳台同胞以及海外侨胞在内的全体中华儿女的责任。一个人只有爱自己的祖国，时刻维护祖国的统一，才可能得到他人的尊重。

可见，发扬爱国主义与弘扬民族精神和弘扬时代精神同样具有一致性。弘扬民族精神是爱国主义的深厚基础，弘扬时代精神是爱国主义的现实体现，它们是一个问题的两个方面。

三是尊重和传承中华民族历史和文化。

中华优秀传统文化是中华民族的精神命脉，其中蕴含着中华民族世世代代形成和积累的思想营养和实践智慧，是中华民族得以延续的文化基因，也是我们在世界文化激荡中站稳脚跟的根基，同时增添了中国人民和中华民族内心深处的自信和自豪。对祖国悠久历史、深厚文化的理解和接受是人们爱国主义情感培育和发展的重要条件，所以我们必须尊重和传承中华民族历史和文化，以时代精神激活中华优秀传统文化的生命力，延续文化基因，汲取思想精华，推进中华优秀传统文化创造性转化和创新性发展，在传承与创新中树立和坚

thought essence and promote the creative transformation and development of Chinese excellent traditional culture, and set up correct historical view, national outlook, national viewpoint and cultural view in the inheritance and innovation, enhance Chinese backbone and confidence.

To respect and inherit Chinese excellent traditional culture, we must resolutely oppose historical nihilism and cultural nihilism. For a long time, some people at home and abroad use the cover of the so-called "review history again" to deny modern Chinese revolutionary history, the history of the Communist Party of China and the People's Republic of China. They smear heroes, denigrate revolutionary leaders, attempting to confuse and disturb Chinese people. They fundamentally deny the guiding position of Marxism and the historical inevitability of Chinese socialism, and object the leadership of the Communist Party of China. We must keep a clear understanding of this, do not forget the past and belittle ourselves. The motherland is the people's most solid reliance, the hero is the most shining coordinates of the nation. "Ancestor LiBei's heroic spirit is full of heaven and earth, and has been respected by thousands of generations." A nation of promise cannot live without heroes, a country of promise cannot live without pioneers. We should hold reverence for the heroes of the Chinese nation, and consciously inherit the splendid history and culture of the Chinese nation.

The fourth one is adhering to the principle of basing on the nation and facing the world.

Adhering to patriotism in the new era re-

持正确的历史观、民族观、国家观、文化观，增强中国人的骨气和底气。

尊重和传承中华优秀传统文化，必须坚决反对历史虚无主义和文化虚无主义。长期以来，国内外一些人打着所谓"重评历史"的幌子，否定近现代中国革命历史、中国共产党历史和中华人民共和国历史，抹黑英雄，诋毁革命领袖，企图混淆视听、扰乱人心，从根本上否定马克思主义的指导地位和中国走向社会主义的历史必然性，否定中国共产党的领导。对此我们必须保持清醒认识，不能数典忘祖、妄自菲薄。祖国是人民最坚实的依靠，英雄是民族最闪亮的坐标。"天地英雄气，千秋尚凛然。"一个有希望的民族不能没有英雄，一个有前途的国家不能没有先锋。我们要对中华民族的英雄心怀崇敬，自觉传承中华民族辉煌灿烂的历史文化。

四是坚持立足民族又面向世界。

坚持新时代的爱国主义，要

quires us to correctly handle the dialectical and unified relationship between basing on the nation and facing the world, and integrate the promotion of patriotism with the expansion of opening up. We should not only respect the historical characteristics and cultural traditions of all countries and the development path chosen by all peoples, seek wisdom and absorb nutrition from different civilizations, and enhance the vitality of Chinese civilization, but also actively advocate seeking common ground while reserving differences, exchanging and learning from each other, promote common progress of different countries and civilizations.

Adhering to the principle of basing on the nation and maintaining the subjectivity of national development requires us to continue to uphold and carry forward the spirit of patriotism in the context of globalization. Economic globalization is the inevitable trend of world economic development, but it is not equal to the integration of global politics and culture. Under the condition of economic globalization, the country is still the supreme organizational form of national existence and an independent subject in international social activities. As long as the country continues to exist, patriotism will have a solid foundation. In the process of participating in economic globalization, we must firmly safeguard the interests of our country, which needs the support of patriotism. Under the background of economic globalization, some western people advocate political integration

求我们正确处理立足民族与面向世界的辩证统一关系，把弘扬爱国主义精神与扩大对外开放结合起来，既要尊重各国的历史特点、文化传统，尊重各国人民选择的发展道路，从不同文明中寻求智慧、汲取营养，增强中华文明的生机和活力，又要积极倡导求同存异、交流互鉴，促进不同国度、不同文明共同进步。

坚持立足民族，维护国家发展主体性，在全球化背景下仍需坚持与弘扬爱国主义精神。经济全球化是世界经济发展的必然趋势，但不等于全球政治、文化一体化。在经济全球化的条件下，国家仍然是民族存在的最高组织形式，是国际社会活动中的独立主体。只要国家继续存在，爱国主义就有坚实的基础。在参与经济全球化的过程中，必须坚定地捍卫自己国家的利益，这就更需要爱国主义的支撑。在经济全球化背景下，西方一些人极力鼓吹政治一体化和文化一体化，实际上是企图借经济全球化推行本国的政治制度和价值观念，损害别国的主权和尊严。世界是丰富多彩的，不能以一个或几个国家的

and cultural integration vigorously. In fact, they are trying to promote their own political system and values by means of economic globalization, thus undermining the sovereignty and dignity of other countries. The world is rich and colorful. We cannot measure the diversity of the world by the political system, values and ideology of one or more countries. To unify the world with a political system, values and ideology is not only an infringement on other countries, but also impossible. It will only endanger the peace and development of the world. In the process of participating in economic globalization, we must keep a clear understanding, not only make full use of the opportunities provided by economic globalization to develop ourselves, but also resolutely safeguard the sovereignty and dignity of the country, and adhere to and develop our own political system and national culture in accordance with our national conditions.

We must face the world and build a community of human destiny. Persisting in promoting the construction of a community of human destiny is an important part of the basic strategy of upholding and developing socialism with Chinese characteristics in the new era. In today's world, no country can meet the challenges facing mankind alone, nor can any country retreat to self-enclosed islands. Jointly building a world of lasting peace, universal security, common prosperity, openness, inclusiveness, cleanliness and beauty is the common interest and common value pursuit of all mankind. The

政治制度、价值观念和意识形态来衡量多样性的世界。用一种政治制度、价值观念和意识形态去统一世界，不仅是对别国的侵害，而且是根本行不通的，只会危害世界的和平与发展。在参与经济全球化的过程中，我们一定要保持清醒的认识，既要充分利用经济全球化所提供的机遇发展自己，又要坚决维护国家的主权和尊严，按照本国国情坚持、发展自己的政治制度和民族文化。

我们必须面向世界，构建人类命运共同体。坚持推动构建人类命运共同体，是新时代坚持和发展中国特色社会主义基本方略的重要内容。当今世界，没有哪个国家能够独自应对人类面临的各种挑战，也没有哪个国家能够退回到自我封闭的孤岛。共同建设一个持久和平、普遍安全、共同繁荣、开放包容、清洁美丽的世界，是全人类的共同利益和共同价值追求。构建人类命运共同体的理念源于中国，属于世界，

idea of building a community of human destiny originates from China and belongs to the world. It is a "Symphony Concerto" between China and the world. The dreams of the Chinese people are closely linked with those of the people of other countries. The realization of the Chinese Dream cannot be separated from a peaceful international environment and a stable international order. Contemporary Chinese patriotism inherits and develops the excellent tradition of Chinese cultural of harmony and peace-loving. It actively advocates socialist patriotism at home, adheres to the principle of international exchanges of equality, mutual benefit and peaceful coexistence abroad, and actively safeguards international peace and civilized harmony. Carrying forward the spirit of world-oriented patriotism in the new era means that we should have a broader world mind and global vision, provide Chinese wisdom for safeguarding the common interests of mankind and promoting the development and progress of human civilization, and always be the builder of world peace, contributor of global development and defender of international order.

2. The Requirement of Patriotism

First, we must love the great rivers and mountains of our motherland.

The great rivers and mountains of the motherland are not only natural scenery, but also the basic carrier of sovereignty, wealth, national development and progress. But with the advent of the industrial age, our ecological

是中国与世界的"交响协奏"。中国人民的梦想同其他国家人民的梦想息息相关，实现中国梦离不开和平的国际环境和稳定的国际秩序。当代中国的爱国主义继承并发扬了中华文化协和万邦、热爱和平的优秀传统，对内积极倡导社会主义的爱国主义，对外主张平等互利、和平共处的国际交往原则，积极维护国际和平与文明和谐。新时代弘扬面向世界的爱国主义精神，意味着我们要有更加宽广的世界胸怀和全球视野，为维护人类共同利益、推动人类文明发展进步提供中国智慧，始终做世界和平的建设者、全球发展的贡献者、国际秩序的维护者。

2. 爱国主义的要求

第一，爱祖国的大好河山。

祖国的大好河山，不只是自然风光，而且是主权、财富、民族发展和进步的基本载体。但随着工业化时代的到来，我们的生态环境遭到了严重破坏，茂密的

environment has been severely damaged. Dense forests have become barren land, the thick green steppes have been degraded into deserts, and rivers and skies are no longer so clear and blue. Let's act in the name of patriotism, love our environment, protect our nature.

Loving the great rivers and mountains of our motherland requires us not only to protect the beautiful environment of our motherland, but also to oppose secession and safeguard the reunification of the motherland. In 2005, China passed the *Anti-Secession Law* to safeguard the territorial integrity and unity of the motherland, which is the sacred mission and duty-bound responsibility of every Chinese.

Second, we must love our own fellow countryman.

The people of all nationalities are the creators of the great motherland. The most fundamental thing to love our motherland is to love the people of all nationalities who have created a long history and splendid civilization. Our country is a united family composed of 56 nationalities. "56 constellations, 56 flowers, 56 ethnic brothers and sisters are one family", Song Zuying's Love Our China is deeply loved by the Chinese people, because it is filled with the passion of loving motherland, brotherly nation.

Third, we must love the splendid culture of the motherland.

The broad concept of nationality is equivalent to the state. If we say the Chinese nation,

森林成为不毛之地，浓绿的草原退化为荒漠，河流和天空也不再那样清澈和蔚蓝。让我们行动起来，以爱国主义的名义，爱护我们的环境，保护我们的自然。

爱祖国的大好河山不仅要求我们保护祖国的美好环境，也要求我们反对分裂，维护祖国统一。2005年我国通过《反分裂国家法》，维护祖国领土的完整和统一，是每个中国人的神圣使命和义不容辞的责任。

第二，爱自己的骨肉同胞。

各族人民都是伟大祖国的创造者，爱祖国最根本的是热爱那些创造悠久历史和灿烂文明的各族人民。我们国家是一个由56个民族组成的团结的大家庭。"56个星座，56枝花，56个民族兄弟姐妹是一家"，宋祖英的这首《爱我中华》深得国人喜爱，就是因为其中洋溢着爱祖国母亲、爱兄弟民族之情。

第三，爱祖国的灿烂文化。

广义的民族概念，等同于国家，如我们所说的中华民族，指

it means China. There are four elements that constitute the nation: a common language; a common territory; a common economic life; and a common psychological and cultural quality. Among them, the common psychological and cultural quality is the most stable and core element of the nation. Our Chinese nation is an ancient nation with 5,000 years of historical civilization. In the historical development of the Chinese nation, Chinese People have made brilliant cultural achievements. The world-famous four inventions, the majestic Great Wall, the profound Confucian culture, the wonderful Tang poetry, Song Ci, Yuan Qu, etc., are just as numerous as the stars in the sky.

Fourth, we must love our own country.

The motherland is not abstract. It is a specific country composed of elements such as land, people, institutions, and culture. To love the motherland must focus on the future and destiny of the country. We must put the interests of the country and the people in the first place, and contribute to the independence and prosperity of the country and the liberation and happiness of the people.

II.The Ways to Become a Loyal Patriot

1.Safeguarding and Promoting the Reunification of the Motherland

Maintaining unity and opposing division are the patriotic traditions of the Chinese nation, and one of the rich connotations of patriotism in the new era. Therefore, to be a loyal patriot, we

的就是中国。构成民族的要素有四个：共同语言、共同地域、共同经济生活、共同心理文化素质。其中，共同心理文化素质是构成民族最稳定、最核心的要素。我们中华民族是一个具有5000多年文明的古老民族，在其历史发展中，华夏儿女取得了光辉灿烂的文化成就。举世瞩目的四大发明，雄伟壮丽的万里长城，博大精深的儒家文化，美妙绝伦的唐诗、宋词、元曲，等等，就像天上璀璨的星星一样数不胜数。

第四，爱自己的国家。

祖国不是抽象的，它是由国土、人民、制度、文化等要素构成的具体的国家。爱祖国就要心系国家的前途和命运，就要把国家和人民的利益摆在首位，为国家的独立和富强、为人民的解放和幸福贡献力量。

二、如何做忠诚的爱国者

1. 维护和推进祖国统一

维护统一、反对分裂是中华民族的爱国主义传统，也是新时期爱国主义的丰富内涵之一。因此，要做一个忠诚的爱国者，就

must do our best to promote the reunification of the motherland and national unity. This is the highest interest of the Chinese nation, and also the responsibility and obligation of each of us. Then, How to maintain and promote the reunification of our motherland?

First, to promote the reunification of the motherland, we must maintain the long-term prosperity and stability of Hong Kong and Macao.

Hong Kong and Macao are always closely linked with the mainland of China. To realize the Chinese dream of the great rejuvenation of the Chinese nation, it is necessary for Hong Kong and Macao to adhere to complementary advantages and common development with the mainland of China. Compatriots of Hong Kong and Macao should adhere to the principle of guarding and helping each other and working hand in hand with the mainland people. We should always accurately grasp the relationship between "one country" and "two systems". "One country" is the essence, and only when it is deep-rooted can it flourish; while "one country" is the root, only when it is solid can it flourish. We should unswervingly implement the principle of "one country, two systems", organically combine maintaining the central government's overall governance over Hong Kong and Macao Special Administrative Regions with safeguarding the high degree of autonomy of the Special Administrative Regions, ensure that the policy of "one country, two systems" remains

必须尽自己所能，促进祖国统一和民族团结，这是中华民族的最高利益所在，也是我们每一个人应尽的责任和义务。那么，如何维护和推进祖国统一？

第一，推进祖国统一，必须保持香港、澳门的长期繁荣稳定。

香港、澳门与内地的命运始终紧密相连，实现中华民族伟大复兴的中国梦，需要香港、澳门与内地坚持优势互补、共同发展，需要港澳同胞与内地人民坚持守望相助、携手共进。要始终准确把握"一国"和"两制"的关系。"一国"是根，根深才能叶茂；"一国"是本，本固才能枝荣。要坚定不移贯彻"一国两制"方针，把维护中央对香港、澳门特别行政区全面管治权和保障特别行政区高度自治权有机结合起来，确保"一国两制"方针不会变、不动摇，确保"一国两制"实践不变形、不走样；要始终依照宪法和基本法办事。《中华人民共和国宪法》和《香港特别行政区基本法》共同构成香港特别行政区的宪制基础。要把中央依法行使权力和特别行政区履行主体责任有机结合起来，不断完善与基本法实施相关的制度和

unchanged and unshakable, and ensure that the practice of "one country, two systems" remains unchanged. We should deal with things in accordance with Law and Basic Law. The Constitution of the People's Republic of China and the Basic Law of the Hong Kong Special Administrative Region constitute the constitutional basis of the Region. We need to integrate the exercise of power by the central government according to the law with the exercise of the principal responsibility of Special Administrative Regions, and constantly improve the systems and mechanisms related to the implementation of the Basic Law. We should organically combine the strong backing role of the mainland of China with enhancing the competitiveness of Hong Kong and Macao to develop the economy and improve people's livelihood. We should always maintain a harmonious and stable social environment. "Harmony leads to auspiciousness, and obedience leads to difference". Under the background of the deep adjustment of the global economic pattern and the increasingly fierce international competition, only by focusing on the overall situation, rational communication, cohesion of common understanding and cooperation, can we gradually solve the problem and let the compatriots of Hong Kong and Macao share the historical responsibility of national rejuvenation and the great glory of prosperity and strength of the motherland.

Second, the peaceful reunification is in the best interests of the Chinese nation, including Taiwan compatriots.

机制。要把发挥内地坚强后盾作用和提高港澳自身竞争力有机结合起来，发展经济，改善民生。要始终维护和谐稳定的社会环境。"和气致祥，乖气致异。"在全球经济格局深度调整、国际竞争日趋激烈的背景下，只有着眼大局，理性沟通，凝聚共识，和衷共济，才能逐步解决问题，让香港、澳门同胞同祖国人民共担民族复兴的历史责任、共享祖国繁荣富强的伟大荣光。

第二，和平统一最符合包括台湾同胞在内的中华民族的根本利益。

We should grasp the overall situation of cross-Straits relations from the perspective of the overall interests of the Chinese nation. and grasp the future of cross-Straits relations under the premise of a clear understanding of historical trends. We should adhere to enhancing mutual trust, benign interaction, seeking common ground while reserving differences, and be pragmatic and enterprising. Thus we can promote the development of cross-strait relations, achieve more positive results, strive to enhance the well-being of the people on both sides of the Straits and improve the cognition of the fate community of cross-Straits, constantly broaden the road of peaceful development of cross-Straits relations.

Third, the one-China principle must be adhered to.

The one-China principle is the political basis of cross-Straits relations. The "1992 Consensus", which embodies the one-China principle, clearly defines the fundamental nature of cross-Straits relations and is the key to ensuring the peaceful development of cross-Straits relations. The two sides should always adhere to the common position of the "1992 Consensus" and form a clearer common understanding on the principle of consolidating and maintaining the one-China framework, and seek common ground while reserving differences on this basis. The fact that the mainland and Taiwan belong to the same China and are inseparable as a whole has never changed and cannot be changed. "Peaceful reunification,

要从中华民族整体利益的高度把握两岸关系大局，在认清历史发展趋势的前提下把握两岸关系的前途，坚持增进互信、良性互动、求同存异、务实进取，促进两岸关系发展取得更多积极成果，努力增进两岸人民福祉，提高对两岸命运共同体的认知，不断拓宽两岸关系和平发展的道路。

第三，坚持一个中国原则。

一个中国原则是两岸关系的政治基础。体现一个中国原则的"九二共识"明确界定了两岸关系的根本性质，是确保两岸关系和平发展的关键。两岸双方应始终坚持"九二共识"的共同立场，在巩固和维护一个中国框架这一原则问题上形成更为清晰的共同认知，并在此基础上求同存异。大陆和台湾同属一个中国，是不可分割的整体，这个事实从未改变，也不可能改变。"和平统一、一国两制"是解决台湾问题的基本方针。两岸双方应本着对历史、对人民负责任的态度，以中华民族整体利益为重，把握好两

one country, two systems" is the basic principle for resolving the Taiwan issue. Both sides of the Straits should take a responsible attitude towards history and the people, put the overall interests of the Chinese nation first, grasp the overall situation of peaceful development of cross-Straits relations, and push forward cross-Straits relations in the right direction.

Fourth, the cross-Straits communication and cooperation must be promoted.

On the basis of the overall stability of cross-Straits relations, there is broad space for cross-Straits communication and cooperation in various fields. The two sides should take more positive measures to deepen cooperation in the fields of economy, science and technology, culture and education, provide more policy support and create more convenient conditions so as to broaden cooperation areas, improve cooperation level, produce greater benefits and open up new prospects for peaceful development of cross-Straits relations.

Fifth, the unity and struggle of compatriots across the Straits must be promoted.

The compatriots on both sides of the Straits are brothers of common destiny. They are a family whose blood is thicker than water. They share common blood, common culture, common connection and common vision. this is an important force to promote mutual understanding, joint efforts and progress of the compatriots on both sides of the Straits. Both sides of the Straits should uphold the concept of "one family on both sides of the Straits" and work together to consolidate and

岸和平发展大局，推动两岸关系沿着正确方向不断迈进。

第四，推进两岸交流合作。

在两岸关系大局稳定的基础上，两岸各领域交流合作有着广阔空间。两岸双方应该为深化经济、科技、文化、教育等领域合作采取更多积极举措，提供更多政策支持，创造更加便利的条件，以拓宽合作领域，提高合作水平，产生更大效益，开创两岸关系和平发展新前景。

第五，促进两岸同胞团结奋斗。

两岸同胞是命运与共的骨肉兄弟，是血浓于水的一家人，有着共同的血脉、共同的文化、共同的联结、共同的愿景，这是推动两岸同胞相互理解、携手同心、一起前进的重要力量。两岸双方应秉持"两岸一家亲"的理念，顺势而为、齐心协力、心心相印、守望相助，巩固和扩大两岸关系发展成果。凡是有利于增

expand the achievements of cross-Straits relations. We should do our best to promote the common well-being of compatriots across the Straits. We should effectively protect the rights and interests of Taiwan compatriots, unite Taiwan compatriots, safeguard and build a common homeland for the Chinese nation.

Sixth, separatist attempts for "Taiwan independence" must be opposed.

Unity leads to being strong, splitting leads to being chaotic". The separatist forces of "Taiwan independence" and their separatist activities remain a real threat to peace in the Taiwan Strait. We must continue to oppose and curb any form of "Taiwan independence" separatist ideas and activities without compromise. The separatist acts of "Taiwan independence" undermine national sovereignty and territorial integrity, destroy peace and stability in the Taiwan Strait, provoke confrontational tensions across the Straits and damage the common interests of compatriots across the Straits, and will inevitably lead to complete failure. We must firmly safeguard national sovereignty and territorial integrity and will never tolerate the repetition of the historical tragedy of national division. All activities aimed at splitting our motherland will be firmly opposed by all the Chinese people. We have firm will, full confidence and sufficient capacity to thwart any form of "Taiwan independence" separatist plot. We will never allow anyone, any organization or any political party to separate any piece of Chinese territory from China at any time or in any form. *The Anti-Secession Law* should be implemented, and all words and deeds

进两岸同胞共同福祉的事情，我们都应尽最大努力做好。要切实保障台湾同胞的权益，团结台湾同胞，维护好、建设好中华民族的共同家园。

第六，反对"台独"分裂图谋。

"统则强、分必乱"。"台独"分裂势力及其分裂活动仍然是对台海和平的现实威胁，必须继续反对和遏制任何形式的"台独"分裂主张和活动，不能有任何妥协。"台独"分裂行径损害国家主权、领土完整，破坏台海和平稳定，挑动两岸对立对抗，损害两岸同胞共同利益，必然走向彻底失败。我们要坚决维护国家主权和领土完整，绝不容忍国家分裂的历史悲剧重演。一切分裂祖国的活动都必将遭到全体中国人民的坚决反对。我们有坚定的意志、充分的信心、足够的能力挫败任何形式的"台独"分裂图谋。我们绝不允许任何人、任何组织、任何政党在任何时候、以任何形式、把任何一块中国领土从中国分裂出去。要贯彻《反分裂国家法》，旗帜鲜明地反对一切损害两岸关系的言行。

harmful to cross—Straits relations should be clearly opposed.

To realize the great rejuvenation of the Chinese nation is the common dream of all Chinese people. As long as all Chinese, including compatriots from Hong Kong, Macao and Taiwan, comply with the historical trend, share the national justice and firmly grasp the national destiny in their own hands, they will surely be able to create a bright future for the great rejuvenation of the Chinese nation. College students should comply with the trend of peaceful development of cross—Straits relations, shoulder the historic task of realizing the great rejuvenation of the nation, and make their own contributions to promote the peaceful development of cross—Straits relations and realize the reunification of the motherland.

2.The Promotion of National Unity

First, we should understand the importance of national issues.

Handling this issue well is a major event concerning the reunification of the motherland, the consolidation of the frontier, national unity, social stability, the long—term stability of the country and the prosperity of the Chinese nation.

Second, we should deepen our understanding of the Party's ethnic theory and policies, earnestly study the state's laws and regulations on ethnic affairs, thoroughly understand the development history of the Chinese nation's "pluralistic integration", and firmly adhere to the ideological concept that "the Han people cannot live without the ethnic minorities, the ethnic minorities cannot live without the Han people, and the ethnic minori-

实现中华民族伟大复兴，是全体中国人共同的梦想。只要包括港澳台同胞在内的全体中华儿女顺应历史大势、共担民族大义，把民族命运牢牢掌握在自己手中，就一定能够共创中华民族伟大复兴的美好未来。大学生要顺应两岸关系和平发展的潮流，担当起实现民族伟大复兴的历史重任，为推动两岸关系和平发展、实现祖国统一做出自己的贡献。

2. 促进民族团结

第一，认识民族问题的重要性。

处理好这一问题，是关系祖国统一和边疆巩固的大事，是关系民族团结和社会稳定的大事，是关系国家长治久安和中华民族繁荣昌盛的大事。

第二，深化对党的民族理论和民族政策的认识，认真学习国家关于民族事务的法律法规，深入了解中华民族"多元一体"的发展历史，坚定"汉族离不开少数民族，少数民族离不开汉族，各少数民族之间也相互离不开"的思想观念。要牢固树立正确的祖国观、民族观，增强对伟大祖

ties cannot live without each other". We should firmly establish a correct view of the motherland and the nation, strengthen the recognition of the great motherland, the Chinese nation, the Chinese culture and the socialist road with Chinese characteristics. We should foster a strong sense of the Chinese nation's community, strengthen communication among all ethnic groups, and promote common unity, struggle, prosperity and development of all ethnic groups. In the daily life of contacting and communicating with compatriots of other nationalities, we should safeguard and develop the equal, solidarity, mutual assistance and harmonious relations among all nationalities. We should respect the traditional culture, customs and religious beliefs of brotherly nationalities, say more words that are conducive to national unity and social stability, and do more things that are conducive to national unity and social stability. We should not say anything harmful to our national feelings or do anything harmful to national unity and social stability.

Third, we should resolutely oppose acts of national separatism. We should recognize the sinister intentions and reactionary nature of various separatist forces, such as "Tibetan independence" and "Xinjiang independence", adhere to principles, distinguish right from wrong, do not believe in rumors, do not spread rumors, do not be incited by separatists, do not participate in illegal and criminal activities, and fight resolutely against acts that undermine national unity. At critical junctures and critical moments, we should stand firm and stand up, dare to fight against various separatist

国的认同、对中华民族的认同、对中华文化的认同、对中国特色社会主义道路的认同。要铸牢中华民族共同体意识，加强各民族交往交流交融，促进各民族共同团结奋斗、共同繁荣发展。在与其他民族同胞接触交往的日常生活中，要维护和发展各民族平等、团结、互助、和谐的关系，要尊重兄弟民族的传统文化、风俗习惯和宗教信仰，多说有利于民族团结、有利于社会稳定的话，多做有利于民族团结、有利于社会稳定的事，不说伤害民族感情的话，不做不利于民族团结和社会稳定的事。

第三，坚决反对民族分裂主义行径。认清"藏独"和"疆独"等各种分裂主义势力的险恶用心和反动本质，坚持原则、明辨是非，不信谣、不传谣，不受分裂分子挑拨煽动，不参与违法犯罪活动，与破坏民族团结的行为作坚决斗争。在危急关头、关键时刻，要立场坚定、挺身而出，敢于同各种分裂活动作斗争，坚决捍卫民族团结进步、共同繁荣发展的大好局面，筑牢各族人民共

activities, resolutely safeguard the good situation of national unity, progress and common prosperity and development, and build a steel wall for the people of all nationalities to jointly safeguard the reunification of our motherland, national unity and social stability.

3. The Enhancement of the National Security Awareness

First, a new concept of national security must be established.

Generally speaking, national security refers to a stable and orderly statement of a country without being threatened or destroyed by internal or external threats. The contents of traditional national security concept include political security and national defense security, namely sovereign independence, territorial security, political stability, etc.

Political security and national defense security are the pillars and cores of national security. Without political security and national defense security, there can be no national security at all. Political security means that the country's political system and political situation are stable and not subverted by hostile forces at home and abroad. The contents of the new national security concept include economic security, scientific and technological security, cultural security, ecological security and social public security.

Second, the obligation of safeguarding national security must be consciously fulfilled.

The first one is to master the knowledge of national security law. According to *The National Security Law of the People's Republic of China*, acts of endangering national security refer to the

同维护祖国统一、维护民族团结、维护社会稳定的钢铁长城。

3. 增强国家安全意识

第一，确立新的国家安全观。

国家安全一般是指一个国家不受内部和外部的威胁、破坏而保持稳定有序的状态。传统的国家安全观的内容包括政治安全和国防安全，即主权独立、领土安全、政治稳定等。

政治安全和国防安全是国家安全的支柱与核心。没有政治安全和国防安全，就根本不可能有国家安全。政治安全是指国家的政治制度和政治形势保持稳定，不受国内外敌对势力的破坏和颠覆。新国家安全观的内容包括经济安全、科技安全、文化安全、生态安全、社会公共安全。

第二，自觉履行维护国家安全的义务。

一是掌握国家安全法律知识。《中华人民共和国国家安全法》规定：危害国家安全的行为，是指境外机构、组织、个人实施

acts endangering the national security of the People's Republic of China, which are carried out by foreign institutions, organizations or individuals, or are directed or aided by others, or are carried out by domestic organizations or individuals in collaboration with foreign institutions, organizations and individuals.

The second one is to consciously fulfill the obligation of safeguarding national security. The Constitution of our country clearly stipulates the basic obligation of citizens to safeguard national security. *The National Security Law the People's Republic of China, The Law on the Conservation of State Secrets the People's Republic of China, The National Defense Law the People's Republic of China* and *The Military Service Law the People's Republic of China* clearly stipulate the specific legal obligations of citizens to safeguard national security.

① The obligation to perform military service and join the militia in accordance with the law. Citizens of the People's Republic of China, regardless of nationality, race, occupation, family origin, religious belief and educational level, are obliged to perform military service in accordance with the provisions of *The Military Service Law of the People's Republic of China*. Persons with serious physical defects or severe disabilities who are not suitable for military service shall be exempted from performing military service. Persons deprived of political rights according to law shall not perform military service.

② The obligation to keep state secrets. The Constitution of our country clearly stipulates that

或者指使、资助他人实施的，或者境内组织、个人与境外机构、组织、个人相勾结实施的危害中华人民共和国国家安全的行为。

二是自觉履行维护国家安全的义务。我国宪法明确规定了公民维护国家安全的基本义务，《中华人民共和国国家安全法》《中华人民共和国保守国家秘密法》《中华人民共和国国防法》《中华人民共和国兵役法》等法律明确规定了公民维护国家安全的各项具体的法律义务。

①依照法律服兵役和参加民兵组织的义务。中华人民共和国公民，不分民族、种族、职业、家庭出身、宗教信仰和教育程度，都有义务依照《中华人民共和国兵役法》的规定服兵役。有严重生理缺陷或者严重残疾不适合服兵役的人，免服兵役。依照法律被剥夺政治权利的人，不得服兵役。

②保守国家秘密的义务。我国宪法明确规定，公民有保守国

citizens have the duty to keep state secrets. *The Law on the conservation of State Secrets of the People's Republic of China, The National Security Law of the People's Republic of China* and *The National Defense Law of the People's Republic of China* specify the obligation of citizens to keep state secrets.

③ The obligation to provide convenience or other assistance. Citizens and organizations shall provide convenient conditions or other assistance for the work of national security.

④ The obligation to report the acts of endengering state security and provide truthful evidence. Citizens who discover acts of endangering state security shall report them directly or through their organizations to the state security organs or public security organs in a timely manner; when the state security organs investigate and understand the situation of endangering state security and collect relevant evidence, citizens and relevant organizations shall provide truthful information and shall not refuse to do so.

⑤ The obligation not to illegally hold and use special spy equipment. Any citizen or organization should keep the state secrets known to them. No individual or organization shall illegally hold documents, materials and other articles belonging to state secrets, no individual or organization shall illegally hold or use special spy equipment such as eavesdropping and secret photographing photographs.

家秘密的义务。《中华人民共和国保守国家秘密法》《中华人民共和国国家安全法》《中华人民共和国国防法》等法律具体规定了公民保守国家秘密的义务。

③提供便利条件或其他协助的义务。公民和组织应当为国家安全工作提供便利条件或者其他协助。

④及时报告危害国家安全的行为，并如实提供证据的义务。公民发现危害国家安全的行为，应当直接或者通过所在组织及时向国家安全机关或者公安机关报告；在国家安全机关调查了解有关危害国家安全的情况、收集有关证据时，公民和有关组织应当如实提供，不得拒绝。

⑤不得非法持有、使用专用间谍器材的义务。任何公民和组织都应当保守所知悉的国家秘密。任何个人和组织都不得非法持有属于国家秘密的文件、资料和其他物品，任何个人和组织都不得非法持有、使用窃听、窃照等专用间谍器材。

Lecture Seven
Let Reform and Innovation Become the Driving Force of Youth Voyage

专题七
让改革创新成为青春远航的动力

Reform and innovation are the most prominent and distinctive features of contemporary China. College students are full of imagination and creativity, and are the fresh force of reform and innovation. They should devote themselves to the motherland, serve the people and realize values in the practice of reform and innovation, so that reform and innovation can become a powerful driving force for the youth voyage.

改革创新是当代中国最突出、最鲜明的特点。大学生富有想象力和创造力，是改革创新的生力军，要在改革创新的实践中奉献祖国、服务人民、实现价值，让改革创新成为青春远航的强大动力。

I. Innovation and Creativity Is the Deepest National Endowment of the Chinese Nation

1.The Chinese Nation Has a National Endowment for Innovation and Creativity

Innovation is the soul of national progress, and the inexhaustible source of a country's prosperity. Early on, our ancestors put forward such ideas as "any circumstance hitting a limit will begin to change, change will in turn lead to an unimpeded state and then lead to continuing". In the long course of history, such ideas as seeking for innovation, changing the profit and loss, reforming the old, keeping pace with the times, and bringing the new with the new have been gradually accumulated as the deepest national endowments of the Chinese nation.

一、创新创造是中华民族最深沉的民族禀赋

1.中华民族具有创新创造的民族禀赋

创新是民族进步的灵魂，是一个国家兴旺发达的不竭源泉。我们的先民很早就提出了"穷则变，变则通，通则久"等与创新创造有关的思想观念。在历史长河中，变通求新、因革损益、革故鼎新、与时俱进、与日偕新等思想观念逐渐积淀为中华民族最深沉的民族禀赋。

On May 4, 2013, Xi Jinping encouraged young people from all walks of life to innovate and create. Among them, "if one can make things better, he will be better every day" is from the Confucian classic "*The Great Learning*". This is the highest level the ancients depict to which gentleman pursue their dreams and constantly perfect themselves. It means "if you can keep it new one day, you should keep it new every day." It emphasizes that we should not stand still and refuse to make progress, and stick to convention. It is the lofty moral character and realm of life that people pursue new things and make a difference.

"Renovating yourself everyday if you can" is a kind of courage. In classical Chinese, the word "gou" means "if". If you can, you need to seek new things every day and have the courage to innovate and create. In the *Book of Documents*, "being a new people" emphasizes the need to create a new generation of people, and points out that "a gentleman should do everything he can", that is to say, a person of high moral character should pursue perfection everywhere. In the *Zhouyi Department of Philosophy*, it says: "the rich are called great cause, and the growing new is called great morality." It means that to have all things is a great cause, and to be continually renewed is a noble virtue. Xi Jinping further pointed out, "Young people are the most dynamic and creative group in society, and they deserve to be at the forefront of innovation and creation" "Young people should have the courage to be the first, to emancipate their minds, to keep pace with the times, to seek truth, to

2013 年 5 月 4 日，习近平同各界优秀青年代表座谈时，鼓励广大青年勇于创新创造。其中"苟日新，日日新，又日新"语出儒家经典《礼记·大学》。这是古人描绘君子追求梦想，不断完善自己要达到的最高境界。意思是"如果能够一天新，就应保持天天新，新了还要更新"，强调不可故步自封，墨守成规，是人们追求新事物革故鼎新的崇高品德和人生境界。

"苟日新"是一种勇气。"苟"字在文言文中意为"如果"。如果可以，就要每日求新，就要勇于创新创造。《尚书》中的"作新民"，强调要造就一代自新的人，指出"君子无所不用其极"，就是说品德高尚的人无处不追求完善。《周易·系辞上传》曰："富有之谓大业，日新之谓盛德。"意思是拥有万物就叫伟大事业，不断更新就叫崇高品德。习近平在讲话中进一步指出，"青年是社会上最富活力、最具创造性的群体，理应走在创新创造前列""广大青年要有敢为人先的锐气，勇于解放思想、与时俱进，敢于上下求索、开拓进取，树立在继承前人的基础上超越前人的雄心壮志，以青春之我，创建青春之国家，青春之

innovate and forge ahead, and build on their ambition to surpass their predecessors on the basis of inheriting them, with youth of themselves to create a country of youth and a nation of youth".

"Renovating yourself from day to day" is a state. It has two meanings: one is the internal self-improvement, another one is the external learning innovation. *The Ancient Text of Zhouyi* said: "The movement of heaven is full of power." This kind of unremitting self-improvement reflects a national character, highlights the spirit of independence, self-esteem, persistent and dauntless. *The analects of Confucius* said: "wasn't it a pleasure to learn and practice often?" We should seek knowledge for pleasure, regard learning as an important way to enrich ourselves and keep moving forward. *The Anthology of Two-Cheng* written by Cheng Hao and Cheng Yi states: "the learning of a gentleman is bound to be new, and the one who learn new things is bound to be improved. The one who does not learn new things will lag behind, and there is no one stand still without moving forward or lagging behind." This is the same as a boat against the current, not to advance is to retreat. "Renovating yourself from day to day" encourages people to strive for new things in the present, never put off till tomorrow what you can do today, and treat everyday with a positive attitude.

"Renovating yourself continuously" is a pursuit. We should not only keep our feet on the ground, but also keep a big dream in our heart, and unify the two in learning practice. "Renovating yourself continuously" lies in reality rather than

民族"。

"日日新"是一种状态,包含两层意思:一是内在的自强不息,二是外在的学习创新。《周易》曰:"天行健,君子以自强不息。"这种自强不息反映了一种民族性格,彰显了独立自主、自尊自强、坚韧不拔、不屈不挠的精神。《论语》云:"学而时习之,不亦说乎?"我们应以求知为愉悦,把学习看作充实自己、不断前进的重要途径。程颢、程颐两兄弟的《二程集》阐述了"君子之学必日新,日新者日进也。不日新者必日退,未有不进而不退者",讲的就是逆水行舟,不进则退的道理。"日日新"激励人们求新于当下,今日事今日做、今日毕,以积极进取之心对待每一天。

"又日新"是一种追求。我们既要脚踏实地,又要心存伟大梦想,将二者统一于学习实践之中。"又日新"在于实而不在于虚,梦在于追而不在于幻。既有

emptiness, and dream lies in pursuit rather than illusion. To have both dream and struggle is the original intention of reform and opening up, the foundation of keeping pace with the times and the essence of scientific development. Major national science and technology projects, such as manned spaceflight, lunar exploration, manned deep-sea submergence and supercomputers, are all fruits of growing talent. Only by growing new every-day, can we deliver the positive energy of youth; only by growing new everyday, can we realize the dream of the great rejuvenation of the Chinese nation.

2.The National Endowment of Innovation and Creativity has Contributed to the Splendid Chinese Civilization

Ancient China made remarkable achieve-ments in astronomy and calendar, mathematics, agriculture, medicine, geography and many other fields. These inventions and creations are close-ly combined with production, providing strong support for the development of agriculture and handicraft industry. British philosopher Bacon once said: printing, gunpowder, the compass these three inventions changed the face and state of the whole world. Data shows that China accounted for 173 of the world's 300 most important inven-tions and discoveries before the 16th century, far more than Europe at that time. In addition, in the fields of literature and art such as poetry, painting and calligraphy, China has also contributed to the world many treasures of human civilization such as Tang poetry, Song Ci and Yuan Qu. In ideology

梦想，又有奋斗，才是改革开放之原意、与时俱进之根本、科学发展之要义。载人航天、探月工程、载人深潜、超级计算机等国家重大科技项目，都是人才日新之果。日新，才能传递青春之正能量；日新，才能实现中华民族伟大复兴之梦想。

2. 创新创造的民族禀赋成就了辉煌灿烂的中华文明

我国古代在天文历法、数学、农学、医学、地理学等众多领域取得了举世瞩目的成就。这些发明创造同生产紧密结合，为农业和手工业发展提供了有力支撑。英国哲学家培根曾说：印刷术、火药、指南针这三项发明改变了整个世界的面貌和状态。资料显示，16世纪以前世界上最重要的300项发明和发现中，我国占173项，远远超过同时代的欧洲。此外，在诗词歌赋、绘画、书法等文学艺术领域，我国也为世界奉献了唐诗、宋词、元曲等诸多人类文明瑰宝。我国在思想文化、社会制度、经济发展、科学技术以及其他许多方面对周边国家和地区发挥了重要的辐射和

and culture, social system, economic development, science and technology and many other aspects, China have played an important role in radiating and guiding its neighbors. The Chinese civilization has made great contributions to the progress of world civilization and a far reaching impact on it. The deep spiritual root lies in the precious spiritual tradition and national endowment of Chinese nation's innovation and creativity.

3.The Communist Party of China has Inherited the Chinese Nation's Endowment for Innovation and Creativity

First, we have fallen far behind the trend of the world's industrial revolution in modern times.

Since modern times, China has gradually turned from a leader to a laggard. One of the important reasons is that China has missed many great development opportunities brought by technological and industrial revolutions. From the middle of the 18th century to the middle of the 19th century, the world industrial revolution began and developed vigorously. At that time, however, China lost the development opportunities in isolation and arrogance, leading to China's economic and technological development greatly lagging behind the pace of world development. From the middle of the 19th century to the middle of the 20th century, China became a semi-colonial and semi-feudal country under the attack of western countries. Under the national survival crisis, the basic material conditions and social and cultural environment for innovation and creation are far from available.

引领作用，中华文明对世界文明进步做出了巨大贡献，产生了深远影响。究其深层精神根源，就在于中华民族创新创造这一宝贵的精神传统和民族禀赋。

3. 中国共产党继承了中华民族创新创造的民族禀赋

第一，近代以来我们远远落后于世界工业革命的浪潮。

近代以来，我国逐渐由领先变为落后，其重要原因之一就是错失了多次科技和产业革命带来的巨大发展机遇。从 18 世纪中叶到 19 世纪中叶的百年间，正是世界工业革命发轫和蓬勃发展的时期，而当时的中国却在闭关锁国、夜郎自大中失去了发展机遇，导致中国经济技术的发展大大落后于世界发展步伐。从 19 世纪中叶到 20 世纪中叶的百年间，在西方坚船利炮的攻击下，中国沦为半殖民地半封建国家，在民族存亡危机之下，根本不具备创新创造的基本物质条件和社会文化环境。

Second, under the leadership of the Communist Party of China, the Chinese people have made great scientific and technological achievements through innovation and creativity.

Since the founding of the People's Republic of China, the central committee of the Communist Party of China has attached great importance to science and technology. It has united and led the scientific and technological workers and the people of all ethnic groups to work hard on their own, and established a comprehensive and independent scientific research system, formed a large-scale scientific and technological team, and made one after another remarkable scientific and technological achievements. Today, the great call of "march to science" is still ringing in our ears, "spring of science" is still spreading sunshine in the sky of the motherland, the strategy of rejuvenating the country through science and education is still providing a powerful drive for the development of science and technology in China.

Some achievements provides a strong support for China's economic and social development, makes a historic contribution to the national defense security, lays an important foundation for our country enhancing the world influence. These achievements are as follows: "Two bombs and one satellite", function theory of several complex variables, theory of terrestrial facies of petroleum, insulin from bovine pancreas artifice, high-temperature superconductivity, abnormal neutrino physics, quantum anomalous Hall effect, nanotechnology, stem cell research, the human genome

第二，中国共产党带领中国人民勇于创新创造，取得了巨大的科技成就。

中华人民共和国成立以来，党中央高度重视科技事业，团结带领广大科技工作者和全国各族人民自力更生、艰苦奋斗，建立起全面独立的科研体系，形成了规模宏大的科学技术队伍，取得了一个又一个举世瞩目的科技成就。今天，"向科学进军"的伟大号召依然在我们的耳畔回响，"科学的春天"依然在祖国的天空播洒阳光，科教兴国战略依然给我国科技事业发展提供着强大的驱动力。

"两弹一星"、多复变函数论、陆相生油理论、人工合成牛胰岛素等成就，高温超导、中微子物理、量子反常霍尔效应、纳米科技、干细胞研究、人类基因组测序等基础科学突破，超级杂交水稻、汉字激光照排、高性能计算机、三峡工程、载人航天、探月工程、移动通信、量子通信、北斗导航、载人深潜、高速铁路、航空母舰等工程技术成果，为我国经济社会发展提供了

sequencing, super hybrid rice, Chinese character laser phototypesetting, high performance computer, Three Gorges Project, manned spaceflight, lunar exploration project, mobile communication, quantum communication, Beidou navigation, manned deep-sea submergence, high-speed rail, aircraft carriers and so on.

II. Reform and Innovation Is the Call of the Times

In contemporary China, social development is inseparable from reform and innovation. Reform and innovation is an important driving force for social development. Adhering to reform and innovation is an urgent requirement of the new era. There are three ways of modernization in the world: increasing national wealth mainly by relying on its abundant natural resources; mainly attached to the capital of developed countries to seek development; take scientific and technological innovation as the basic strategy and substantially improve its capacity for independent innovation.

China's national conditions determine that it is impossible to choose resource-based and dependent development model. Only through comprehensive reform and innovation, taking the innovation-oriented development path, and comprehensively improving the independent innovation ability of the nation, can our country be in an invincible position in the increasingly fierce international competition.

Since the reform and opening up, Chinese people's awareness of innovation has been generally enhanced and their innovation ability has

有力支撑,为国防安全做出了历史性贡献,也为我国提高世界影响力奠定了重要基础。

二、改革创新是时代要求

在当代中国,社会发展离不开改革创新,改革创新是社会发展的重要动力,坚持改革创新是新时代的迫切要求。世界上有三种现代化道路:主要依靠自身丰富的自然资源增加国民财富;主要依附发达国家的资本谋求发展;把科技创新作为基本战略,大幅度提高自主创新能力。

我国的国情决定了不可能选择资源型和依附型发展模式,只有通过全面的改革创新走创新型发展道路,全面提高民族的自主创新能力,才能在日趋激烈的国际竞争中立于不败之地。

改革开放以来,我国人民的创新意识普遍增强,创新能力普遍提高,但与世界发达国家相

been generally improved. However, compared with developed countries, there is still a big gap. Since the third scientific and technological revolution, the world science and technology has developed rapidly. Everything is changing fast. The cultivation of reform innovation ability has become the strong driving force for the development of all countries. Under such international and domestic background, China has followed the pace of the times and established the development concept of independent innovation. To build an innovation-oriented country, China needs to take scientific and technological progress and innovation as the primary driving force for economic and social development, and take the improvement of the capacity for independent innovation as the central link in adjusting the economic structure, changing the economic growth pattern and improving national competitiveness. This is our major development strategy for the future.

1. Innovation has Always been the Primary Driving Force for the Development of Human Society

Since the 16th century, human society has entered an unprecedented period of innovation. In the past few hundred years, mankind has made more innovative achievements in science and technology than in the past several thousand years combined. In particular, since the 18th century, the world has witnessed several major scientific and technological revolutions, such as the birth of modern physics, steam engines and machinery, electricity and transportation, relativity and quan-

比，还存在较大差距。第三次科技革命以来，世界科学技术迅猛发展，可谓瞬息万变，改革创新能力的培养已成为各国发展的强大动力。在这样的国际国内背景下，中国紧跟时代步伐，确立了自主创新的发展理念。我国要建设创新型国家，就要把科技进步和创新作为经济社会发展的首要推动力量，把提高自主创新能力作为调整经济结构、转变经济增长方式、提高国家竞争力的中心环节。这是我们面对未来的重大发展战略。

1. 创新始终是推动人类社会发展的第一动力

16 世纪以来，人类社会进入前所未有的创新活跃期，几百年间，人类在科学技术方面取得的创新成果超过过去几千年的总和。特别是 18 世纪以来，世界发生了几次重大科技革命，如近代物理学诞生、蒸汽机和机械、电力和运输、相对论和量子论、电子和信息技术发展等。在此带动下，世界经济发生多次产

tum theory, and the development of electronics and information technology and so on. Driven by this, the world economy has witnessed many industrial revolutions, such as mechanization, electrification, automation and informatization. Each scientific and technological and industrial revolution has profoundly changed the development landscape and power structure of the world. Some countries have seized the opportunity, and their economic and social development has entered a fast lane. Their economic strength, scientific and technological strength and military strength have increased rapidly, and they have even become world powers. The first industrial revolution originated in Britain, led Britain to the world hegemony. America seized the opportunity of the second industrial revolution to overtake Britain as the world's number one. In a sense, innovation determines changes in the balance of political and economic forces in the world, as well as the future and destiny of countries and nations.

2. Innovation Ability is a Concentrated Manifestation of the New Advantages in Today's International Competition

"In the fierce international competition, only the innovator advances, only the innovator is strong, only the innovator wins." Since the beginning of the 21st century, a new round of scientific and technological revolution and industrial transformation is emerging. Global science and technology innovation presents new development trend and characteristics. Interdisciplinary integration is accelerating, and emerging disciplines keep

业革命，如机械化、电气化、自动化、信息化。每一次科技和产业革命都深刻改变了世界发展面貌与力量格局。一些国家抓住机遇，经济社会发展驶入快车道，经济实力、科技实力、军事实力迅速增强，甚至一跃成为世界强国。发端于英国的第一次产业革命，使英国走上了世界霸主地位；美国抓住了第二次产业革命机遇，赶超英国成为世界第一。从某种意义上说，创新决定着世界政治经济力量对比的变化，也决定着各国各民族的前途命运。

2. 创新能力是当今国际竞争新优势的集中体现

"在激烈的国际竞争中，惟创新者进，惟创新者强，惟创新者胜。"进入21世纪以来，新一轮科技革命和产业变革正在孕育兴起，全球科技创新呈现出新的发展态势和特征。学科交叉融合加速，新兴学科不断涌现，前沿领域不断延伸，物质结构、宇宙演化、生命起源、意识本质等基

emerging, the frontier field continues to expand, basic scientific fields such as material structure, evolution of the universe, origin of life, and nature of consciousness are being made or are expected to make major breakthroughs. Information technology, biotechnology, new materials technology, and new energy technologies have been widely infiltrated, driving a group-based technological revolution characterized by green, intelligent, and ubiquitous in almost all fields. In the traditional sense, the boundaries of basic research, applied research, technology development and industrialization are becoming increasingly blurred. The chain of technological innovation is more dexterous. Technology updates and fruits are transformed more quickly. Industrial upgrading is accelerating. Technological innovation activities continue to break through the boundaries of geography, organization, and technology, and evolve into the competition of innovation systems. The role of innovation strategy competition in the competition of comprehensive national strength is increasingly important.

Today, the new advantages of international competition are increasingly concentrated in the ability of innovation. In today's world, who has taken the "the nose of an ox" of technological innovation, who can take the lead and win the advantage; and who takes the lead in technological innovation, who can have the initiative to lead development. Faced with the new trends of technological innovation and industrial revolution, the world's major countries are actively adjusting,

础科学领域正在或有望取得重大突破性进展。信息技术、生物技术、新材料技术、新能源技术广泛渗透，带动几乎所有领域发生了以绿色、智能、泛在为特征的群体性技术革命。传统意义上的基础研究、应用研究、技术开发和产业化的边界日趋模糊，科技创新链条更加灵巧，技术更新和成果转化更加快捷，产业更新换代不断加快。科技创新活动不断突破地域、组织、技术的界限，演化为创新体系的竞争，创新战略竞争在综合国力竞争中的地位日益重要。

今天，国际竞争的新优势越来越集中体现在创新能力上。当今世界，谁牵住了科技创新这个"牛鼻子"，谁就能占领先机，赢得优势；谁在科技创新上先行一步，谁就能拥有引领发展的主动权。面对科技创新和产业革命新趋势，世界主要国家都在积极调整应对，努力寻找创新的突破口，抢占发展先机，纷纷出台新

striving to find breakthroughs in innovation, seize the opportunities of development, and introduce new innovation strategies, increase investment, leading to the increasingly fierce competition for strategic innovation resources such as talents, patents, and standards.

Reform and innovation are the inevitable requirements for China to win the future. To grasp innovation is to grasp development, and to seek innovation is to seek the future. At present, although China's economic aggregate has leapt to the second place in the world, the problem of "big but not strong" is quite prominent. The main manifestations are that the innovation ability is not strong, the development level of science and technology is generally not high, the support ability of science and technology to economic and social development is insufficient, and the contribution rate of science and technology to economic growth is far lower than that of developed countries. In the new round of scientific and technological revolution and industrial transformation, whether China can catch up with others depends on whether it can take tangible steps in the innovation-driven development. Innovation must be the first driving force for development, talents should be the first resource to support development, innovation should be placed at the core of the country's overall development, innovation-driven development strategy should be regarded as a major national strategy. We should continuously promote theoretical innovation, institutional innovation, scientific and technological innovation, and cultural innova-

的创新战略，加大投入，使人才、专利、标准等战略性创新资源的争夺日益激烈。

改革创新是我国赢得未来的必然要求。抓创新就是抓发展，谋创新就是谋未来。目前，虽然我国经济总量跃居世界第二，但大而不强的问题相当突出，主要体现在创新能力不强，科技发展水平总体不高，科技对经济社会发展的支撑能力不足，科技对经济增长的贡献率远低于发达国家水平。在新一轮科技革命和产业变革中，我国能否后来居上，主要取决于能否在创新驱动发展上迈出坚实的步伐。必须把创新作为引领发展的第一动力，把人才作为支撑发展的第一资源，把创新摆在国家发展全局的核心位置，把创新驱动发展战略作为国家重大战略，不断推进理论创新、制度创新、科技创新、文化创新等各方面创新，让创新贯穿党和国家的一切工作，让创新在全社会蔚然成风。

tion, and so on, let innovation run through all the work of the Party and the country, so that innovation can become a common practice in the whole society.

If we compare scientific and technological innovation to the new engine of China's development, then reform is the indispensable ignition system to ignite this new engine. To implement the innovation-driven development strategy, the most fundamental thing is to enhance the ability of independent innovation, the most urgent thing is to break down the barriers of the system and mechanism, and to maximize the liberation and stimulation of the enormous potential of science and technology as the primary productive force, open up a channel from strong science and technology to strong industry, strong economy, and strong national power, so that the reform will release innovation vitality, and all sources of innovation will flow fully. Only by deepening the reform in an all-round way, can we accelerate the transformation of the mode of economic development, promote the strategic adjustment of economic structure and actively create a good atmosphere for encouraging bold innovation, daring innovation and inclusive innovation in the whole society. In this way, the new engine driven by innovation will be launched at full speed to provide unprecedented strong impetus for China's economic and social development.

There is no end to reform and innovation. College students should consciously set up the ambition and confidence to be the first in the

如果把科技创新比作我国发展的新引擎，那么改革就是点燃这个新引擎必不可少的导火索。实施创新驱动发展战略，最根本的是要增强自主创新能力，最紧迫的是要破除体制机制障碍，最大限度地解放和激发科技作为第一生产力所蕴含的巨大潜能，打通从科技强到产业强、经济强、国家强的通道，让改革释放创新活力，让一切创新源泉充分涌流。只有通过全面深化改革，才能加快转变经济发展方式，推进经济结构战略性调整，在全社会积极营造鼓励大胆创新、勇于创新、包容创新的良好氛围，把创新驱动的新引擎全速发动起来，为我国经济社会发展提供前所未有的强劲动力。

改革创新永无止境。大学生要自觉树立敢为天下先的志向和信心，敢于担当、勇于超越，在

world, have the courage to take responsibility and go beyond, pursue excellence in overcoming difficulties, and lead the trend in reform and innovation.

III. College Students Should be the New Force of Reform and Innovation

The scale of China's science and technology team is the largest in the world, but it also facing severe challenges. The main manifestations are that the contradiction between the structural defects of innovative science and technology talents is prominent, the world-class science and technology masters are lacking, the leading talents and the top talents are insufficient, and the training of engineering and technical personnel is out of touch with production and innovation practices. "A year is for planting grains, a decade is for planting trees, a lifelong time is for cultivating people." We must place human resources development at the top of technological innovation, reform the mechanisms for talent cultivation, introduction, and employment. We should strive to create a group of world-class scientists, leading talents in science and technology, engineers, and high-level innovation teams, and focus on cultivating first-line innovative talents and young scientific and technological talents.

At present, the young and middle-aged talent group has become the main force for technological innovation of our country. For example, this year, among the winners who won the National Natural Science Award, the Technology Invention Award and the Science and Technology Progress

攻坚克难中追求卓越，在改革创新中引领潮流。

三、大学生应做改革创新的生力军

我国科技队伍规模是世界上最大的，但是也面临着严峻挑战，这主要表现在创新型科技人才结构性不足矛盾突出，世界级科技大师缺乏，领军人才、尖子人才不足，工程技术人才培养同生产和创新实践脱节。"一年之计，莫如树谷；十年之计，莫如树木；终身之计，莫如树人。"我们要把人才资源开发放在科技创新的优先位置，改革人才培养、引进、使用等机制，努力造就一批世界水平的科学家、科技领军人才、工程师和高水平创新团队，注重培养一线创新人才和青年科技人才。

当前，中青年人才群体已经成为我国科技创新的主要力量。例如，近年，在国家自然科学奖、技术发明奖和科技进步奖获得者中，45岁以下中青年科研人员比例达到44.2％；在航天科技

Award, the proportion of young and middle-aged researchers under the age of 45 reached 44.2%; among the 150,000 employees of the Aerospace Science and Technology, the proportion of the young and middle-aged people under the age of 35 is more than 54%; among the chief designers and chief conductors, the number of the young and middle-aged people under 45 has already accounted for 46%.

Youth is a precious period of innovation and creation. Under the torrent of the era of realizing the great rejuvenation of the Chinese nation, college students in the new era should shoulder the mission of the times, grasp the pulse of the times, meet the challenges of the times, enhance the ability of innovation and creation, and be practitioners of reform and innovation, make the spirit of reform and innovation run through practice and reflected in action.

1.The Establishment of the Consciousness of Reform and Innovation

Reform and innovation first require people to consciously enhance the sense of responsibility for reform and innovation, establish ideas and ideologies that dare to break through stereotypes, boldly explore the unknown, and dare to innovate and create, have the courage to face difficulties in practice, and the spirit of breaking through the difficulties, forge ahead, and strive to move forward.

First, colledge students must enhance the sense of responsibility for reform and innovation.

Reform and innovation manifests itself as a sense of responsibility and mission of unwill-

行业 15 万员工中，35 岁以下中青年超过 54%，型号总设计师、总指挥中，45 岁以下中青年占 46%。

青年时期是创新创造的宝贵时期。新时代的大学生身处实现中华民族伟大复兴的时代洪流之中，应当肩负时代使命，把握时代脉搏，迎接时代挑战，增强创新创造的能力和本领，勇做改革创新的实践者，将弘扬改革创新精神贯穿于实践中、体现在行动上。

1. 树立改革创新的自觉意识

改革创新，首先要求人们自觉增强改革创新的责任感，树立敢于突破陈规、大胆探索未知、勇于创新创造的思想观念，具有在实践中直面困难的勇气和突破难关的精神，锐意进取，奋力前行。

第一，增强改革创新的责任感。

改革创新表现为一种不甘落后、奋勇争先、追求进步的责任

ing to lag behind, and striving for progress. In the tide of the times, some people choose to satisfy with the current situation, do not want to forge ahead, drift with the tide, while some other people are high-spirited, strive for the upstream, work hard and make progress. In addition to confidence and courage, the root cause of these two different choices lies in whether they have a sense of responsibility and mission to contribute to social development and progress. Reform and innovation are full of hardships, dedication and even sacrifice. Without a strong sense of responsibility and mission, it is difficult to support people in overcoming the difficult twists and turns in the process of reform and innovation. Li Dazhao once wrote the warning words: "Strong shoulders load morality and justice, while skilled artists write articles." In here, "shoulders" and "morality" is the responsibility and mission. College students should continue to intensify the lofty sense of responsibility and mission of promoting social progress through reform and innovation, dedicating themselves to serving the society and realizing their life values, be committed to the practice of reform and innovation with a sense of urgency.

Responsibility is the soul of innovation. Achieving the great rejuvenation of the Chinese nation requires a steady strength of youth. Innovation and entrepreneurship is the mission given to this generation of young people by times and history.

Second, college students must establish a sense of daring to break through the outmoded

感和使命感。在时代大潮中，有人选择安于现状、不思进取、随波逐流，有人则意气风发、力争上游、拼搏进取。这两种不同选择的根源，除了信心和勇气外，更在于是否具有为推动社会发展进步贡献力量的责任感和使命感。改革创新充满艰辛、奉献甚至牺牲，没有强烈的责任感和使命感，很难支撑人们克服和战胜改革创新过程中的艰难曲折。李大钊曾写下"铁肩担道义，妙手著文章"的警语，"铁肩""道义"讲的就是责任与使命。大学生要不断增强以改革创新推动社会进步，在改革创新中奉献和服务社会、实现人生价值的崇高责任感和使命感，以时不我待、只争朝夕的紧迫感投身改革创新的实践。

责任担当是创新之魂。实现中华民族伟大复兴需要源源不断的青春力量，创新创业是时代和历史赋予这一代青年的使命。

第二，树立敢于突破陈规的意识。

conventions.

The outmoded conventions have the easiest way to tie people's minds and hands and feet. The process of innovation and creation is often full of hardships. To innovate, we must have a strong sense of innovation, and have the strength to "break the cover to seek the truth". We should dare to question the existing conclusions, dare to open up new directions, overcome difficulties, and pursue excellence. We should dare to boldly break through stereotypes and even routines, dare to explore and try boldly, be good at observing and discovering, thinking and criticizing, not basing on books and superiors, but on reality, this is an important pre-requisite for college students to innovate and create in learning and practice.

Second, college students must build up the confidence to boldly explore the unknown realms.

Innovation means going the way no one has gone before. To innovate, we must have strong confidence in innovation. If we always follow the imitation, it is neither innovative nor having a way out. The unknown realms may be the blind area of human knowledge, and are often daunting, stop people to explore and seek for new steps. However, the unknown realms also contain fertile soil for discovery and opportunities for innovation. Just as Wang Anshi said in the "*The Diary of Visiting Bao Chan Mountain*": "The wonderful and magnificent scenery is often in a steep and remote place. Since it is a place where people are inaccessible, it is difficult to reach without a will." Young people should always be innovative and dare to create,

陈规最易束缚人的思维和手脚，创新创造的过程往往充满艰辛。要创新，就要有强烈的创新意识，凡事要有"打破砂锅问到底"的劲头，敢于质疑现有定论，勇于开拓新的方向，攻坚克难，追求卓越。敢于大胆突破陈规甚至常规，敢于大胆探索尝试，善于观察发现、思考批判，不唯书、不唯上，只唯实，这是大学生在学习与实践中创新创造的重要前提。

第三，树立大胆探索未知领域的信心。

创新就是要走前人没有走过的路。要创新，就要有强烈的创新自信。如果总是跟踪模仿，既谈不上创新，也没有出路。未知领域可能是人类认识的盲区，常常令人心生怯意，使人们因此停下探索和求新的脚步，但未知领域也往往蕴含着发现的沃土和创新的机遇。正如王安石在《游褒禅山记》中所言："而世之奇伟、瑰怪，非常之观，常在于险远，而人之所罕至焉，故非有志者不能至也。"青年应是常为新、敢创造的，理当锐意创新创造，不等待、不观望、不懈怠，勇做改

and they should be determined to innovate and create, not waiting, not watching, not slacking, but bravely being the new force of reform and innovation.

2. The Enhancement of the Capacity for Reform and Innovation

First, college students must tamp a solid foundation for innovation.

Any reform and innovation is based on the accumulated professional knowledge of predecessors. Why reform and innovation can bring forth the new from the old, put forward new ideas that have not been put forward by predecessors, and introduce new creations that are admired by the world? An important reason is that reformers and innovators have a solid foundation of professional knowledge. Lack of profound accumulation of professional knowledge and blind pursuit of reform and innovation are often prone to unrealistic fantasies or "fearless ignorant" brutality. If we ignore or despise professional knowledge learning, it is impossible for us to shoulder the responsibility of reform and innovation. As a fresh force of reform and innovation, college students should start with a solid and systematic study of professional knowledge, rather than aiming too high, and talking about reform and innovation emptily.

Second, college students must cultivate innovative thinking.

The difference between innovative thinking and conservative thinking lies in that conservative thinking tends to seek common ground and imitate, while innovative thinking pays attention to seeking

革创新的生力军。

2. 增强改革创新的能力

第一，夯实创新基础。

任何一项改革和创新都是建立在前人积累的专业知识的基础之上的。改革创新之所以能够推陈出新，提出前人不曾提出的新思想，推出令世人敬仰的新创造，一个重要的原因就在于改革创新者具有扎实的专业知识基础。缺乏深厚的专业知识积淀，盲目追求改革创新，往往容易流于不切实际的空想，或者"无知者无畏"的蛮干。无视或轻视专业知识学习，就不可能担负起改革创新的重任。大学生作为改革创新的生力军，应从扎实系统的专业知识学习起步，而不能好高骛远，空谈改革，坐论创新。

第二，培养创新思维。

创新思维与守旧思维的区别在于，守旧思维往往求同、模仿，创新思维则注重求异、批判而不甘落入窠臼和俗套；守旧思

differences and criticizing and refuses to fall into the beaten track and routine; conservative thinking passively answers questions, while innovative thinking is good at finding problems; conservative thinking is often mechanical, linear, closed, while innovative thinking is flexible and open, divergent and multi-dimensional; the ideas put forward by conservative thinking are often acceptable to people because of familiarity, while innovative thinking is often suspected because of "Fantasy". In the professional study and social practice, college students should consciously cultivate innovative thinking, be diligent in thinking, be good at discovering, and be brave in innovation.

Third, the diligent thinking is the foundation of innovation.

"It is difficult to grow without learning, and it is difficult to learn without willpower." Erudition is an inevitable requirement of innovation, and it will not be innovated by enthusiasm alone. Without thick accumulation, it is impossible to break forth vastly. Throughout the ages, all those who have created new doctrines are those who are thirsty for knowledge. College students should strive to absorb knowledge, cherish time like gold, be tireless, change from "passive acceptance" to "active inquiry", insist on the combination of learning and thinking, think in learning, understand in thinking, dare to criticize, dare to question, so as to flow the source of innovative ideas fully.

Fourth, college students must devote themselves to innovative practice.

Knowledge comes from practice, talent

维被动回答问题，创新思维善于发现问题；守旧思维往往机械、线性、封闭，创新思维则灵活而开放，发散而多维；守旧思维提出的观点，人们往往因熟悉而易于接受，创新思维则常常因"异想天开"而被怀疑。大学生在专业学习与社会实践中应自觉培养创新思维，勤于思考，善于发现，勇于创新。

第三，勤学善思是创新之基。

"非学无以广才，非志无以成学。"博学是创新的必然要求，仅凭一腔热情，断不会推陈出新；没有厚积，不可能薄发。古往今来，大凡创立新说者，莫不是求知若渴之人。大学生要努力汲取知识，惜时如金、孜孜不倦，由"被动接受"向"主动探究"转变，坚持学与思相结合，在学习中思考、在思考中领悟，敢于批判、勇于质疑，使创新的思想源泉充分涌流。

第四，投身创新实践。

实践出真知，实践长才干。

comes from practice. Contemporary college students are not only in the historical opportunity period of the new round of scientific and technological revolution and the rise of industrial revolution in the world, but also in the new historical journey of China's great modernization. We should deeply understand the spirit of reform and innovation in the great practice of comprehensively deepening reforms, enhance the awareness of reform and innovation, temper the will of reform and innovation, enhance the ability to reform and innovation, and be practitioners and new force in reform and innovation.

Fifth, the unity of knowledge and action is the foundation of innovation.

"Without action, thoughts can never be matured and turned into truth." Countless practices tell us that no innovation can be achieved overnight and move smoothly. In the process of innovation, there are a lot of suffering. College students should keep the faith, dare to think, dare to try, dare to be a pioneer, combine learning with practice, let innovation become the driving force of youth voyage, let youth glow in the dedication to the country and the people.

Young people are often full of vigor and vitality, with active thinking, strong curiosity, thirst for knowledge and the courage to try new things. All these are important conditions conducive to innovation and creation. Throughout the history of the world, many important creations have come from the youth of the creators when they are in their prime and have the most agile thinking. It can

当代大学生既置身于全球新一轮科技革命和产业变革兴起的历史机遇期，又置身于我国迈向现代化强国的历史新征程，应当在全面深化改革的伟大实践中深刻体悟改革创新精神，增强改革创新意识，锤炼改革创新意志，增强改革创新能力，勇做改革创新的实践者和生力军。

第五，知行合一是创新之本。

"没有行动，思想永远不能成熟而化为真理。"无数实践告诉我们，任何创新都不是一蹴而就、一帆风顺的，在创新的过程中会有诸多磨难。大学生要坚定信念，敢想敢试敢为，敢于做先锋，知行合一，让创新成为青春远航的动力，让青春年华在为国家、为人民的奉献中焕发出绚丽光彩。

青年往往朝气蓬勃、思维活跃，好奇心强、求知欲盛，敢于尝试新生事物，这些都是有利于创新创造的重要条件。纵观世界历史，许多重要创造都产生于创造者风华正茂、思维最敏捷的青年时期。可以说，青年身上蕴藏着巨大的创造能量和活力。大学

be said that the youth has enormous creative energy and vitality. College students should cherish the precious period in their life when they have the most innovative and creative vitality. They should have the courage to be the first to forge ahead and the will to bridge mountains and rivers, and continue to accumulate experience, make achievement and perform wonderfully in innovation and creation.

生应当珍惜人生中最具创新创造活力的宝贵时期，有敢为人先、开拓进取的锐气，有逢山开路、遇河架桥的意志，在创新创造中不断积累经验、取得成果、演绎精彩。

Lecture Eight
The Socialist Core Values is the Common Value Pursuit of Chinese People

In this topic, the connotation of value, values and socialist core values will be discussed, as well as the significance and the implementation of socialist core values.

I.The Connotation of the Socialist Core Values

1. The Meanings of the Concept of Value and Values

Value is a very complex category with different meanings in different contexts. In philosophy, the general essence of value is that it is a relationship between the needs of real people and the attributes of things. As for value, Marx expounded as follows: "The universal concept of value arises from the way people relate to external that meet their needs." In this exposition, "external objects" mainly refer to objects, including any objects, people, phenomena and relations that deal with people; the concept of "people" refers to the main body, including individual, collective, class, nation, state and other realistic forms. Generally speaking, value refers to the relationship between object attributes and subject needs. In daily life, value is a problem that people often encounter, such as

专题八
社会主义核心价值观是中国人民的共同价值追求

本专题探讨价值观的含义、社会主义核心价值观的内涵、重要意义以及如何践行社会主义核心价值观。

一、社会主义核心价值观的内涵

1. 价值和价值观的含义

价值是一个含义十分复杂的范畴，在不同的语境中具有不同的含义。在哲学中，价值的一般本质在于它是现实的人的需要与事物属性之间的一种关系。关于价值，马克思是这样论述的："价值这个普遍的概念是人们对待满足他们需要的外界物的关系中产生的。"在这个论述中，"外界物"主要是指"客体"，包括与人打交道的任何物、人、现象和关系；"人们"这个概念指的是主体，包括个人、集体、阶级、民族、国家等现实形态。一般来说，价值就是指客体属性满足主体需要的关系。在日常生活中，

"whether it is worth it" "whether it is beneficial" and so on, which is a value judgment. People's understanding and practice are closely related to value judgment.

Values are fundamental ideas of people about what is value, how to judge value, and how to create value. The content of values, on the one hand, expresses value orientation, value pursuit, and condenses into certain value goals; on the other hand, it is expressed as value scales and norms, and becomes the evaluation standard for people to judge whether things have value or not, whether they are glorious or shameful.

2. Socialist Core Values and Socialist Core Value System

First, the connotation of core values.

Core values is a concentrated expression of a certain social nature. It is in a dominant position in a social ideological system, embodying the basic principles of social systems, social operations, and the basic direction of social development. Since the founding of, especially since the reform and opening up, the Communist Party of China has led the people of the whole country to establish a set of relatively mature basic systems and institutions in economic, political and cultural and social aspects, and successfully explored a socialist road with Chinese characteristics. Compatible with these basic systems and institutions, it is inevitable to have a core values that dominates the ideological, moral, and behavioral patterns of the whole society.

"价值"是人们经常遇到的问题，如做事说话时经常要考虑"值不值得""有没有益处"等，这就是一种价值判断。人们的认识和实践与价值判断密切相关。

价值观是人们关于什么是价值、怎样评判价值、如何创造价值等问题的根本观点。价值观的内容，一方面表现为价值取向、价值追求，凝结为一定的价值目标；另一方面表现为价值尺度和准则，成为人们判断事物有无价值及价值大小的评价标准。

2. 社会主义核心价值观和社会主义核心价值体系

第一，核心价值观的含义。

核心价值观是一定社会性质的集中体现，在一个社会的思想观念体系中处于主导地位，体现着社会制度、社会运行的基本原则和社会发展的基本方向。中华人民共和国成立以来，特别是改革开放以来，中国共产党带领全国人民在经济、政治、文化和社会等方面建立了一套比较成熟的基本制度和体制，成功探索出了一条中国特色社会主义道路。与这些基本制度和体制相适应，必然要求有一个主导全社会思想道德观念和行为方式的核心价值观。

Second, the connotation of socialist values?

The 18th National Congress of the Communist Party of China proposed to advocate prosperity, democracy, civilization and harmony, advocate freedom, equality, justice and the rule of law, advocate patriotism, dedication, integrity and friendliness, and actively cultivate and practice socialist core values. This is in line with the development requirements of socialism with Chinese characteristics, and is in line with the excellent Chinese traditional culture and outstanding achievements of human civilization. It is an important conclusion made by the Communist Party of China to unite the consensus of the whole party and the whole society. The introduction of the socialist core values clearly sets the core values of contemporary China and vividly demonstrates the high value self-confidence and value consciousness of the Communist Party of China and the Chinese nation.

The socialist core values integrate the value requirements of the state, society and citizens, embody the essential requirements of socialism, inherit the fine traditional Chinese culture, absorb the beneficial results of world civilization, embody the spirit of the times. They are profound answers to major issues such as what kind of country we should build, what kind of society we should build and what kind of citizens we should cultivate.

In March 2018, the first session of the 13th National People's Congress passed a constitutional amendment to officially write the state's socialist core values into the Constitution, further high-

第二，社会主义核心价值观的内涵。

党的十八大提出，要倡导富强、民主、文明、和谐，倡导自由、平等、公正、法治，倡导爱国、敬业、诚信、友善，积极培育和践行社会主义核心价值观。这与中国特色社会主义发展要求相契合，与中华优秀传统文化和人类文明优秀成果相承接，是中国共产党凝聚全党全社会价值共识做出的重要论断。社会主义核心价值观的提出，鲜明地确立了当代中国的核心价值理念，生动展现了中国共产党和中华民族高度的价值自信与价值自觉。

社会主义核心价值观把涉及国家、社会、公民的价值要求融为一体，体现了社会主义本质要求，继承了中华优秀传统文化，吸收了世界文明中的有益成果，体现了时代精神，是对我们要建设什么样的国家、建设什么样的社会、培育什么样的公民等重大问题的深刻解答。

2018年3月，十三届全国人大一次会议通过宪法修正案，把"国家倡导社会主义核心价值观"正式写入宪法，进一步凸显了社

lighting the great significance of the socialist core values.

Third, the connotation of socialist core value system?

In October 2006, the *Decision of the Central Committee of the Communist Party of China on Several Major Issues Concerning the Construction of a Harmonious Socialist Society* adopted by the Sixth Plenary Session of the 16th Central Committee of the Communist Party of China clearly stated the major proposition and strategy of "building a socialist core value system" for the first time and expounded the connotation of the socialist core value system. The socialist core value system mainly includes the guiding ideology of Marxism, the common ideal of socialism with Chinese characteristics, the national spirit with patriotism as the core, the spirit of the times with reform and innovation as the core, and the socialist concept of honor and disgrace.

3. The Inherent Logical Relationship Between the Socialist Core Values and the Socialist Core Value System

To promote the socialist core values and the construction of the socialist core value system is to carry forward the common ideals, to unite the spiritual forces to lead the morality, and to form the spiritual ties of the whole nation to strive for progress, unity and harmony, so that our country, nation and people are ideologically and mentally stronger, and could better adhere to the Chinese road, carry forward the Chinese spirit, and unite China's strength. The socialist core value system

会主义核心价值观的重大意义。

第三，社会主义核心价值体系的内涵。

2006 年 10 月，党的十六届六中全会通过的《中共中央关于构建社会主义和谐社会若干重大问题的决定》第一次明确提出了"建设社会主义核心价值体系"这个重大命题和战略任务，提出了社会主义核心价值体系的内涵。社会主义核心价值体系主要包括马克思主义指导思想、中国特色社会主义共同理想、以爱国主义为核心的民族精神和以改革创新为核心的时代精神、社会主义荣辱观。

3. 社会主义核心价值观和社会主义核心价值体系的内在逻辑关系

推进社会主义核心价值观与社会主义核心价值体系建设，就是要弘扬共同理想、凝聚精神力量，引领道德风尚，形成全民族奋发向上、团结和睦的精神纽带，使我们的国家、民族、人民在思想上和精神上强大起来，更好地坚持中国道路、弘扬中国精神、凝聚中国力量。社会主义核心价值体系与社会主义核心价值

and the socialist core values are both different and related.

First, the socialist core value system and socialist core values are different.

The socialist core values cover the four major levels of economy, politics, culture and society. They not only reflect the lofty ideals and highest values of communism, but also reflect the grand goals and overall layout of the state's socialist modernization at the present stage, reflecting the party's unity of the highest program and the minimum program, and embody the organic unity of socialist material civilization, political civilization, spiritual civilization, social civilization and ecological civilization.

The socialist value system is a multi-level system with rich content, which has its core value, its basic value and specific value. The socialist value system not only contains the ideal value appeal, but also reflects the realistic value requirements; it not only has the advanced value concept that inspires people to continuously ascend, but also has the universal value that most people can accept and practice. It is expressed through the corresponding core values and specific values in various fields of economy, politics, culture and society.

First, the socialist core value system and the socialist core values are interconnected with each other.

The socialist core value system is the necessary condition, basis and important carrier for

观既有区别又有联系。

第一，社会主义核心价值体系与社会主义核心价值观是有区别的。

社会主义核心价值观涵盖了经济、政治、文化、社会四大层面，既体现了共产主义的远大理想和最高价值，又反映了现阶段我国社会主义现代化建设的宏伟目标和总体布局，体现了党的最高纲领和最低纲领的统一，体现了社会主义物质文明、政治文明、精神文明、社会文明和生态文明的有机统一。

社会主义价值体系是一个包含丰富内容的多层次体系，既有其核心价值，又有其基本价值、具体价值。社会主义价值体系既包含着理想性的价值诉求，又体现着现实性的价值要求；既有感召人们不断递升的先进性价值理念，又有大多数人可以接受并实践的广泛性价值体现。它通过经济、政治、文化、社会各个领域相应的核心价值和具体价值表现出来。

第二，社会主义核心价值体系和社会主义核心价值观是相互联系的。

社会主义核心价值体系是社会主义核心价值观形成和发展的

the formation and development of socialist core values. On the one hand, without the socialist core value system, there will be no emergence, development and evolution of socialist core values, and socialist core values will have no support and no place to live. On the other hand, the socialist core values are the core, high generalization and highest abstraction of the socialist core value system, embody the value nature of socialism, determine the fundamental nature, basic direction and basic characteristics of the socialist core value system, and lead the construction of the socialist core value system.

II.The Significance of Socialist Core Values

1. The basis of Value of the Adherence to and Development of Socialism with Chinese Characteristics

Socialism with Chinese characteristics is a socialist with all-round development and all-round progress. It not only needs to constantly improve the systems of economy, politics, culture, society and ecological civilizations, but also needs to constantly explore the essential provisions of socialism at the spiritual and value levels; it not only needs to portray the future goals of material life in society, but also needs to point out the fate of future social spiritual values. In the whole society, we should vigorously carry forward the socialist core values, clarify what the socialist cause with Chinese characteristics pursues and oppose in the end, what direction it goes in, what direc-

必要条件、基础和重要载体。一方面，没有社会主义核心价值体系，就不会有社会主义核心价值观的产生、发展和演进，社会主义核心价值观就无所依托、无所寄寓。另一方面，社会主义核心价值观是社会主义核心价值体系的内核、高度概括和最高抽象，体现了社会主义的价值本质，决定社会主义核心价值体系的根本性质、基本方向和基本特征，引领和主导社会主义核心价值体系的建构。

二、社会主义核心价值观的重大意义

1.坚持和发展中国特色社会主义的价值基础

中国特色社会主义是全面发展、全面进步的社会主义。它既需要不断完善经济、政治、文化、社会和生态文明等各方面的制度，也需要不断探索社会主义在精神和价值层面的本质规定性；既需要为人们描绘未来社会物质生活方面的目标，也需要为人们指出未来社会精神价值的归宿。在全社会大力弘扬社会主义核心价值观，明确中国特色社会主义事业到底追求什么、反对什么，要朝着什么方向走、不能朝着什么方向走，坚守我们的价值

tion it should not go in, adhere to our standpoint of values, and strengthen the road self-confidence, theoretical self-confidence, institutional self-confidence and cultural self-confidence of socialism with Chinese characteristics, provide clear value criteria for the orderly operation and benign development of society, and ensure that the cause of socialism with Chinese characteristics always advances in the right direction. This is the soul-casting project of socialism with Chinese characteristics.

2. The Urgent Requirements for Improving the Cultural Soft Power

"The core values are the soul of cultural soft power and the focus of cultural soft power construction. This is the deepest factor that determines the nature and direction of culture." In today's world, culture has increasingly become an important factor in the competition of comprehensive national strength and has become an important support for economic and social development. Cultural soft power has increasingly become the key to competing for the commanding heights of development and morality. The power of culture, in the final analysis, comes from the influence and appeal of the core values condensed therein; the competition of cultural soft power is essentially the competition of the core values represented by different cultures. Nowadays, more and more countries have established the promotion of cultural soft power as a national strategy, and the dispute over values has become increasingly intense. Cultivating and practicing the socialist core values and

观立场，坚定中国特色社会主义的道路自信、理论自信、制度自信和文化自信，为社会的有序运行、良性发展提供明确价值准则，保证中国特色社会主义事业始终沿着正确方向前进，是中国特色社会主义的铸魂工程。

2. 提高文化软实力的迫切要求

"核心价值观是文化软实力的灵魂、文化软实力建设的重点。这是决定文化性质和方向的最深层次要素。"当今世界，文化越来越成为综合国力竞争的重要因素，成为经济社会发展的重要支撑，文化软实力越来越成为争夺发展制高点、道义制高点的关键所在。文化的力量，归根到底来自凝结其中的核心价值观的影响力和感召力；文化软实力的竞争，本质上是不同文化所代表的核心价值观的竞争。现在，越来越多的国家把提升文化软实力确立为国家战略，价值观之争日趋激烈。培育和践行社会主义核心价值观，用最简洁的语言介绍和说明中国，有利于增进国际社会对中国的理解，扩大中华文化的影响力，展示社会主义中国的

introducing and explaining China in the most concise language will help enhance the international community's understanding of China, expand the influence of Chinese culture, demonstrate the good image of socialist China; enhance the competitiveness of socialist ideology, grasp the right to speak and win the initiative, gradually break the monopoly of discourse and public opinion in the West, safeguard national cultural interests and ideological security, and constantly improve our country's cultural soft power.

3. The Greatest Common Denominator for the Enhancement of Social Harmony

History and reality have repeatedly shown that only by establishing a common value goal, can a country and a nation rely on a spiritual bond to maintain a unified will and action, and have a strong cohesive force and centripetal force. At present, China is in the accelerated period of economic transition and social transformation. The ideological field is increasingly multielement, diverse and changeable. Various trends of thought are coming and going. Various concepts are mixed and different values are coexisting. All of these manifest the dispute of interests and ideas, but reflect the differences in values. Xi Jinping pointed out: "China is a big country with more than 1.4 billion people and 56 nationalities. establishing the value of 'the greatest common denominator' that reflects the common identity of the people of all nationalities in the country, to make all the people forge ahead in unity, is related to the future of the country and about the happiness and well-be-

良好形象；有利于增强社会主义意识形态的竞争力，掌握话语权，赢得主动权，逐步打破西方的话语垄断、舆论垄断，维护国家文化利益和意识形态安全，不断提高我国的文化软实力。

3. 增进社会和谐的最大公约数

历史和现实一再表明，只有建立共同的价值目标，一个国家和民族才会有赖以维系的精神纽带，才会有统一的意志和行动，才会有强大的凝聚力、向心力。当前，我国正处在经济转轨和社会转型的加速期，思想领域日趋多元、多样、多变，各种思潮此起彼伏，各种观念交相杂陈，不同价值取向并存，所有这些表现出来的是具体利益、观念观点之争，但折射出来的是价值观的分歧。习近平指出："我国是一个有着 14 亿多人口、56 个民族的大国，确立反映全国各族人民共同认同的价值观'最大公约数'，使全体人民同心同德、团结奋进，关乎国家前途命运，关乎人民幸福安康。"培育和践行社会主义核心价值观，能够在具体利

ing of the people." Cultivating and practicing the core values can form a broad consensus on the contradictions of specific interests and differences in various ideas, effectively lead, integrate the complex social ideology, effectively avoid the ideological opposition and confusion that may be brought about by the adjustment of interest patterns, and form a strong spiritual force of unity and struggle.

III.Adhering to the Self-Confidence of Socialist Core Values

1.The Necessity to the Adherence to the Self-Confidence of Socialist Core Values

First, the socialist core values have a deep historical profoundity.

The Chinese excellent traditional culture is the spiritual lifeline of the Chinese nation and an important source of socialist core values.

General Secretary Xi Jinping pointed out: "Chinese excellent traditional culture has become the gene of the Chinese nation, rooted in the hearts of the Chinese people, and subtly affecting the way of thinking and conducting of the Chinese people. Today, to advocate and carry forward the socialist core values, we must draw rich nutrition from it, otherwise there will be no vitality and influence."

The Chinese civilization has been stretching for thousands of years and has its own unique value system. China has always stressed the importance of knowledge, sincerity and integrity, self-cultivation, governing the country and the world. This kind of responsibility ethic, which takes the world as its own responsibility, em-

益矛盾、各种思想差异上最广泛地形成价值共识，有效引领、整合纷繁复杂的社会思想意识，有效避免利益格局调整可能带来的思想对立和混乱，形成团结奋斗的强大精神力量。

三、坚定社会主义核心价值观自信

1. 坚定社会主义核心价值观自信的必要性

第一，社会主义核心价值观具有深厚的历史底蕴。

中华优秀传统文化是中华民族的精神命脉，是涵养社会主义核心价值观的重要源泉。

习近平总书记指出："中华优秀传统文化已经成为中华民族的基因，植根在中国人内心，潜移默化影响着中国人的思想方式和行为方式。今天，我们提倡和弘扬社会主义核心价值观，必须从中汲取丰富营养，否则就不会有生命力和影响力。"

中华文明绵延数千年，有其独特的价值体系。中国历来讲格物致知、诚意正心、修身齐家、治国平天下。这种以天下为己任的责任伦理强调个人、家庭的命运与社会、国家、天下的命运紧密相连，要求每个人都承担个

phasizes that the fate of individuals and families is closely linked with that of society, the country and the world, and requires everyone to assume multiple responsibilities of individuals, society, and the country. From a certain point of view, the knowledge, sincerity and self-cultivation are the requirements of the individual level, managing the family well is the requirement of the social level, and governing the country and the world is the requirement of the national level. The socialist core values integrate the value requirements of the state, society and citizens, inherit the excellent Chinese traditional culture, and embody the essential requirements of socialism and the spirit of the times. Chinese culture emphasizes "the people are the foundation of the state, the "harmony between man and nature" "harmony but not uniformity"; stresses that- "people should be self-reliant and tenacious " and " a public spirit will rule all under the heaven when the great way prevails"; stresses that " every man has a share of responsibility for the fate of his country"; emphasizes that everyone should be honest; emphasize "the benevolent lover" "do not do what you want, don' t do it to others" "to respect the old and cherish the young of other families as if they were our own" "to help each other when they are in troubles"; Etc. These thoughts and ideas with distinctive national characteristics have a profound impact on different levels of socialist core values.

In his report to the 19th National Congress of the Communist Party of China, Xi Jinping stressed that we should tap into the ideas and concepts, hu-

人、社会与国家的多重责任。从某种角度看，格物致知、诚意正心、修身是个人层面的要求，齐家是社会层面的要求，治国平天下是国家层面的要求。社会主义核心价值观把涉及国家、社会、公民的价值要求融为一体，继承了中华优秀传统文化，体现了社会主义本质要求和时代精神。中华文化强调"民惟邦本""天人合一""和而不同"；强调"天行健，君子以自强不息""大道之行也，天下为公"；强调"天下兴亡，匹夫有责"；强调"君子喻于义""诚者，天之道也；思诚者，人之道也""言必信，行必果""人而无信，不知其可也"；强调"仁者爱人""己所不欲，勿施于人""老吾老以及人之老，幼吾幼以及人之幼""出入相友，守望相助""扶贫济困""不患寡而患不均"；等等。这些具有鲜明民族特色的思想和理念对社会主义核心价值观的不同层面都有着深刻影响。

习近平在党的十九大报告中强调，深入挖掘中华优秀传统文化蕴含的思想观念、人文精神、

manistic spirits and ethical norms in the Chinese fine traditional culture, inherit and make innovations in line with the needs of the times, so that Chinese culture will display its enduring appeal and charm of the times. This provides a fundamental understanding and action guide for us to correctly understand and accurately grasp the internal relationship between the socialist core values and the Chinese excellent traditional culture, and continue to deepen the construction of the socialist core values in the new era.

Second, the socialist core values have a firm realistic foundation.

The socialist core values that we actively promote and practice are not only compatible with the long and splendid history and culture of the Chinese nation, but also have a profound historical and cultural heritage, and combined with our ongoing struggles, and with the issues of the times we are trying to solve，which have a solid realistic foundation. In a nutshell, this solid realistic foundation is the most magnificent and unique practice of socialist construction with Chinese characteristics in human history carried out by the Chinese nation in current era.

Third, the construction of socialism with Chinese characteristics is the practical basis of socialist core values.

Values are what human beings produce and play their roles in the process of recognizing and transforming nature and society. Different nationalities and countries have different characteristics of core values that are generated and formed due to

道德规范，结合时代要求继承创新，让中华文化展现出永久魅力和时代风采。这为我们正确认识和准确把握社会主义核心价值观与中华优秀传统文化的内在关系，立足新时代持续深入地推进社会主义核心价值观建设提供了根本遵循和行动指南。

第二，社会主义核心价值观具有坚实的现实基础。

我们所积极弘扬和践行的社会主义核心价值观，不仅与中华民族悠久灿烂的历史文化相契合，具有深厚的历史文化底蕴，而且同我们正在进行的奋斗相结合，同我们所要解决的时代问题相适应，具有坚实的现实基础。概括而言，这一坚实的现实基础，就是当今时代中华民族所进行的人类历史上最为宏伟而独特的中国特色社会主义建设实践。

第三，中国特色社会主义建设是社会主义核心价值观的实践根据。

价值观是在人类认识、改造自然和社会的过程中产生与发挥作用的。不同民族、不同国家由于其自然条件和发展历程不同，产生和形成的核心价值观也各有

their different natural conditions and development processes. Building a prosperous, strong, democratic, civilized, harmonious and beautiful socialist modernization and realizing the great rejuvenation of the Chinese nation is the greatest dream of the Chinese people. It is the highest interest and fundamental interest of the Chinese nation, which carries the ideals and explorations of several generations of Chinese Communists and entrusted with the will and expectation of countless people with lofty ideals. It embodies the struggle and sacrifice of thousands of revolutionary martyrs. It is the inevitable choice for the development of Chinese society in modern times, the choice of history and people, and embodies the struggle and practice of the people of all nationalities in the country. The facts also eloquently prove that to develop China, stabilize China, build a well-off society in an all-round way, accelerate the modernization of socialism, and realize the great rejuvenation of the Chinese nation, we must unswervingly adhere to and develop socialism with Chinese characteristics. Advancing the building of socialism with Chinese characteristics will inevitably require its own bright spiritual banner, with clear and powerful value. The socialist core values are generated in the practice of building socialism with Chinese characteristics, and are compatible with the most distinctive theme of the times in China today. They are the concentrated expression of the contemporary Chinese spirit and the value expression of the essence of socialism with Chinese characteristics. From the perspective of values, they clearly

特点。建设富强民主文明和谐美丽的社会主义现代化强国，实现中华民族伟大复兴，是中国人民最伟大的梦想，是中华民族的最高利益和根本利益，承载着几代中国共产党人的理想和探索，寄托着无数仁人志士的意愿和期盼，凝聚着千千万万革命先烈的奋斗和牺牲，是近代以来中国社会发展的必然选择，是历史和人民的选择，凝聚着全国各族人民的奋斗和实践。事实也雄辩地证明，要发展中国、稳定中国，要全面建成小康社会、加快推进社会主义现代化，要实现中华民族伟大复兴，必须坚定不移地坚持和发展中国特色社会主义。推进中国特色社会主义建设，必然要求有自己鲜明的精神旗帜，有明确有力的价值引领。社会主义核心价值观生成于中国特色社会主义建设实践，同当今中国最鲜明的时代主题相适应，是当代中国精神的集中体现，是中国特色社会主义本质规定的价值表达。它从价值观的层面，清晰地展现了我们所推进的中国特色社会主义建设的基本特征和根本追求，引领着中国特色社会主义建设铿锵前行。

demonstrate the basic characteristics and funda-mental pursuits of socialist construction with Chinese characteristics that we promote, and lead the construction of socialism with Chinese character-istics to steady advance.

The construction of socialism with Chinese characteristics also vividly demonstrates the vitality of socialist core values with irrefutable facts. Since the reform and opening up, we have adhered to the path of socialism with Chinese character-istics. Under the complicated domestic and in-ternational situation, we have seized the period of strategic opportunities for China's development. China's comprehensive national strength, people's living standards, international competitiveness and international influence have all stepped to a new level, demonstrating the great superiority and strong vitality of socialism with Chinese charac-teristics. Many countries follow the Western model that reflects the core values of capitalism. "Passive learning" and "imitate other and thus lose one's own individuality" have not presented the so-called "democratic grandeur" "developmental grandeur", "prosperous grandeur", but have led to quarrels between the parties and social unrest. On the contrary, the road of socialism with Chi-nese characteristics that has been explored since China's reform and opening up has allowed China to realize a miracle in the history of human devel-opment. Socialism with Chinese characteristics is not a replica or an imported product, which has its own unique qualities. The value of Chinese char-acteristics is the core of it.

中国特色社会主义建设也以无可辩驳的事实生动展示着社会主义核心价值观的生机和活力。改革开放以来，我们坚持走中国特色社会主义道路，在复杂的国内外形势下，抓住我国发展的战略机遇期，使我国的综合国力、人民的生活水平、国际竞争力和国际影响力都迈上了新台阶，彰显了中国特色社会主义的巨大优越性和强大生命力。许多国家沿袭反映资本主义核心价值观的西方模式，"被动学习""邯郸学步"，非但没有实现所谓的"民主盛景""发展盛景""繁荣盛景"，反而党争纷起、社会动荡。相反，中国改革开放以来探索出的中国特色社会主义道路却让中国实现了人类发展史上的奇迹。中国特色社会主义不是复制品、舶来品，而是有其自身的独特品质，中国特色的价值理念就是其核心内容。

Fourth, the socialist core values have great moral strength.

The power of truth combined with the power of morality can go on for a long time. The socialist core values have a strong moral force occupying the high point of value of human society with their advanced nature, people character and authenticity.

The advanced nature of the socialist core values is reflected in the core values that the socialist system adheres to and pursues. The socialist system is based on the public ownership of the means of production, eliminates the system of exploitation thus the working people become the true masters of the country. Up to date, it is the most advanced social system in human society. The socialist system with Chinese characteristics is a creative combination of the principles of scientific socialism and China's reality. It is still undergoing continuous reform, improvement and development. The pioneering achievements of socialism with Chinese characteristics have made scientific socialism glow a powerful vitality in China in the 21st century, and provided valuable Chinese wisdom and China's plan for mankind to explore a better social system. The socialist core values reflect the essential requirements of China's socialist basic system and penetrate into all aspects of economic, political, cultural, social and ecological construction. They are the inner spirit of China's socialist system.

The people character of the socialist core values is embodied in the fundamental interests of the overwhelming majority of the people it rep-

第四，社会主义核心价值观具有强大的道义力量。

社会主义核心价值观以其先进性、人民性和真实性而居于人类社会的价值制高点，具有强大的道义力量。

社会主义核心价值观的先进性体现为它是社会主义制度所坚持和追求的核心价值理念。社会主义制度建立在生产资料公有制的基础之上，消灭了剥削制度，劳动人民成为国家的真正主人，是人类社会迄今为止最先进的社会制度。中国特色社会主义制度是科学社会主义原则与中国实际的创造性结合，至今仍在不断地改革、完善和发展之中。中国特色社会主义所取得的开创性成就使得科学社会主义在 21 世纪的中国焕发出强大的生机和活力，为人类探索更加美好的社会制度提供了宝贵的中国智慧和中国方案。社会主义核心价值观反映着我国社会主义基本制度的本质要求，渗透于经济、政治、文化、社会、生态建设的各个方面，是我国社会主义制度的内在精神之魂。

社会主义核心价值观的人民性体现在它所代表的最广大人民的根本利益，反映的是最广大

resents, reflecting the value demands of the over-whelming majority of the people, and guiding the broadest people to strive for the realization of a better social ideal. The most fundamental polit-ical standpoint of Marxism is to always stand on the standpoint of the working people and take the liberation of the working people as the purpose, and do everything in its power to seek welfare and profit for the people. *The Communist Manifesto* solemnly proclaimed: "All movements in the past are a minority, or a movement for the benefit of the few. The movement of the proletariat is the inde-pendent movement of the vast majority of people, for the interests of the vast majority of people." Correspondingly, the people character is also the fundamental characteristic of the socialist core values based on Marxism and the practice of the socialist movement. In the process of guiding the building of socialism with Chinese characteris-tics, the Communist Party of China has repeatedly stressed that the people are the creators of history, must practice the fundamental purpose of serving the people wholeheartedly, persist in taking the people as the center and the masters of the country, and take the people's yearning for a better life as the goal of struggle; emphasizing that the original intention and mission of the Communists of Chi-na is to seek happiness for the Chinese people and revival for the Chinese nation; emphasize that the Communist Party of China is a party that seeks happiness for the Chinese people and strives for the cause of human progress, and has always taken the greater contributions to mankind as its mission.

人民的价值诉求，引导着最广大人民为实现美好的社会理想而奋斗。马克思主义最根本的政治立场就是始终站在广大劳动人民的立场上，以广大劳动人民的解放为旨归，竭尽全力为人民求福利、谋利益。《共产党宣言》庄严宣告："过去的一切运动都是少数人的，或者为少数人谋利益的运动。无产阶级的运动是绝大多数人的，为绝大多数人谋利益的独立的运动。"与此相适应，人民性也是以马克思主义为理论基础、以社会主义运动为实践根据的社会主义核心价值观的根本特性。在引导中国特色社会主义建设的进程中，中国共产党也反复强调，人民是历史的创造者，要践行全心全意为人民服务的根本宗旨，坚持以人民为中心、坚持人民当家作主，把人民对美好生活的向往作为奋斗目标；强调中国共产党人的初心和使命就是为中国人民谋幸福，为中华民族谋复兴；强调中国共产党是为中国人民谋幸福的政党，也是为人类进步事业而奋斗的政党，始终把为人类做出新的更大贡献作为自己的使命。鲜明的人民性使得社会主义核心价值观具有强大的道义感召力。

The distinct people character makes the socialist core values have a strong moral appeal.

The moral power of socialist core values also stems from its authenticity. "A name is not made in heaven, but in fact." In the process of the development of human society, many ruling classes have proposed many values that look very good, and some of them have played a very positive role in history, but because of their class and historical limitations, these good values have not been fully and truly realized. Democracy, freedom, fraternity, etc. are the value propositions that the bourgeoisie always talks about, but as Lenin pointed out: "Compared with the medieval system, bourgeois democracy is a great progress in history, but it has always been a narrow, incomplete, hypocritical and deceptive democracy under the capitalist system, a paradise for the rich, a trap and a trick for the exploited and the poor. However, the socialist system in which the people are the masters of the country provides the foundational premise and system for the real realization of the socialist core values, making the values of freedom, democracy and justice become a truly, concrete and extensive reality.

2. How to Practice the Socialist Core Values

First, college students should buckle the first button of life.

Both the world today and contemporary China are undergoing major change. This kind of change is reflected in people's ideas and concepts,

社会主义核心价值观的道义力量还源于它的真实性。"名非天造，必从其实。"在人类社会发展进程中，许多统治阶级都曾提出了不少看上去非常美好的价值理念，其中有些在历史上也发挥了很大的积极作用，但由于其阶级和历史局限性，这些美好的价值理念并未能彻底地、真正地实现。民主、自由、博爱等便是资产阶级时刻挂在嘴边的价值主张，但正如列宁所指出的那样："资产阶级民主同中世纪制度比较起来，在历史上是一大进步，但它始终是而且在资本主义制度下不能不是狭隘的、残缺不全的、虚伪的、骗人的民主，对富人是天堂，对被剥削者、对穷人是陷阱和骗局。"而人民当家作主的社会主义制度为社会主义核心价值观的真正实现提供了根本的制度前提和保障，使得自由、民主、公正等价值观成为真切、具体、广泛的现实。

2. 如何践行社会主义核心价值观

第一，扣好人生的第一粒扣子。

当今世界和当代中国都处于大变革之中。这种变革反映到人们的思想观念中，自然会产生多

and naturally it will produce a variety of ideas and values. Facing the new situation of various ideological and cultural exchanges in the world, facing the new characteristics of the ideological values of the whole society, which are diverse, complex and changeable, the growth of college students into talents requires the guidance of correct values. Correct values can guide college students to integrate the pursuit of life value into the cause of the country and the nation, always stand on the position of the people, work hard with the people, advance with the motherland, serve the people, contribute to the society, and strive to become qualified builders and reliable successors of the socialism with Chinese characteristics. Colledge students should adhere from easy to difficult, from near to far, from now on, start from, try to turn the requirements of core values into daily behavioral norms, form a consciously pursued value concept, and vigorously promote it to the whole society, so as to gather powerful youth energy to realize the Chinese dream of national prosperity, national rejuvenation and people's happiness.

First, college students should study hard, cultivate morality, distinguish right from wrong, and be down-to-earth.

The first one is that college students should study hard. Knowledge is an important foundation for building the socialist core values. College students are in the golden age of learning scientific knowledge, they should make great efforts to acquire true knowledge, regard learning as a spiritual pursuit and a way of life, with dogged persererance, strive to expand the radius of knowledge,

种多样的思想理论和价值理念。面对世界范围内各种思想文化交流交融交锋的新形势，面对整个社会思想价值观念呈现出的多元多样、复杂多变的新特点，大学生成长成才更加需要正确价值观的引领。正确价值观能够引导大学生把人生价值追求融入国家和民族事业，始终站在人民大众立场，同人民一道拼搏、同祖国一道前进，服务人民、奉献社会，努力成为中国特色社会主义事业的合格建设者和可靠接班人。大学生要坚持由易到难、由近及远，从现在做起，从自己做起，努力把核心价值观的要求转变为日常的行为准则，形成自觉奉行的价值理念，并身体力行，将其推广到全社会，为实现国家富强、民族振兴、人民幸福的中国梦凝聚强大的青春能量。

第二，勤学、修德、明辨、笃实。

一是勤学。知识是树立社会主义核心价值观的重要基础。大学生正处于学习科学知识的黄金时期，要下得苦功夫，求得真学问，把学习作为一种精神追求、一种生活方式，以顽强的毅力，努力扩大知识半径，既读有字之书，也读无字之书，提高道德品

read both books with words and books without words, improve their moral quality, master real talents and practical learning, and strive to develop skills. Colledge students should strive to master Marxist theory, form a correct world view and scientific methodology, and deepen the recognition of socialist core values. College students should pay attention to internalizing the knowledge they have learned, form their own opinions, and strive to master the real talents that serve the motherland and the people, so that diligent study and sensitivity to knowledge can become the driving force for youth voyage.

The second one is that college students should cultivate morality. The most important thing for living and working is the cultivation of virtue and morality. "Morality and cultivation are the origins of being human being." Cai Yuanpei once said: "If one has no morality, although his body is strong and intelligence is developed well, these strengths can only help him do something evil and harmful." Morality has fundamental meanings for both individuals and society. "The core values are actually a kind of morality, which is not only a personal virtue, but also a great virtue,that is, the morality of the country and the society. The country cannot prosper without morality and people cannot get improved without morality." Only through the understanding of great virtue,the obedience of social morality and strict attitude to personal virtue, the talents can get worthy use. To cultivate morality, we should establish lofty ambitions while studying and working steadfast.College students should be determined to serve the motherland and the peo-

质，掌握真才实学，练就过硬本领。要努力掌握马克思主义理论，形成正确的世界观和科学的方法论，深化对社会主义核心价值观的认知和认同。要注重把所学知识内化于心，形成自己的见解，努力掌握为祖国、为人民服务的真才实学，让勤于学习、敏于求知成为青春远航的动力。

二是修德。做人做事的第一位是崇德修身。"德者，本也。"蔡元培曾经说过："若无德，则虽体魄智力发达，适足助其为恶。"道德之于个人、之于社会，都具有基础性意义。"核心价值观，其实就是一种德，既是个人的德，也是一种大德，就是国家的德、社会的德。国无德不兴，人无德不立。"一个人只有明大德、守公德、严私德，其才方能用得其所。修德，既要立志高远，又要立足平实。要立志报效祖国、服务人民，这是大德，养大德者方可成大业。同时，要从做好小事、管好小节开始，"见善则迁，有过则改"，踏踏实实修好公德、私德，学会劳动、学会勤俭、学会感恩、学会助人、学会谦让、学会宽容、学会自省、学会自律。

ple because this is a great virtue. Only those who owns great virtue can make achievements.At the same time, we must start from doing small things and managing the small details well. "Seeing good moves, one should follow them and study hard ,but when making mistakes one should correct them soon", and one should cultivate both social and private morality steadfast, learn to work, be diligent, be grateful, help others, be modest, be tolerant, be introspective, and be self−disciplined.

The third one is that college students should distinguish right from wrong. To cultivate and practice the socialist core values, we must strengthen our ability of value judgment and sense of moral responsibility, identify what is true, good and beautiful, what is false, evil and ugly, and consciously cultivate good morality, nurse good thoughts and always do good deeds. At present,in some fields and among some people,the value judgment has no boundaries, losts the bottom line, and some people even mix the false things with those genuine, and pride themselves on being ugly and shameful. College students must face up to the choice of views on values and moral responsibility, strengthen judgment, be good at distinguishing between right and wrong, be good at decision−making, carry forward the true, good and beautiful things and demote false,evil and ugly things, establish correct orientation, clarify vague understanding, correct improper behaviors, and form ideological and moral paradox of eliminating vice and exalting virtue, and of pressing the evil and supporting the good, and consciously be a builder of good morality and a promoter of social

三是明辨。培育和践行社会主义核心价值观，要增强自己的价值判断力和道德责任感，明辨什么是真善美、什么是假恶丑，自觉做到常修善德、常怀善念、常做善举。当前，在一些领域和一些人当中，价值判断没有了界限、丧失了底线，甚至以假乱真、以丑为美、以耻为荣。大学生一定要正视价值观选择和道德责任感，强化判断，善于明辨是非，善于决断选择，旗帜鲜明地弘扬真善美、贬斥假恶丑，树立正确导向，澄清模糊认识，匡正失范行为，形成激浊扬清、抑恶扬善的思想道德舆论，自觉做良好道德风尚的建设者、社会文明进步的推动者。

civilization progress.

The fourth one is that college students should be down-to-earth. We cannot sit to talk empty of morality. We must take small things as big things to do and go step by step. Some people say "The Sage are mediocre people who are willing to make efforts, and mediocre people are the sage who are not willing to make efforts." The meaning is: A person with high intelligence is a mediocre person who is diligent and hard-working, and a mediocre person who does nothing is a sage who refuses to work hard. This shows that as long as you are willing to work hard, even a mediocre person can be a sage; but if you refuse to work hard, the sage will also become a mediocre person.

Only through applying force to implementation, making efforts according to the combination of knowing and doing, can the core values be internalized into people's spiritual pursuits, and externalized into people's conscious actions. *Book of Rites* said: "study extensively,inquire prudently,think carefully,distinguish clearly,and practice earnestly." Teenagers have great opportunities, it's key for them to take a steady step, lay a solid foundation, and work hard and unceasingly. And it's the biggest taboo to be impatient and fickle in both studying and starting a business ,such as dropping learning something before starting just for a while or giving up a job very soon after starting engaging in it. "Difficult things in the world are developed from the easy ones, and the great things in the world are formed from the tiny points." It will always be hard work behind the

四是笃实。道不可坐论，德不能空谈。要把小事当作大事干，一步一个脚印往前走。有人说："圣人是肯做工夫的庸人，庸人是不肯做工夫的圣人。"意思是：智能高的人是勤奋肯干的庸人，而那些无所作为的庸人则是不肯用功的圣人。这说明只要肯用功，即便是庸人也能成为圣人；如果不肯用功，就是圣人也会变成庸人。

于实处用力，从知行合一上下功夫，社会主义核心价值观才能内化为人们的精神追求，外化为人们的自觉行动。《礼记·中庸》中说："博学之，审问之，慎思之，明辨之，笃行之。"青年有着大好机遇，关键是要迈稳步子、夯实根基、久久为功。心浮气躁、朝三暮四，学一门丢一门，干一行弃一行，是为学和创业最忌讳的。"天下难事，必作于易；天下大事，必作于细。"成功的背后，永远是艰辛努力。青年要把艰苦环境作为磨炼自己的机遇，只要坚韧不拔，百折不挠，就一定能取得成功。

success. Young people should take the hard environment as an opportunity to temper themselves. As long as they are tough and unyielding, success will definitely wait for them in the front.

In short, the active cultivation and practice of socialist core values and active promotion of the common values pursued by the broad masses of people is the inherent requirement for realizing the goal of building a well-off society in an all-round way and persisting in and developing socialism with Chinese characteristics. The world today is in the period of great development, great change, great adjustment, ideological and cultural exchanges, blends and bouts are more frequent, the strategic position of culture in the competition of comprehensive national strength is more and more prominent, and the lifeline role of the core value system in social development and national security is more and more outstanding.

总之，积极培育和践行社会主义核心价值观，积极推动广大人民形成共同的价值追求，是实现全面建成小康社会奋斗目标、坚持和发展中国特色社会主义的内在要求。当今世界正处在大发展大变革大调整时期，思想文化交流交融交锋更加频繁，文化在综合国力竞争中的战略地位越来越凸显，核心价值体系在社会发展和国家安全中的生命线作用越来越突出。

Lecture Nine
The Inheritance of Chinese Traditional Virtues and the Promotion of Chinese Revolutionary Morality

I. The Brief Introduction to Morality

1.The Connotation, Origin, Essence, Function and Role of Morality and its Change and Development

First, the connotation of morality.

Morality belongs to the category of superstructure, and it is a special form of social consciousness,which is standardized by good and evil,is the combination of behavioral norms mainly relying on public opinion, traditional customs and people's inner beliefs to play a role. The complete definition of morality has three meanings: Morality is determined by certain social and economic foundation, and serves certain social and economic foundation; morality uses good and evil as evaluation criteria to adjust the relationship and behavior between people, and sets standards and guidelines for what people should and should not do; morality works primarily through social opinion, traditional customs and inner beliefs rather than through legal coercion.

Second, the origin of morality.

The non-Marxist theory of moral origin includes "the doctrine of divine providence" "the

专题九
传承中国传统美德和发扬中国革命道德

一、道德概述

1. 道德的含义、起源、本质、功能、作用及变化发展

第一，道德的含义。

道德属于上层建筑的范畴，是一种特殊的社会意识形式，以善恶为标准，主要依靠社会舆论、传统习俗和人们的内心信念来发挥作用的行为规范的总和。道德这一完整定义包含三层含义；道德由一定的社会经济基础决定，并为一定的社会经济基础服务；道德以善恶为评价标准来调整人们之间的关系和行为，它规定着人们应该做什么和不应该做什么的标准和准则；道德主要通过社会舆论、传统习俗和内心信念来发挥作用，而不是靠法律的强制手段来维持。

第二，道德的起源。

非马克思主义的道德起源论有"天意神启论""先天人性

theory of innate human nature" "the theory of emotional desire" and "the theory of animal instinct" and so on.

Marxist moral view holds that labor is the primary premise of the origin of morality, social relations are the objective conditions on which morality depends, and man's self-consciousness is the subjective condition of morality.

Third, the essence of morality.

Morality is a special ideology that reflects social and economic relations. The emergence, development and change of morality are ultimately rooted in social and economic relations.

Morality is a special way of regulating social interests, and is a special code of conduct that regulates the relationship between people, people and society, people and nature, and people and themselves.

Morality is a spirit of practice, and is a social consciousness that aims to regulate people's behaviors through the understanding of the world's phenomena of good and evil and is reflected through people's practical activities.

In short, morality, as a kind of practical spirit, is the sum of special consciousness and beliefs, codes of conduct, evaluation choices, etc., and is the driving force for regulating social relations, developing personal qualities, and improving spiritual realms.

Fourth, the function of morality.

The function of morality generally refers to the effect and ability of morality as a special form of social consciousness for social development. The function of morality can be divided into the

论""情感欲望论"和"动物本能论"等。

马克思主义道德观认为,劳动是道德起源的首要前提,社会关系是道德赖以产生的客观条件,人的自我意识是道德产生的主观条件。

第三,道德的本质。

道德是反映社会经济关系的特殊意识形态。道德的产生、发展和变化,根源于社会经济关系。

道德是社会利益关系的特殊调节方式,是一种调整人与人、人与社会、人与自然以及人与自身之间关系的特殊的行为规范。

道德是一种实践精神,是一种旨在通过把握世界的善恶现象来规范人们的行为并通过人们的实践活动体现出来的社会意识。

总之,道德作为一种实践精神,是特殊的意识信念、行为准则、评价选择等方面的总和,是调节社会关系、发展个人品质、提高精神境界等活动的动力。

第四,道德的功能。

道德的功能一般是指道德作为社会意识的特殊形式,对于社会发展所具有的功效与能力。道德的功能分为认识功能、规范功

cognitive function, the normative function and the regulatory function.

The cognitive function of morality refers to the effect and ability of morality to reflect social relations, especially to reflect social and economic relations.

The normative function of morality refers to the effect and ability of morality to regulate social members' behavior in the social public field, occupational field, and family field under the guidance of correct views of good and evil, and regulate the cultivation of personal morality, and guide and promote people's admiration of good deeds.

The regulatory function of morality refers to the effect and ability of morality to guide and correct people's behaviors and practices, and coordinate social relations and relationships between people through evaluation and other means.

Fifth, the role of morality.

The role of morality refers to the social influence and actual effects of the realization of the function of morality such as understanding, regulation, adjustment, encouragement, orientation, and education.

Morality is an important spiritual force for the formation, consolidation and development of economic foundation.

Morality has a major impact on the existence of other social ideologies, and maintains social order and stability by regulating the relationship between people.

Morality is the internal power to improve people's spiritual realm, promote people's

道德的认识功能是指道德反映社会关系，特别是反映社会经济关系的功效与能力。

道德的规范功能是指道德在正确善恶观的指引下，规范社会成员在社会公共领域、职业领域、家庭领域的行为，并规范个人品德的养成，引导并促进人们崇德向善的功效与能力。

道德的调节功能是指道德通过评价等方式，指导和纠正人们的行为和实践活动，协调社会关系和人们之间关系的功效与能力。

第五，道德的作用。

道德的作用是指道德的认识、规范、调节、激励、导向、教育等功能的发挥和实现所产生的社会影响及实际效果。

道德为经济基础的形成、巩固和发展服务，是一种重要的精神力量。

道德对其他社会意识形态的存在有着重大的影响，通过调节人与人之间的关系维护社会秩序和稳定。

道德是提高人的精神境界、促进人的自我完善、推动人的全

self-improvement, and people's all-round development.

In a class society, morality is an important tool for regulating class contradictions and carrying out class struggle between opposing classes.

We should oppose the two extreme views of "the theory of moral omnipotence" and "the theory of moral uselessness".

"The theory of moral omnipotence" exaggerates the role of morality unilaterally, believing that morality decides everything, is above everything and dominates everything. As long as the moral level is high, all social problems can be easily solved. The fundamental error of this view is that it reverses the determining and being determined relationships between the social existence and the social consciousness and between the economic base and the superstructure, and denies the decisive role of the mode of production of material materials in social development.

"The theory of moral uselessness" denies the role of morality, either by emphasizing the role of non-moral factors to deny the positive role of morality, or by emphasizing the negative factors of morality to deny the positive role of morality.

The nature of moral function is linked to the different historical stages of social development, determined by the economic foundation reflected by morality and the class interests represented by morality. Only the morality that reflects the requirements of the development of advanced productive forces and the interests of the progressive class will positively promote the development of

面发展的内在动力。

在阶级社会中，道德是调节阶级矛盾和对立阶级之间开展阶级斗争的重要工具。

我们要反对"道德万能论"和"道德无用论"这两种对道德的极端看法。

"道德万能论"片面夸大道德的作用，认为道德决定一切、高于一切、支配一切，只要道德水平高，一切社会问题都可以迎刃而解。这种观点的根本错误在于，颠倒了社会存在和社会意识、经济基础同上层建筑之间的决定与被决定的关系，否定了物质资料的生产方式在社会发展中的决定作用。

"道德无用论"从根本上否认道德的作用，或者通过强调非道德因素的作用来否定道德的积极作用，或者通过强调道德的消极因素来否定道德的积极作用。

道德发挥作用的性质与社会发展的不同历史阶段相联系，由道德所反映的经济基础、代表的阶级利益所决定。只有反映先进生产力发展要求和进步阶级利益的道德，才会对社会的发展和人的素质的提高产生积极的推动作用，否则就不利于甚至阻碍社会

society and the improvement of human quality. Otherwise, it will not help or even hinder the development of society and the improvement of human quality.

Sixth, the change and development of morality.

The development of human morality is a historical process rising tortuously and the general trend of moral development is upward and forward.

The main manifestation of moral progress is that morality plays an increasingly important role in social life, and its role in promoting social harmony and the overall and free development of human beings is becoming more and more prominent; the scope of moral regulation is constantly expanding, and the means or methods of regulation are continuously enriched and more scientific and reasonable. The development and advancement of morality has also become an important measure of the degree of social civilization. Socialist and communist morality are the inevitable outcome of human morality development in accordance with laws. It is a new type of morality in the history of human morality development. It is a criticism and inheritance of human morality tradition, and must keep pace with the times with the progress of social and the development of practice.

II.Inheriting the Achievements of Chinese Excellent Morality, Carrying forward Chinese Revolutionary Morality

Chinese traditional morality takes Confucian ethics and morality as the main content, including

的发展和人的素质的提高。

第六，道德的变化发展

人类道德的发展是一个曲折上升的历史过程，道德发展的总趋势是向上的、前进的。

道德进步主要表现为道德在社会生活中所起的作用越来越重要，对促进社会和谐与人的全面自由发展的作用越来越突出；道德调控的范围不断扩大，调控的手段或方式不断丰富且更加科学合理。道德的发展和进步也成为衡量社会文明程度的重要尺度。社会主义和共产主义道德，是人类道德合乎规律发展的必然产物，是人类道德发展史上的一种崭新类型的道德，是对人类道德传统的批判与继承，并必然随着社会的进步和实践的发展而与时俱进。

二、传承中国优秀道德成果，发扬中国革命道德

中国传统道德以儒家伦理道德为主要内容，还包括墨家、道

the traditional ethical and moral thoughts such as Mohism, Taoism and Legalism. The construction of socialist morality must inherit the excellent moral tradition in history critically.

1. Inheriting Chinese Traditional Virtues

First, the basic spirit of Chinese traditional virtues

The overall interest is attached importance to, and the responsibility and devotion is emphasized. The principles of "benevolence and love" are respected, and that harmony is the most valuable is attached importance to. The spiritual realm is pursued and the ideal personality is yearned for. The moral cultivation is emphasized and the moral practice is attached importance to.

Second, the creative transformation and innovative development of Chinese traditional virtues.

The first one is that the excavation and elucidation of the Chinese traditional virtues must be strengthened. Any morality is the product of a specific historical era. The Chinese traditional virtues have been formed through a long period of social development and are inevitably marked with traditional society. There exists more or less content and form that is incompatible with today's real life. To carry forward the Chinese traditional virtues, we must eliminate the elements of class nature and the limitations of the times through scientific analysis and identification, and excavate the moral spirit with contemporary values, sum up the rich ideological and moral resources of traditional virtues, interpret and activate the virtues and

家、法家等传统伦理道德思想。社会主义道德建设，无疑要批判地继承历史上优秀的道德传统。

1. 传承中华传统美德

第一，中华传统美德的基本精神。

重视整体利益，强调责任奉献。推崇"仁爱"原则，注重以和为贵。追求精神境界，向往理想人格。强调道德修养，注重道德践履。

第二，中华传统美德的创造性转化和创新性发展。

一是加强对传统美德的挖掘和阐发。任何道德都是具体历史时代的产物。中华传统美德是经过漫长的社会发展而形成的，不可避免地带有传统社会的印记，在内容和形式上或多或少地存在着与今天的现实生活不相适应的地方。弘扬中华传统美德，必须通过科学的分析和鉴别，剔除其中带有阶级性和时代局限性的成分，把其中具有当代价值的道德精神发掘出来，总结传统美德中丰富的思想道德资源，对中华传统美德的德目、观点进行新的诠释和激活，结合现代生活赋予其

viewpoints of Chinese traditional virtues from a new way, and strive to promote the creative transformation and innovative development of Chinese traditional virtues combining with a new era connotation given by modern life. For example, the answer to how to treat parents, friends, teachers, strangers, etc. should be rooted in local cultural resources; filial piety, family stability, cohesiveness, emphasis on education and faithfulness are still the most important value chosen by the people. For the values of benevolence, righteousness, rites, wisdom, faith, loyalty, filial piety, sincerity, and forgiveness advocated by Confucianism, after eliminating their histoyical negativity, We can completely refine and revitalize their rational factors, and penetrate them into today's life, let them participate in the modernization as a positive and healthy force.

The second one is that traditional virtues are used to nourish the construction of socialist morality. To realize the creative transfoemation of traditional virtues, we should regard traditional morality as an important resource and reliance of contemporary Chinese socialist morality, realize new morality's direct inheritance and continuation of traditional virtues. The construction of our new morality is not only inseparable from its "source" of changed social life practice, but also inseparable from the "flow" of traditional virtues.

Traditional ethics is a complex system with multiple levels, whose roles and meanings in modern society are different. As far as the content of Confucian ethics is concerned, it can be roughly

的新的时代内涵，努力推动中华传统美德的创造性转化和创新性发展。例如，怎么对待父母、朋友、师长、陌生人等，应根植于本土文化资源；孝敬、家庭的稳定性、凝聚力、重视教育和忠信，仍然是老百姓选择的最主要的价值。对于儒家所提倡的仁、义、礼、智、信、忠、孝、诚、恕等价值观，在剔除它们的历史负面性之后，完全可以提炼、活化它们的合理因素，并得其渗透到今天的生活中，让其作为正面的、积极的、健康的力量参与现代化建设。

二是用传统美德滋养社会主义道德建设。实现传统美德的创造性转化，就是要把传统道德作为当代中国社会主义道德的重要资源和凭借，实现新道德对传统美德的直接继承和延续。我们的新道德建设，既离不开变化了的社会生活实践这个"源"，也离不开传统美德这个"流"。

传统伦理道德是一个多层次的复杂体系，不同层次在现代社会中的作用和意义是不同的。就儒家伦理的内容而言，其大致可

divided into three levels: Core spirit, i.e. the doc- trine of "benevolence", which is the most general value spirit of Confucianism about the relationship between people; the specific social moral values, including "three principles and five virtues", the family standard, the loyalty and filial piety; the general rules of conduct of people in daily life, including righteousness, wisdom, humility, toler- ance, honesty, acumen, moderation and so on.

For the flow of traditional moral resources in China, we should inherit what can be and should be inherited in it, and mainly abandon the dross of political ethics in its feudal state and transform the rational elements of individual morality, family morality and social morality to guide the daily life of people in modern society.

It is necessary to combine the requirements of the times to persist in the principle of using the past to serve the present and keeping innovating, provide rich moral resources for the construction of socialist morality and give socialist and com- munist morality distinct national characteristics according to whether it is conducive to promoting the construction cause of socialism with Chinese characteristics, building a socialist moral system with Chinese characteristics, cultivating and prac- ticing the standards of socialist core values. And it is necessary to play the role of catalysis and edu- cation of the Chinese traditional virtues in every- day life based on facing the public and serving the people,so that the traditional virtues and the daily life can be blended, and the ethical spirit contained in the traditional virtues can be introduced into the

分为三个层次：核心精神，即"仁"学，这是儒家关于人与人之间关系的最一般的价值精神；特定的社会伦理价值观，如"三纲五常"、家族本位、忠孝等；日常生活中为人处世的一般行为准则，如义、智、恭、宽、信、敏、中庸等。

对于我国传统道德资源主流中能继承的和要继承的，我们主要是抛弃其封建国家政治伦理的糟粕，转化为个体道德、家族道德与社会道德中的合理成分，以指导现代社会民众的日常生活。

要结合时代要求，按照是否有利于推动中国特色社会主义的建设事业，是否有利于建设中国特色社会主义道德体系，是否有利于培育和践行社会主义核心价值观的标准，坚持古为今用、推陈出新的原则，为社会主义道德建设提供丰富的道德资源，赋予社会主义道德和共产主义道德以鲜明的民族特色。要立足于面向大众、服务人民，发挥中华传统美德人伦日用的化育功能，使传统美德与日常生活水乳交融，让传统美德中蕴含的伦理精神点点滴滴地导入人们的生活，生根发酵，产生化育的功能，不断丰富人们的精神世界，增强人们的精

roots of people's life and fertilize,thus the function of catalyzing and education are produced,which will constantly enrich people's spiritual world and enhance people's spiritual strength.

2.Carrying Forward Chinese Morality

First, the connotation of chinese revolutionary morality.

The Chinese revolutionary morality refers to the fine morality formed by Chinese communists, the people's army, all advanced people and the masses in the new democratic revolution and socialist revolution, construction and reform in China. It is the product of the combination of Marxism and the great practice of Chinese revolution, construction and reform, an important theoretical achievement of the Sinicization of Marxist ethics, a succession and development of China's fine moral tradition, a new sublimation and a qualitative leap of Chinese traditional virtues and the premise and foundation of socialist morality and the extremely precious moral wealth of the Chinese nation.

Second, the ancient traditional morality, the modern revolutionary morality and the Party's practices of the new democratic revolution and the socialist revolution lay the foundation of Chinese revolutionary morality.

The first one is that the ancient traditional morality is the historical premise of the emergence and formation of Chinese revolutionary morality. The ancient traditional morality mainly refers to the ethics accumulated and passed down from the pre-Qin period to the Revolution of 1911, including the morality of slave society and the morality

神力量。

2. 发扬中国革命道德

第一，中国革命道德的内涵。

中国革命道德是指中国共产党人、人民军队、一切先进分子和人民群众在中国新民主主义革命和社会主义革命、建设与改革中所形成的优良道德。它是马克思主义与中国革命、建设和改革的伟大实践相结合的产物，是马克思主义伦理思想中国化的重要理论成果，是对中国优良道德传统的继承和发展，是中华传统美德新的升华和质的飞跃，是社会主义道德的前提和基础，是中华民族极其宝贵的道德财富。

第二，古代传统道德、近代革命道德以及新民主主义革命与社会主义革命实践是中国革命道德形成与发展的基础。

一是古代传统道德是中国革命道德产生和形成的历史前提。古代传统道德主要是指从先秦到辛亥革命时期所积淀和流传下来的伦理道德，包括奴隶社会和封建社会的道德。从一定意义上来说，没有中华传统美德的长期发

of feudal society. In a certain sense, Chinese revolutionary morality cannot be formed and developed without the long-term development and rich accumulation of Chinese traditional virtues. The Chinese revolutionary morality ,which inherits the essence of Chinese traditional morality and abandons its dross, is the continuation and development of Chinese fine traditional morality, and is a brand-new morality formed beyond the limitations of the times of the Chinese traditional virtues.

The second one is that the modern revolutionary morality is the historical basis of the emergence of Chinese revolutionary morality.

During the Revolution of 1911, the bourgeois-democratic revolutionary school represented by Sun Yat-sen combined the critique of feudal ethics with the practical actions of the revolution, and used the ideas of freedom, equality, and fraternity from the West as a weapon to gave a fatal blow to the ideas of "divine right of kings" and "ruler guides subjects" and the ethics associated with feudal despotism. At the same time, the standard of "loyalty" and "filial piety" norms and the concepts of "personality" and "nationality" in traditional ethics were reinterpreted and endowed with revolutionary content. Eight virtues of loyalty, filial piety, benevolence, love, trustworthiness, righteousness, harmony, and peace proposed by him are Sun Yat-sen's new attempts to replace the ideological system of feudal ethics , and have taken a valuable step in transforming the old morality. Due to the lack of scientific critical weapons and strong weapon criticism, the historical mission of

展和丰厚积淀，就不可能有中国革命道德的形成和发展。中国革命道德继承了中国传统道德的精华，摒弃了传统道德的糟粕，是中国优良传统道德的延续和发展，是超越了中华传统美德时代局限而形成的一种崭新的道德。

二是近代革命道德是中国革命道德产生的历史基础。

辛亥革命时期，以孙中山为代表的资产阶级民主革命派，把对封建礼教的批判与革命的实际行动相结合，以西方自由、平等、博爱的思想为武器，对"君权神授""君为臣纲"以及与封建专制主义相联系的道德规范给予致命打击。同时，对传统伦理道德中的"忠""孝"规范和"人格""国格"观念重新进行解释，并赋予其革命内容。孙中山提出的八德，即忠、孝、仁、爱、信、义、和、平是他试图以此代替封建纲常伦理思想体系的新尝试，在变革旧道德上迈出了可贵的一步。由于缺乏科学的批判武器和强有力的武器批判，这一尝试随着革命成果被篡夺而失败，未能完成批判旧道德、重建新道德的历史使命。

criticizing old morality and rebuilding new morality has not been completed as the revolutionary achievements have been defeated and the revolution has failed.

During the "May 4th" New Culture Movement, the radical democratic fighters raised the banner of democracy and science and issued the slogan of "Down with the Confucianism" to promote new morality , break the old ethics and launched a fierce attack on feudal ethics in response to the retro-revolutionary trend of "worshiping the Confucianism and restoring the ethics in the ancient time" at that time. This "ethical revolution" which is based on individual liberation reversed the retrogression in ideological and cultural fields, and brought the feudal ethics that lasted for thousands of years into crisis, and opened the way for the spread of Marxism in China. At the same time, in the face of the international situation and domestic realities, some advanced elements felt that learning Western bourgeois democracy would never work and could not solve China's problems, and it was impossible to truly realize the "ethical revolution" .

The third one is that the Party's practices of the new democratic revolution and the socialist revolution are the practice foundation for the generation of Chinese revolutionary morality.

Chinese revolutionary morality sprouted before and after the "May 4th" Movement in 1919, originated from the worker and peasant movement after the founding of the Communist Party of China and gradually formed after the Agrarian

五四新文化运动期间，激进的民主主义斗士们针对当时十分猖獗的"尊孔复古"思潮，举起民主和科学的旗帜，提出"打到孔家店"的口号，提倡新道德，破除旧道德，向封建礼教发起猛烈攻击。这场以个性解放为主的"伦理革命"扭转了思想文化领域的倒退局面，使延续几千年的封建伦理道德陷入危机，也为马克思主义在中国的传播打开了通道。与此同时，面对国际形势和国内现实，一些先进分子感到学习西方资产阶级民主主义的是行不通的，解决不了中国的问题，也不可能真正实现"伦理革命"。

三是新民主主义革命和社会主义革命实践是中国革命道德产生的实践基础。

中国革命道德萌芽于1919年五四运动前后，发端于中国共产党成立以后的工人运动和农民运动，经过土地革命战争、抗日战争、解放战争以及社会主义革

Revolutionary War, the War of Resistance Against Japanese Aggression, the War of Liberation, and the practice of socialist revolution. Revolutionary morality was formed under the guidance of Marxism. It belongs to the Communist moral system and has fundamentally different characteristics from ancient traditional morality.

When the Communist Party of China was founded in 1921, the Chinese proletariat independently entered the political arena and became the core force leading the Chinese revolution. The Chinese Communists represented by Mao Zedong insisted on combining the basic principles of Marxism with the concrete practices of the Chinese revolution and had led the Chinese people to acquire the victory of the new democratic revolution and the socialist revolution. In the great historical process of revolution defeating reaction, progress beating reversal, the ideological and moral field has undergone a revolutionary transformation. And the epochal achievements and main signs of the development of ethical thoughts are the emergence and formation of revolutionary morality, thus creating a new era of Chinese ethical development.

① This transformation established the guiding position of Marxism in China's ethical and moral construction. Revolutionary morality is formed under the guidance of the Marxist outlook on world and methodology. It is not only opposed to the feudal ethics and morality based on the theory of "destiny", but also completely demarcated from the bourgeois ethics based on abstract theory of human nature and humanitarianism, sweeping

命的实践逐渐形成。革命道德是在马克思主义指导下形成的,属于共产主义道德体系,具有与古代传统道德截然不同的特点。

1921 年,中国共产党成立,中国无产阶级独立地走上政治舞台,成为领导中国革命的核心力量。以毛泽东为代表的中国共产党人,坚持把马克思主义的基本原理同中国革命的具体实践相结合,领导中国人民夺取了新民主主义革命和社会主义革命的胜利。在这个革命战胜反动、进步战胜倒退的伟大历史进程中,思想道德领域合乎逻辑地发生了革命性变革。伦理思想发展的时代性成果和主要标志就是产生和形成了革命道德,从而开创了中国伦理道德发展的新时代。

①这次变革确立了马克思主义在中国伦理道德建设中的指导地位。革命道德是在马克思主义世界观和方法论的指导下形成的。它既同以"天命论"为理论依据的封建伦理道德相对立,又与建立在抽象的人性论和人道主义基础上的资产阶级伦理道德彻底划清了界限,扫除了笼罩在伦

away the fog of theory in the field of ethics. In the process of formation, has solved a series of major social ethical issues through the way of the combination of theory and practice with the dialectical materialist historical view, and formed a systematic revolutionary moral theory. Mao Zedong's works of *On Correcting the Wrong Thoughts in the Party*, *Serving the People*, *Commemorating Bethune*, Liu Shaoqi's works of *On the Cultivation of Communists* and Zhou Enlai's works of *My Cultivation Principles*, etc. are all classic works about Chinese revolutionary morality.

② This transformation has achieved the sublation and transcendence of ancient traditional morality. Revolutionary morality is a new achievement of the criticism, inheritance, transformation and innovation of ancient traditional morality. On the issue of treating ancient traditional morality, it opposes the historical nihilism that denies traditional culture and the cultural conservatism that affirms everything, and adopts the scientific method of critical inheritance. That is "removing its feudal dross and absorbing its essence of democracy" through digesting and decomposing, making the essence a fresh nutrient and summarizing the moral categories and ethics that suit the needs of the times. It is through the sublation of the combination of criticism, inheritance and innovation that revolutionary morality realized the transformation from the old quality to the new one, and the revolutionary leap of the new quality surpassing the old one.

③ This transformation has created revolu-

理道德领域的理论迷雾。在生成过程中，它用辩证唯物主义历史观从理论与实践的结合上解决了一系列重大的社会伦理问题，形成了系统的革命道德理论。毛泽东的《关于纠正党内的错误思想》《为人民服务》《纪念白求恩》，刘少奇的《论共产党员的修养》，周恩来的《我的修养要则》等都是有关中国革命道德的经典之作。

②这次变革实现了对古代传统道德的扬弃和超越。革命道德是对古代传统道德批判、继承、改造和创新的崭新成果。在对待古代传统道德的问题上，它反对否定传统文化的历史虚无主义和肯定一切的文化保守主义，采取批判继承的科学方法，即通过消化和分解，"剔除其封建性糟粕，吸取其民主性精华"，使精华成为新鲜营养，概括出适合时代需要的道德范畴和道德规范。正是通过这种批判、继承和创新有机结合的扬弃，革命道德才实现了从旧质向新质的转化和新质超越旧质的革命性跃升。

③这次变革铸就了富有民族

tionary ethics and fine moral traditions with national characteristics. The Chinese revolutionary morality has not only the core of scientific thought and theory, but also the profound cultural heritage of the Chinese nation,and its connotation is extremely rich, such as the firm socialist and communist ideals and beliefs, the ruling purpose and outlook on life of serving the people wholeheartedly, the adherence to the collectivist moral principles of the proletariat, advocacy of the spirit of revolutionary heroism of self-improvement, hard work and being not afraid of suffering and death, the patriotic tradition of the devotion to national rejuvenation, the reunification ,prosperity and strength of the motherland, and the social customs of unity and friendship, and that when troubles occurs at one spot, helps comes from all quarters and so on. These noble qualities and spirits not only inherit the excellent Chinese traditional moral spirit, but also vividly reflect the proletarian outlook world, life and values, and become a powerful spiritual force that unites and inspires the Chinese nation to build a new society. They have also laid the foundation and pointed out the direction for the construction of socialist morality and new culture in the era of reform and opening up.

Third, the main content of Chinese revolutionary morality.

The Chinese revolutionary morality has rich and unique connotations, including the principles, requirements, attitudes, cultivation, and fashion of Chinese revolutionary morality, as well as the revolutionary ideals and spirits. In the long-term

特色的革命道德规范和优良道德传统。中国革命道德既有科学的思想理论内核，又有深厚的中华民族文化底蕴，内涵极为丰富。例如，坚定的社会主义和共产主义理想信念，全心全意为人民服务的执政宗旨和人生观，坚持无产阶级的集体主义道德原则，倡导自强不息、艰苦奋斗、一不怕苦二不怕死的革命英雄主义精神，致力于民族振兴和祖国统一、富强的爱国主义传统，团结友爱、一方有难八方支援的社会风尚，等等。这些高尚品德和精神既继承了中华优秀传统道德精神，又生动地体现了无产阶级世界观、人生观和价值观，成为凝聚和激励中华民族建设新社会的强大精神力量，也为改革开放时代的社会主义道德建设、社会主义新文化建设奠定了基础，指明了方向。

第三，中国革命道德的主要内容。

中国革命道德具有丰富而独特的内涵，既包括革命道德的原则、要求、态度、修养、风尚等方面，也包括革命理想、革命精神等方面。在长期革命实践中，

revolutionary practice, the revolutionaries with the Chinese Communists as the main representative have become the models of practicing revolutionary morality by their own actions and even sacrificing their lives.

The first one is that we should strive for the realization of socialist and communist ideals. Lenin pointed out: "To fight for the consolidation and completion of the communist cause is the basis of communist morality." The unyielding spirit of adhering to the ideals and beliefs of socialism and communism is the soul of revolutionary morality. Countless revolutionary martyrs did not hesitate to sacrifice their own lives just to achieve such a lofty ideal. Xia Minghan wrote the brave words in "Poetry before being executed for championing a just cause" that "As long as the Communism I believe in is a truth which is worthy of faith, I am not afraid to be headed. After killing Xia Minghan, there will be thousands of revolutionary descendants who will inherit my path". In *Lovely China*, Fang Zhimin wrote the firm oath that "the enemy can only cut ours skulls, but will never shake our faith". The reason why these revolutionary martyrs are able to rule out all difficulties, persist in struggling, be selfless and fearless, and not afraid to sacrifice is that they have firm socialist and communist ideals and beliefs.

The second one is that we should serve the people wholeheartedly. It is the self-requirement of all the revolutionary advanced elements to truly seek benefits for the masses. As early as 1939, Mao Zedong proposed that "serving the people" is

以中国共产党人为主要代表的革命者，以自己的行动甚至生命成为率先践履革命道德的典范。

一是为实现社会主义和共产主义理想而奋斗。列宁指出："为巩固和完成共产主义事业而斗争，这就是共产主义道德的基础。"坚持社会主义、共产主义理想和信念的不屈不挠的精神，是革命道德的灵魂。无数革命先烈，正是为了实现这样一个崇高的理想，毫不犹豫地献出了自己的生命。夏明翰在《就义诗》中写下"砍头不要紧，只要主义真。杀了夏明翰，还有后人来人"这样的豪言壮语；方志敏在《可爱的中国》中发出"敌人只能砍下我们的头颅，决不能动摇我们的信仰"这样的坚定誓言。这些革命先烈之所以能够排除万难、坚持斗争、无私无畏、不怕牺牲，就是因为他们有坚定的社会主义、共产主义理想和信念。

二是全心全意为人民服务。真心实意为群众谋利益是一切革命先进分子对自己的要求。早在1939年毛泽东就提出，是否"为人民服务"是区别革命道德和

the fundamental boundary between revolutionary morality and all exploiting class morality. In 1944 when commemorating the revolutionary warrior Zhang Side, Mao Zedong clearly defined "serving the people" as a generalization of the lofty qualities of all revolutionaries such as Zhang Side, emphasizing that all revolutionaries should think of the interests of the majority and work wholeheartedly for the benefit of the people. "Serving the people wholeheartedly" ,as a red line implicating the Chinese revolutionary morality, is a great creation of the Communist Party of China in the practice of the Chinese revolution and has played a major role in promoting China's revolution, construction and moral construction.

The third one is that we should always put the interests of the revolution in the first place. The purpose of Communists and revolutionaries being engaged in revolutionary activities is to fight for the interests of the revolution. When there is a contradiction between personal interests and revolutionary interests, we must "take revolutionary interests as the first life, personal interests should obey the revolutionary interests", and "all advanced elements who have revolutionary consciousness should sacrifice their own interests when necessary". Always putting the interests of revolution in the first place has greatly inspired the revolutionaries' dedication to the collective, and made the revolutionary team form unprecedented centripetal and cohesive force.

The fourth one is that the new social atmosphere and the new type of interpersonal relation-

一切剥削阶级道德的根本界限。1944 年，在纪念革命战士张思德时，毛泽东明确以"为人民服务"作为对张思德等一切革命者的崇高品质的概括，强调一切革命者都要想到大多数人的利益，全心全意地为人民的利益工作。"全心全意为人民服务"作为贯穿中国革命道德始终的一根红线，是中国共产党在中国革命实践中的一个伟大创造，对中国的革命、建设事业和道德建设产生了重要的推动作用。

三是始终把革命利益放在首位。共产党人和革命者从事革命活动的目的就是为革命利益而奋斗，在个人利益与革命利益发生矛盾时，要"以革命利益为第一生命，以个人利益服从革命利益"，"一切有革命觉悟的先进分子必要时都应当牺牲自己的利益"。始终把革命利益放在首位，极大地激发了革命者为集体而献身的斗志，使革命队伍形成了前所未有的向心力和凝聚力。

四是树立社会新风，建立新型人际关系。任何道德规范都要

ship should be established. Any ethical code must be oriented towards life practice. Establishing a new social atmosphere and establishing a new type of interpersonal relationship reflects the significance of Chinese revolutionary morality on the level of social life. The spread of Chinese revolutionary morality broke the idea of hierarchy and privilege, the old moral concept of defying labor and working people, established equality awareness, protected the legitimate rights and interests of women, children and the elderly, guided the establishment of new family relationships and the cultivation good family tradition,which has played an important role in raising the civilized standards and moral outlook of the people and establishing a new social trend.

The fifth one is that we should cultivate,discipline ourselves and stay unchaste. The Communist Party of China attaches great importance to the personal moral cultivation of party members, and regards strengthening personal moral cultivation as a major event that can affect the success or failure of the revolution. Therefore, an important part of practicing Chinese revolutionary morality is that the Communists are self-disciplined and stay unchaste. Specifically, it is necessary to focus on the cause of the Chinese revolutionary cause and be open and aboveboard; always be noble in morality and conduct to show the lofty power of personality.

III.The Reference of the Excellent Moral Achievements of Human Civilization

1. Absorbing the Excellent Moral Achieve-

面向生活实践。树立社会新风，建立新型人际关系，体现了中国革命道德在社会生活层面的重要意义。中国革命道德的传扬破除了等级观念和特权思想，破除了鄙视劳动和劳动人民的旧道德观念，树立了平等意识，保护了妇女、儿童和老人的合法权益，引导建立了新型家庭关系和培育良好家风，对提升人民群众的文明水准和道德风貌、树立社会新风尚发挥了重要的作用。

五是修身自律，保持节操。中国共产党非常重视党员的个人道德修养，把加强个人道德修养看作能够影响革命成败的大事，因而践履中国革命道德的重要环节就是共产党人修身自律、保持节操。具体来说，就是要以中国革命事业为重，光明磊落；始终保持高风亮节，展现出高尚的人格力量。

三、借鉴人类文明的优秀道德成果

1. 以开放的胸怀和视野吸收

ments of Human Civilization with an Open Mind and Vision

The civilization development and moral progress of any nation and country today will inevitably be affected by the achievements of the culture and moral civilization of other nations or countries, and it is impossible to break away from the road of human civilization development. Many nations in the world have contributed to human civilization in different periods of human development. Many western thinkers have explored the origin and essence, the principles and norms ,quality, evaluation, education and cultivation of morality,among which there are many insights that have greatly enriched the common civilization achievements of human society. We must uphold the Marxist standpoint, viewpoints, and methods, adhere to the principle of bringism "foreign culture for our own use", not only oppose the whole Westernization, mechanical copying, but also oppose total negation, blind exclusion, and absorb the essence which have positive significance for today's China on the basis of criticism. comtemporary college students not only must have a global vision, the worldwide consciousness, but also cannot dispel the national self-esteem and self-confidence, and cannot lose recognition of our national culture.

2. Opposing the Two Wrong Views on Chinese Traditional Morality

First, the theory of restoring ancient ways completely.

The theory of restoring ancient ways completely is a wrong theory that inherits a nation's

人类文明的优秀道德成果

当今任何民族和国家的文明发展和道德进步都不可能不受到其他民族或国家的文化和道德文明成果的影响，都不可能脱离人类文明发展的大道。世界上许多民族都在人类发展的不同时期对人类文明做出过贡献。西方许多思想家对道德的起源和本质、道德的原则和规范、道德品质、道德评价、道德教育和修养等进行了探讨，其中不乏真知灼见，极大地丰富了人类社会共同的文明成果。我们要坚持马克思主义的立场、观点和方法，坚持"以我为主，为我所用"的原则，既反对全盘西化、机械照搬，又反对全盘否定、盲目排外，在批判的基础上借鉴吸收其对今天的中国有积极意义的精华。当代大学生不但要有全球眼光、世界意识，而且不能消解民族自尊心和自信心，不能失去对我们民族文化的认同。

2. 反对两种对待中国传统道德的错误观点

第一，全盘复古论。

全盘复古论就是不加分析地全面继承一个民族的文化思想的

cultural thought comprehensively without analysis. Those who hold this view think that the reason of moral decline in our country is the loss of our traditional culture, especially the Confucian traditional morality. Therefore, the ultimate goal of moral construction is to restore China's "inherent culture", form a moral system with Chinese traditional culture as the main body, and derive modern scientific democracy through the revival of this traditional morality, namely the so-called "returning to the original and opening up the new".

Second, the historical nihilism.

Historical nihilism is a kind of ideological trend that negates the traditional morality completely without analysis. Its main performance is that it does not distinguish between the essence and the dross of chinese cultural heritage of thousands of years, denies all of them and advocates the whole westernization.

The above two trends of thought adopt a metaphysical attitude towards traditional morality, divided the relationship between the history and development of morality, and denied the historical progress of morality. It is extremely harmful to the development of the fine moral tradition of the Chinese nation and the construction of new socialist morality. We must establish a high degree of cultural consciousness and cultural self-confidence, safeguard the basic elements of national culture, strengthen the construction of an excellent traditional moral inheritance system, and make the Chinese traditional virtues a spiritual force that encourages the people to advance in the new era.

错误理论。持此观点的人认为我国之所以出现道德滑坡，就是因为我们的传统文化特别是儒家传统道德的失落，所以道德建设的最终目标就是恢复中国"固有文化"，形成以中国传统文化为主体的道德体系，并通过这种传统道德的复兴衍生出现代的科学民主，即所谓的"返本开新"。

第二，历史虚无主义。

历史虚无主义就是对传统道德不加分析地全面否定的一种思潮，主要表现为对中国几千年的文化遗产不区分精华和糟粕，全盘加以否定，主张全盘西化。

以上两种思潮对传统道德均采取形而上学的态度，割裂了道德的历史与发展的关系，否定了道德的历史进步性，对于发展中华民族的优良道德传统和建设社会主义新道德极端有害。我们要树立高度的文化自觉和文化自信，维护民族文化基本元素，加强对优秀传统道德传承体系的建设，使中华传统美德成为新时代鼓舞人民前进的精神力量。

Lecture Ten
The Moral Requirements
of College Students' Public Life

This Lecture Eleven mainly expounds the core and principle of the construction of socialist morality, the public life, the main content of Social public morality and the moral requirements in network life.

I.The Core and Principle of the construction of Socialist Morality

1.Serving the People is the Core of the Construction of Socialist Morality

As the core of the construction of socialist morality,serving the people is a remarkable sign of distinction and superiority of socialist morality to the morality of other social forms. Serving the people is the objective requirement of the socialist economic basis and interpersonal relationship, is the requirement for the healthy development of the socialist market economy, is the unity of the requirements of the advancement and the requirements of the universality. College students' practice of serving the people is to carry forward the spirit of serving the people, respect people, understand people, care for people, do more good things for the people and for the society, and contribute more. Marx once said: "If we choose the profession that does good for human happiness, then, the

专题十
大学生公共生活的
道德要求

本专题主要阐述了社会主义道德建设的核心和原则、公共生活、社会公德的主要内容以及网络生活中的道德要求四个问题。

一、社会主义道德建设的核心和原则

1. 为人民服务是社会主义道德建设的核心

为人民服务作为社会主义道德建设的核心，是社会主义道德区别和优越于其他社会形态道德的显著标志。为人民服务是社会主义经济基础和人际关系的客观要求，是社会主义市场经济健康发展的要求，是先进性要求和广泛性要求的统一。大学生践行为人民服务，就是要弘扬为人民服务的精神，尊重人、理解人、关心人，为人民、为社会多做好事、多做贡献。马克思曾说过："如果我们选择了最能为人类幸福而劳动的职业，那么，重担就不能把我们压倒……我们的幸福将属于千百万人，我们的事业将

burden cannot overwhelm us... our happiness will belong to millions of people and our cause will exist silently but play a role eternally. Faced with our ashes, people with noble traits will shed tears."

2.Collectivism is the Principle of the Construction of Socialist Morality

Collectivism emphasizes the dialectical unity of national interests, overall interests of society and personal interests. In social life , people exist as individuals and also as members of the collective, so collective and individual are inseparable. In a socialist society, national interests, overall interests of society, and personal interests are also inseparable.The national interest and the overall interests of the society embody the fundamental and long-term interests of the individual and are the unity of the common interests of all members of society.Meanwhile, the legitimate interests of every citizen are inseparable components of national interests and the overall interests of society. The rise and decline of the nation and the society is closely related to the gain and loss of personal interests.In real life, national interests, overall interests of society and personal interests are mutually reinforcing. It doesn't mean suppressing one party to develop the other, but striving for common development, mutual benefit, and mutual complementation.Collectivism emphasizes that national interests and overall interests of society are more significant than personal interests.In real life, personal interests will inevitably go against national interests and overall interests of society. Some of these contradictions can be mitigated and resolved,

无声息地存在下去，但是它会发挥作用，而面对我们的骨灰，高尚的人们将洒下热泪。"

2. 集体主义是社会主义道德建设的原则

集体主义强调国家利益、社会整体利益和个人利益的辩证统一。在社会中，人既作为个体而存在，又作为集体中的一员而存在，集体和个人是不能分割的。在社会主义社会中国家利益、社会整体利益和个人利益也是不能分割的。国家利益、社会整体利益体现着个人根本的、长远的利益，是所有社会成员共同利益的统一。同时，每个人的正当利益，又都是国家利益、社会整体利益不可分割的组成部分。国家和社会的兴衰与个人利益得失息息相关。在现实生活中，国家利益、社会整体利益和个人利益是相辅相成的，不是靠抑制一方来发展另一方，而是要力求做到共同发展、相互增益、相得益彰。集体主义强调国家利益、社会整体利益高于个人利益。在实际生活中，个人利益和国家利益、社会整体利益难免会发生矛盾。这种矛盾，有的是可以缓和、化解的，有的则会导致或大或小的冲突。但是，集体主义强调，在个人利益与国家利益、社会整体利

while others may cause severe or negligible conflicts.However, collectivism emphasizes that when personal interests go against national interests and the overall interests of society, especially in a fierce conflict, we must adhere to the principle that national interest and overall interests of society are more significant than personal interests. That is to say,Individuals should focus on the overall situation, where personal interests are subject to national interests and the overall interests of society, and even make sacrifices if necessary.It is not arbitrary that collectivism requires individuals to make sacrifices for the country and society. Only when the national interests and the overall interests of the society cannot be preserved without sacrificing personal interests, will individuals be required to sacrifice for the national interest and the overall interests of the society. In the final analysis, the reason why socialist collectivism emphasizes that personal interests should obey the national interests and the overall interests of the society, is to safeguard the common interests of the state and society, and ultimately to safeguard the fundamental interests and long-term interests of individuals. Collectivism promotes and guarantees the realization of the legitimate interests of individuals, so that the abilities and values of individuals can be fully exerted,which is not contradictory to collectivism, but catch the appropriate meaning of collectivist thinking. Only in the country and society can individuals achieve comprehensive development and freedom.The idea of treating collectivism as a suppression of the individual and

益发生矛盾冲突，尤其是发生激烈冲突的时候，必须坚持国家利益、社会整体利益高于个人利益的原则，即个人应当以大局为重，使个人利益服从国家利益、社会整体利益，在必要时做出牺牲。集体主义要求个人为国家、社会做出牺牲并不是任意的，只有在不牺牲个人利益就不能保全国家利益、社会整体利益的情况下，才要求个人为国家利益、社会整体利益做出牺牲。社会主义集体主义强调个人利益要服从国家利益、社会整体利益，归根到底，既是为了维护国家、社会的共同利益，也是为了维护个人的根本利益和长远利益。集体主义促进和保障个人正当利益的实现，使个人的才能、价值得到充分的发挥。这不但与集体主义不矛盾，而且正是集体主义思想的应有之义。只有在国家、社会中个人才能获得全面发展，才可能有个人自由。那种把集体主义看作对个人的压制、对个性的束缚的思想，是与集体主义的本意相违背的。事实上，正是集体主义为培养个人的健全人格、鲜明个性和创新精神提供了道义保障。对于集体主义来说，只有个人的价值、尊严得到实现，个人的正当利益得到保证，集体才能有更强大的生命力和凝聚力。集体主

a bondage to the personality is contrary to the real intention of collectivism. In fact, it is the collectivism that provides guarantee for the cultivation of a person's sound personality, distinctive character and innovative spirit.For collectivism, only when the individual's value and dignity are realized, and the individual's legitimate interests are guaranteed, can the collective have more vitality and cohesiveness.There is no doubt that collectivism pays attention to the realization of personal interests, but this does not mean that any individual needs should be unconditionally satisfied regardless of occasion and time. What the socialist collectivism values and guarantees is the legitimate interests of individuals, rather than personal interests of any nature.Collectivism does not protect the interests of those who harm others to benefit themselves even at the expense of public interests, and strongly opposes and forbids this act.With the development of the socialist market economy, China's economic life and moral life went through profound changes. There are many new problems emerging in the field of ethics, so we must adapt to real changes and constantly supplement, enrich and improve the principles of collectivism.Under the conditions of a socialist market economy, collectivism still and should be the basic principle of socialist morality. The development of a socialist market economy requires collectivism because it helps to overcome the weaknesses and negative aspects of the market itself, and helps to form a good social atmosphere to pursue nobleness and encourage advancement, and guarantees the orderly and healthy develop-

义重视个人利益的实现，这是毫无疑义的，但这并不意味着任何个人不分场合、不分时间的利益需求都应该无条件得到满足。社会主义集体主义所重视和保障的是个人的正当利益，而不是任何性质的个人利益，对于损人利己、损公肥私的行为，集体主义不但不保护，而且强烈反对和禁止。随着社会主义市场经济的发展，我国的经济生活和道德生活发生了深刻的变化，在道德领域出现了许多新问题，我们必须适应实际变化，不断补充、丰富和完善集体主义原则。在社会主义市场经济条件下，集体主义仍然而且应当成为社会主义道德的基本原则。发展社会主义市场经济之所以需要集体主义，是因为其有助于克服市场自身的弱点和消极方面，有助于形成追求高尚、激励先进的良好社会风气，保证社会主义市场经济的有序健康发展。

ment of the socialist market economy.

According to the reality of China's current economic and social life and people's ideology and morality, the moral requirements of collectivism can be divided into three levels.

The first one is selfless dedication with the belief of serving the public. This is the highest level of collectivism and the moral goal that communists and advanced people should strive to achieve.

The second one is to put others before yourself, and public affairs befor private affairs, and then to consider self interests. This is a requirement that people with higher socialist moral consciousness can achieve.

The third one is to take the overall situation seriously, obey the laws and rules, love our motherland, and work diligently. This is the basic requirement for every citizen. Collectivism is not far away from us, which exists in the specific life of study and work. Everyone can and should practice the principles of collectivism and climb up the ladder of morality step by step. Contemporary college students should correctly understand and deal with the interests of the state, the collective and the individual, consciously insist that personal interests obey the collective interests, partial interests obey the overall interests, current interests obey the long-term interests, and oppose small groupism, selfish departmentalism and ultra-individualism.

根据我国现阶段经济社会生活和人们思想道德的实际，可将集体主义的道德要求分为三个层次。

一是无私奉献、一心为公。这是集体主义的最高层次，是共产党员、先进分子应努力达到的道德目标。

二是先公后私、先人后己。这是已经具有较高社会主义道德觉悟的人能够达到的要求。

三是顾全大局、遵纪守法、热爱祖国、诚实劳动。这是对公民最基本的道德要求。集体主义离我们并不遥远，就存在和体现于具体的学习工作生活之中。人人都可以而且应当践行集体主义原则，沿着道德的阶梯循序渐进地向上攀登。当代大学生应正确认识和处理国家、集体、个人的利益关系，自觉坚持个人利益服从集体利益、局部利益服从整体利益、当前利益服从长远利益，反对小团体主义、本位主义和极端个人主义。

II.The Generalization of Public Life

1.The Connotation of Public Life

Public life refers to the activities and life of people in the public environment. Public life is relative to private life.The main area of private life is family internal activities, which are characterized by privacy, closure and independence.Public life surpasses the limits of private life and is characterized by versatility, openness, complexity and diversity.

2.The Characteristics of Public Life

First, the scope of activities in public life has universality.

The public places and fields of communication continue to expand. The communication between villages and towns used to be through letters, packages, long-distance telephone calls and long journey life. At present, it is the most convenient communication among countries through advanced Email, QQ, video, plane, bullet train and subway.

Second, the content of activities in public life has openness.

Public life is the most common and basic life in social life, which is enjoyed by all members of society without exclusivity. There is no secret in public life through timely media reports.

Third, the object of communication in public life has complexity.

With the continuous expansion of social public life, the objects of communication in public life

二、公共生活

1. 公共生活的内涵

公共生活是指人们在公共环境中的活动和生活。公共生活是相对于私人生活而言的。私人生活往往以家庭内部活动为主要领域，具有私密性、封闭性和独立性等特点。公共生活超越了私人生活局限，具有广泛性、开放性、复杂性和多样性的特点。

2. 公共生活的特征

第一，活动范围的广泛性。

交流的公共场所和领域不断扩展。从前是村镇之间的交流，大家的联系方式是书信、包裹、长途电话和漫长的旅途生活；现在是国家与国家之间的交流，交流方式是先进的 E-mail、QQ、视频、飞机、动车和地铁等。

第二，活动内容的开放性。

公共生活是社会生活中最普遍、最基本的公众性生活，为社会全体成员所享有，不具有排他性，通过媒体的及时报道，公共生活没有秘密可言。

第三，交往对象的复杂性。

社会公共生活领域的不断扩大使人们在公共生活中的交往对

are no longer limited to acquaintances, but anyone who enters public places.

Fourth, the way of activity in public life has diversity.

With the development of society, many new changes have taken place in people's way of life. Therefore, more public places and facilities have been added, and the content of public life has been more abundant, such as online shopping, fitness and entertainment.

3. The Public Life Requires the Public Order

Every society has its norms and requirements for the public life. The larger the area of public life, the higher the demand for public life order. Public order is an ordered state of people's public life maintained by certain rules, such as work order, teaching order, business order, traffic order, entertainment order, network order and so on.

4. The Significance of Orderly Public Life

First, orderly public life is an important foundation for social productive activities.

Second, orderly public life is an important condition for promoting social harmony.

Third, orderly public life is a basic guarantee for improving the quality of life of members of society.

Fourth, orderly public life is an important symbol of social civilization.

III. The Main Content of Social Public Morality

The code of morality in public life, namely social morality, refers to the code of conduct that

象不再局限于熟人，而是进入公共场所的任何人。

第四，活动方式的多样性。

社会的发展使人们的生活方式发生了很多新的变化，因此增加了更多的公共场所和设施，公共生活内容也更加丰富，如网络购物、健身娱乐等活动。

3. 公共生活需要公共秩序

任何一个社会都有它的公共生活规范和要求。公共生活领域越大，对公共生活秩序的要求就越高。公共秩序是由一定规则维系的人们公共生活的一种有序化状态，如工作秩序、教学秩序、营业秩序、交通秩序、娱乐秩序、网络秩序等。

4. 有序公共生活的意义

第一，有序公共生活是社会生产活动的重要基础。

第二，有序公共生活是促进社会和谐的重要条件。

第三，有序公共生活是提高社会成员生活质量的基本保障。

第四，有序公共生活是社会文明的重要标志。

三、社会公德的主要内容

公共生活中的道德规范，即社会公德，是指人们在社会交往

people should abide by in social communication and public life. It is the minimum code of conduct of maintaining public interests, public order and social harmony and stability, covering the relationship between people, people and society, people and nature. Every member of society, including college students, should abide by the social morality with the civility and politeness, helpfulness, the public property protection, the environmental protection and the law and discipline observation as the main content.

1. Civility and Politeness

Civility and politeness is the code of conduct for adjusting and standardizing interpersonal relations, which is closely related to everyone's daily life. Civility and politeness is the smile when you meet somebody on the road, the respect when you get along with others, and the bridge of communication. It reflects a person's moral cultivation, reflects the overall quality of a nation. College students should consciously be civilized and polite, keep etiquette, and create a good image of sincerity, comity and tolerance.

2.Helpfulness

In public life, everyone can encounter difficulties and problems, so the need of help and concerns from others will arise at times. "Give rose ,leave grace." regarding the act of helping others as what should be done is the social morality that every member of society should have and embodies the meaning of love. College students should do their part to help others, actively participate in public welfare undertakings, care for and concern

和公共生活中应该遵守的行为准则，是维护公共利益、公共秩序、社会和谐稳定最起码的道德要求，涵盖了人与人、人与社会、人与自然之间的关系。包括大学生在内的每一个社会成员，都应遵守以文明礼貌、助人为乐、爱护公物、保护环境、遵纪守法为主要内容的社会公德。

1. 文明礼貌

文明礼貌是调整和规范人际关系的行为准则，与我们每个人的日常生活密切相关。文明礼貌是路上相遇时的微笑，是与人相处时的尊重，是沟通感情的桥梁。它反映着一个人的道德修养，体现着一个民族的整体素质。大学生应当自觉讲文明、懂礼貌、守礼仪，塑造真诚待人、礼让宽容的良好形象。

2. 助人为乐

在公共生活中，每个人都会遇到困难和问题，总有需要他人帮助和关心的时候。"赠人玫瑰，手有余香。"把帮助他人视为自己应做之事，是每个社会成员应有的社会公德，是有爱心的表现。大学生应当尽自己的努力帮助他人，积极参与公益事业，以力所能及的方式关心和关爱他

others in ways they can, and gain happiness of realizing the value of life in the care and help of others.

3. The Public Property Protection

It is the social responsibility and obligation that every citizen should undertake to cherish and care the common achievements of social labor. It not only shows the level of personal moral cultivation, but also an important symbol of the level of social civilization. If social public property are destroyed, the interests of society will be lost. College students should strengthen the sense of being the social masters by their practical behaviors to cherish the property of the country and collectives, and protect public property. Particularly, they must protect social public facilities and resolutely fight against those who damage the public property and assets.

4.The Environmental Protection

The protection of environment is a career that should be carried out in this generation and conducive to our offspring. The nature would go back at our human beings if we didn't respect it, conform to it, and protect it during the activities of human development. College students should regard the ecological environment as important as their lives, put this into practice, advocate a simple and moderate, green and low-carbon lifestyle, and make their own contribution to the production and living environment with blue sky, green ground, and clear water, most importantly, to build a beautiful country.

5.The Law and Discipline Observation

The law and discipline Observation is a ba-

人，并在对他人的关心和帮助中收获实现人生价值的快乐。

3. 爱护公物

对社会共同劳动成果的珍惜和爱护是每个公民应该承担的社会责任和义务，它既显示出个人的道德修养水平，也是社会文明水平的重要标志。如果社会公共财物遭到破坏，社会的利益就会受到损害。大学生要增强主人翁责任感，珍惜国家、集体财产，爱护公物，特别要保护社会公共设施，坚决同损害公共财产、破坏公物的行为作斗争。

4. 保护环境

环境保护是功在当代、利在千秋的事业。人类发展活动必须尊重自然、顺应自然、保护自然，否则就会遭到大自然的报复。大学生要像对待生命一样对待生态环境，身体力行，倡导简约适度、绿色低碳的生活方式，为留下天蓝、地绿、水清的生产生活环境，为建设美丽中国做出自己应有的贡献。

5. 遵纪守法

遵纪守法是全体公民都必须

sic code of conduct that all citizens must obey, and also an important condition for maintaining public order. In social life, every member of society must comply with the relevant laws and regulations promulgated by the state, as well as the relevant disciplinary regulations of specific public places and units. Comprehensively pushing forward the rule of law requires everyone to abide by disciplines and laws, and to establish a sense of observing rules. College students should fully understand the laws and regulations in the field of public life, be familiar with disciplines and rules in school, and firmly establish the concept of legislative rules. What's more, they must be proud of observing laws and disciplines, be ashamed of breaking these rules, and consciously abide by them.

IV.Moral Requirements in Network Life

The Internet is a large platform for social information, and hundreds of millions of netizens obtain information and exchange information on it, which will not only affect people's way of seeking knowledge, thinking modes, values, but also affect people's views on the country, society and life. In essence, network interaction is still a real communication between people, and it is also a person's real life.The moral requirements in network life are the basic ethical principles that people need to abide by in order to maintain the normal network public order in network life, which embodies the application and expansion of social morality in cyberspace. College students should correctly ob-

遵循的基本行为准则，是维护公共生活秩序的重要条件。在社会生活中，每个社会成员既要遵守国家颁布的有关法律、法规，也要遵守特定公共场所和单位的有关纪律规定。全面依法治国需要每个人都遵纪守法，树立规则意识。大学生应当全面了解公共生活领域的各项法律法规，熟知校纪校规，牢固树立法治观念，以遵纪守法为荣，以违法乱纪为耻，自觉遵守有关的纪律和法律。

四、网络生活中的道德要求

互联网是一个社会信息大平台，亿万网民在上面获得信息、交流信息，这既会影响人们的求知途径、思维方式、价值观念，也会影响人们对国家、社会、人生的看法。从本质上说，网络交往仍然是人与人的现实交往，网络生活也是人的真实生活。网络生活中的道德要求是人们在网络生活中为了维护正常的网络公共秩序需要共同遵守的基本道德准则，是社会公德在网络空间的运用和扩展。大学生应当遵守网络生活中的道德要求，成为营造清

serve the moral requirements in network life, and become a positive energy for creating a clean cyberspace.

1.The Proper Use of Network Tools

Nowadays, science and technology are advancing rapidly. Modern information technologies such as the Internet, cloud computing, and big data have profoundly changed the way of human thinking, producing, living, and study, which demonstrate the prospects of world development. It is more convenient and diverse for those who obtain information through the Internet. Therefore, people, especially young people, are increasingly relying on the Internet to obtain information. At the same time, there are omnipresent false, vulgar and even reactionary, obscene, and violent behaviors in the Internet, especially some malicious attacks and thought penetration behaviors organized online, which have seriously affected the order of network life. College students should use the Internet correctly, improve their ability for new information, strengthen their ability to identify information, increase their ability to apply information, and make the Internet become an important tool for broadening their horizons and improving their capabilities.

2. The Healthy Internet Communication

The Internet has become an important medium and tool for interpersonal communication. Some popular applications like QQ, WeChat, Weibo, live webcast and other Apps provide people with different ways to send and receive mails, chat in real time, and make friends online. College

朗网络空间的正能量。

1. 正确使用网络工具

当今世界，科技进步日新月异，互联网、云计算、大数据等现代信息技术深刻改变着人类的思维、生产、生活、学习方式，展示了世界发展的前景。人们通过网络获取信息的方式更加方便、多样，大部分人特别是年轻人越来越主要地依靠网络获取信息。与此同时，网络也充斥着越来越多的虚假、低俗甚至反动、淫秽和暴力等内容，特别是一些有组织的网络恶意攻击和思想渗透行为，严重地影响了网络生活秩序。大学生应当正确使用网络，提高信息的获取能力，加强信息的辨识能力，增进信息的应用能力，使网络成为开阔视野、提高能力的重要工具。

2. 健康地进行网络交往

网络已成为人际交往的重要媒介和工具。QQ、微信、微博、网络直播等各种应用为人们提供了邮件收发、实时聊天、网上交友等的平台。大学生应通过网络开展健康有益的人际交往，树立

students should conduct healthy and beneficial interpersonal communication through the Internet, establish a sense of self-protection, consciously be vigilant to netizens, avoid being deceived, and avoid harming their personal and property safety. At the same time, although the Internet has shortened the distance between ourselves and strangers, it may alienate us from the people around us, such as your family, classmates, friends, etc. This will also weaken the ability of actual interpersonal communication to a certain extent. Therefore, network communication cannot be used to replace face-to-face communication.

3. The Self-conscious Avoidance of Internet Addiction

College students can have access to a vast and unprecedented space through the Internet, and can effectively and widely acquire information, learn knowledge, exchange emotions, and understand our society. However, in reality, there are also some teenagers who are addicted to the Internet, especially online games, which can impede their study and even make them drop out of school. A person's time and energy are limited. More time is spent online, and less time is invested in other activities. It is not always the good thing that you get more from the Internet because the more information you receive, the more likely you are to interfere with your thinking and actions. College students must reasonably arrange online time, restrict online behaviors, in order to avoid being addicted to the Internet.

自我保护意识，不要轻易相信网友，避免上当受骗，避免给自己的人身和财产安全带来危害。同时，网络虽然拉近了我们与陌生人的距离，却有可能使我们疏远家人、同学、朋友等身边的人。这也会在一定程度上弱化现实的人际交往能力，因此不能以网络交往代替现实交往。

3. 自觉避免沉迷于网络

大学生通过网络可以接触到前所未有的广阔空间，能更加有效和广泛地获取信息、学习知识、交流情感和了解社会。但是，现实中也存在着一些青少年沉迷于网络，尤其是网络游戏不能自拔，导致耽误学业甚至放弃学业的现象。一个人的时间和精力都是有限的，在网络上消耗的时间多，在其他方面投入的时间就少。从网络上得到的信息也并非越多越好，接受越多的信息越有可能干扰自己的思维和行动。大学生应当合理安排上网时间，约束上网行为，避免沉迷于网络。

4.The Strengthening of Network Moral Self-Discipline

Cyberspace, like real society, must promote freedom and maintain order. The fictitious nature of the network and the concealment of the behavioral subject are not conducive to the role of public opinion in monitoring, and significantly reduce the external binding force of the moral code. If enjoying the freedom of the Internet is an inalienable right of Internet users, then strengthening moral self-discipline should become an inescapable obligation of Internet users. In this case, the individual's moral self-discipline has become the basic guarantee for maintaining the network ethics. College students should cultivate the spirit of self-discipline in online life, and in a cyberspace that lacks external supervision, achieve self-discipline and "do not go beyond the rules" to promote the health and harmony of network life.

5.The Active Guidance of Network Public Opinion

If the complicated online utterance is not properly guided, it will inevitably lead to various social problems. The society needs positive public opinion to inspire people, and the guidance of network public opinion needs to eliminate detriment and promote the righteousness. College students in the new era should take the lead in guiding network public opinion, clear up vague understanding, resolve grievances and complaints, and guide and correct misperceptions in a timely manner to actively create a clear cyberspace. As for the acts that endanger network security, the Criminal Law of our country gives clear definition.

4. 加强网络道德自律

网络空间同现实社会一样，既要提倡自由，也要保持秩序。网络的虚拟性以及行为主体的隐匿性不利于发挥社会舆论的监督作用，使道德规范所具有的外在约束力明显降低。如果说享受互联网的自由是网民不可剥夺的权利，那么加强道德自律就应该成为网民不可推卸的责任。在这种情况下，个体的道德自律成为维护网络道德规范的基本保障。大学生应当在网络生活中培养自律精神，在缺少外在监督的网络空间里做到自律而"不逾矩"，促进网络生活的健康与和谐。

5. 积极引导网络舆论

纷繁复杂的网络言论如果得不到正确引导，势必会引发各种社会问题。社会需要正向舆论来鼓舞和温暖人心，网络舆论引导需要激浊扬清，弘扬正气。新时代的大学生应当带头引导网络舆论，对模糊认识要及时廓清，对怨气怨言要及时化解，对错误看法要及时引导和纠正，积极营造清朗网络空间。针对危害网络安全的行为，我国刑法做了明确的界定。

Lecture Eleven
The Correct Outlook on Career Choice,Love and Family of College Students

I.The Establishment of College Students' Correct Outlook on Career Choice and Entrepreneurship

Employment plays an important role for people's livelihood. Employment involves the interests of college students and millions of families, and also affects the development of the country and society. Every college student has to face the reality of employment. Establishing a correct outlook on career choice and entrepreneurship is of great significance for college students to enter into professional life. There are three major characteristics in current employment situation: high employment pressure, long duration, and pessimistic prospects. We must master the current employment situation from two perspectives: supply and demand of labor, economic development and structural changes.

1.The Establishment of College Students' Correct Outlook on Career Choice

First, Professional activities are not only a means for people to make a living, but also a necessary condition for people to contribute to society and improve themselves. Marx wrote about career choices when he was young: "If we choose the

专题十一
大学生正确的择业观、恋爱观和家庭观

一、树立正确的择业观和创业观

就业是最大的民生。就业牵涉大学生自身和千家万户的利益，也影响国家和社会的发展。每个大学生都要面临就业的现实。树立正确的择业观和创业观，对于大学生顺利走进职业生活具有重要的现实意义。当前的就业形势具有三大特点：就业压力大、持续时间长、前景不乐观。我们要从两个角度把握当前的就业形势：劳动力供需情况、经济发展和结构变化情况。

1. 树立正确的择业观

第一，职业活动不仅是人们谋生的手段，也是人们奉献社会、完善自身的必要条件。青年马克思在谈到选择职业理想时曾经写道："如果我们选择了最能

profession that does good for human happiness, then, the burden cannot overwhelm us, because it is a sacrifice for everyone; then we are not enjoying poor, limited, selfish pleasures, our happiness will belong to millions of people, our cause will exist silently but play a role eternally, and noble people will shed tears in the face of our ashes." Marx' slofty career ideal is worth studying and pursuing for college students when they are choosing a career or starting a business.

Second, the compliance with social demand.

It is certain that we must take personal interests and wishes into account when choosing a job, but we have to consider the possibility of reality and the needs of society, and combine our own professional expectations with social needs and realistic possibilities. At present, grass-roots positions in many places, especially the central and western regions, have a very strong demand for talents, which can provide college students with a broad space to exert their talents and abilities. College students should actively respond to the call of the country, adapt to the needs of social development, choose their future careers at the grass-roots and the first line of national construction, and contribute wisdom and strength to economic and social development.

Third, the full preparation for the career choices.

Quality is Quality is the foundation of conducting yourself in society, so as skills to careers.

为人类幸福而劳动的职业，那么，重担就不能把我们压倒，因为这是为大家作出的牺牲；那时我们所享受的就不是可怜的、有限的、自私的乐趣，我们的幸福将属于千百万人，我们的事业将悄无声息地存在下去，但是它会永远发挥作用，而面对我们的骨灰，高尚的人们将洒下热泪。"马克思这种崇高的职业理想值得大学生择业和创业时去学习和追求。

第二，服从社会的需要。

择业固然要考虑个人的兴趣和意愿，但也要充分考虑现实的可能性和社会的需要，把自己对职业的期望与社会的需要、现实的可能结合起来。目前，许多地方的基层单位特别是中西部地区的人才需求十分强烈，能够为大学生提供施展才华的广阔空间。大学生应该积极响应国家号召，适应社会发展需求，面向基层、面向国家建设第一线去选择自己未来的职业，为经济社会发展贡献智慧和力量。

第三，做好充分的择业准备。

素质是立身之基，技能是立业之本。大学生有了真才实学，

College students must have real talent and ability to enable them to adapt to a variety of positions in the future. To have real talent and ability, we must be diligent in study, learning culture, science, skills, and all aspects of knowledge, constantly improve comprehensive ability, and acquire strong skills; not only learn from books, but also learn from the masses, and from practice. College students should realize that all workers, regardless of their abilities, must be able to create a bright life as long as they are dedicated and keep improving.

2.The Establishment of College Students' Correct Outlook on Entrepreneurship

Entrepreneurship is a practical process of creating new jobs, expanding the scope of professional activities, and creating new performance through exerting initiative and creativity. College students should not only establish a correct outlook on career choice, but also establish a correct outlook on entrepreneurship, have the mental preparation for active entrepreneurship pay more attention to the trend of economic and social development, know the relevant policies for encouraging college students to start their own businesses, and lay a good foundation for future business. College students should have the courage of entrepreneurship. Only when you bravely accept the challenge of starting business and overcome the dependence and timidity, can you become a real entrepreneur with good quality and skill to start your business. We must give full consideration to various realistic factors such as our self abilities and the environment for starting a business, and

才能在未来适应多种岗位。要有真才实学就要勤于学习，学文化、学科学、学技能、学各方面知识，不断提高综合素质，练就过硬本领；既要向书本学习，也要向群众学习、向实践学习。大学生应认识到，任何一名劳动者，无论从事的劳动技术含量如何，只要兢兢业业、精益求精，就一定能够造就闪光的人生。

2. 树立正确的创业观

创业是通过发挥自己的主动性和创造性，开辟新的工作岗位、拓展职业活动范围、创造新业绩的实践过程。大学生不仅要树立正确的择业观，还应当树立正确的创业观。要有积极创业的思想准备，积极关注经济社会发展的趋势，了解国家鼓励大学生自主创业的有关政策，为今后自主创业打下良好的基础。要有敢于创业的勇气，只有勇敢地接受创业的挑战，破除依赖心理和胆怯心理，才能敢于创业、善于创业，做一个真正的创业者。要充分考虑自身条件、创业环境等各种现实因素，努力提高自主创业的能力。

work hard to improve our ability to start a business independently.

3. The Voluntary Compliance of Professional Ethics

Whether the professional life is smooth or successful depends not only on the individual's professional knowledge and skills, but also on the individual's professional ethics. The moral status of people in professional activities is directly related to the moral status of all walks of life and even the entire society. College students are the premium among the young people. We must deeply understand the importance of improving professional ethics and pay attention to cultivation and exercise in this regard.

First, college students must learn the norms of professional ethics.

It is especially important for young people to know the basic principles and purpose of professional activities by learning the norms of professional ethics in order to improve their abilities of professional cognition, judgment and establish correct values. The college period is a stage of preparing knowledge, morality and ability for career choice, employment, and entrepreneurship. The professional ethics knowledge that college students should learn is multifaceted, including both general professional ethics knowledge and professional ethics knowledge for specific industries. College students should incorporate professional ethics into their planning for learning and becoming talented, and plan to study purposefully, laying a good foundation for future employment.

3. 自觉遵守职业道德

职业生活是否顺利、是否成功，既取决于个人的专业知识和技能，更取决于个人的职业道德素质。人们在职业活动中的道德状况直接关系着各行各业乃至整个社会的道德状况。大学生是青年人中的佼佼者，要深刻认识提高职业道德素质的重要性，注重这方面的修养和锻炼。

第一，学习职业道德规范。

通过学习职业道德规范，明确职业活动的基本规范和目的，从而提高自己的职业认知能力、判断能力和树立正确的价值理念，对青年人来说尤为重要。大学阶段是为择业、就业、创业准备知识、品德、能力的阶段。大学生应学习的职业道德知识是多方面的，既包括一般的职业道德知识，也包括特定行业的职业道德知识。大学生应当将职业道德修养纳入学习与成才的规划，有计划、有目的地学习，为今后走上工作岗位打下良好的基础。

Second, college students must improve the awareness of professional ethics.

To improve professional ethics, college students should internalize the professional ethics into their own qualities and raise it to the level of consciousness. Although college students have not formally entered the vocational field, they can still find a way to improve their awareness of professional ethics in their study and life. College students should take a model of professional ethics as example, cultivate good awareness of professional ethics that is aggressive, dedicated, and serving the society, and prepare for future profession.

Third, college students must improve the ability of practicing professional ethics.

The university is not an ivory tower isolated from society, but is closely connected with society through various ways. Although studying at university is not a career, college students can also experience professional life through work-study, part-time, internship and other channels. Many college student volunteers walk into the west, into the community, and into the countryside, and use knowledge and love to serve the people in need. They have gained growth and progress in serving others and contributing to the society, and they have also accumulated practical experience for smoothly moving to work in the future. College students should actively take advantage of various opportunities to carry out social practice, and participate more in social voluntary service activities, so that the knowledge they have learned can be used and sublimated in the process of serving society.

第二，提高职业道德意识。

大学生要提高自己的职业道德素质，就应当将其内化为自身的素质，提高到自觉意识的层面。虽然大学生尚未正式进入职业领域，但是仍然可以在学习生活中找到提高职业道德意识的路径。大学生应当以职业道德模范为榜样，培养积极进取、甘于奉献、服务社会的良好职业道德意识，为未来的职业生活做准备。

第三，提高践行职业道德的能力。

大学不是与社会隔绝的象牙塔，而是通过多种渠道与社会紧密联系。在大学学习虽然不是一种职业，但是也可以通过勤工助学、兼职、实习等途径体验职业生活。许多大学生志愿者走进西部、走进社区、走进农村，用知识和爱心为需要帮助的群众热情服务。他们在服务他人、奉献社会中收获了成长和进步，也为将来顺利走上工作岗位积累了实践经验。大学生应当积极利用各种机会开展社会实践，多参与社会志愿服务活动，使自己学到的知识在服务社会的过程中得到运用和升华。

II. Moral Norms in Love, Future Marriage and Family

1. The Moral Norms in Love

Based on certain social foundations and common ideals of life of a man and a woman, love is a strong, innocent, and single-minded relationship that the couple infatuate each other and wish to live together until death. The so-called love is the process of cultivating love between men and women or their mutual interaction activities based on love. As an interpersonal relationship, love must also be bound by morals. Love is the prelude to the establishment of a happy marriage and family. Adhering to the moral norms in love is closely related to the happiness of future marriage and family life. The moral norms in love are mainly reflected in the following aspects.

First, respecting the equality of personality.

The mutual respect between couples is mainly refer to respecting the independence of their partners and the equality of them. Couples in love are independent in personality. If they treat their partners as their vassal, or lose themselves because of over-relying on their lovers, It is a distortion of the essence of love. Couples in love are equal in their relationship, and they both have the freedom to give, accept, and reject love. It is not in line with the moral requirements of love by indulging one's emotions or restraining or forcing one another.

Second, self-consciously taking responsibility.

The voluntary dedication to take responsibility for each other is the embodiment of the essence

二、恋爱、婚姻家庭中的道德规范

1. 恋爱中的道德规范

爱情是一对男女基于一定的社会基础和共同的生活理想，在各自内心形成的相互倾慕，并渴望对方成为自己终身伴侣的一种强烈、纯真、专一的感情。男女双方培养爱情的过程或在爱情基础上进行的相互交往活动就是人们日常所说的恋爱。恋爱作为一种人际交往，也必然要受到道德的约束。恋爱是建立幸福婚姻家庭的前奏，恪守恋爱中的道德规范关系到未来婚姻家庭生活的幸福。恋爱中的道德规范主要体现在以下几个方面。

第一，尊重人格平等。

恋人间彼此尊重人格的表现主要是尊重对方的独立性和重视双方的平等。恋爱双方在人格上都是独立的，如果把对方当作自己的附庸或依附对方而失去"自我"，都是对爱情实质的曲解。恋爱双方在相互关系上是平等的，都有给予爱、接受爱和拒绝爱的自由。放纵自己的情感或者对对方予以束缚或强迫，都不符合恋爱的道德要求。

第二，自觉承担责任。

自愿地为对方承担责任是爱情本质的体现。无论对方处在顺

of love. If you pursue or accept one's love, you must consciously take responsibility for him regardless of whether he is in advantageous or tough times, whether he is rich or poor, health or disease. The responsibility is not simply the repeated chant of "I only have you in my heart", but the consciousness that requires real action. Taking responsibility is often reflected in every aspects of life: love is an umbrella held up together in rainstorms, is an eager expect for the return of lover in the twilight, and also a cup of warm tea in the lamplight at a cold night.

Thirdly, loving each other civilly.

Civilization in love is often the infatuation and closeness of both parties, and also good manners and mutual respect, which is not vulgar and indulgent attitude, manner, language, etc. Lovers who go in and out of public places must abide by social morality and never adversely affect the lives of others. When lovers live together, they must also attach importance to civilization and morals. To abide by the morals of love is to maintain true love in real life. This is the secret to maintaining love for a long time.

Fourth, the outlook on love college students should have.

Love is a way of personality reinvention, changes people's thinking, psychology, and behavior to a large extent. In the process of love, couples have a positive attitude to please each other and get deep love from each other. Therefore, they often need to take the initiative to correct their own shortcomings, manifest their own advantages,

境还是逆境，是富裕还是贫穷，是健康还是疾病，爱一个人或接受一个人的爱，就要自觉地为对方承担责任。责任的担当，不是单纯的"我的心中只有你"的反复吟唱，而是见诸行动的自觉。责任常常体现在生活的点点滴滴之中：爱情是风雨中共同撑起的一把伞，是暮色里急切盼归的一种情，是寒夜灯影下温暖的一杯茶。

第三，文明相亲相爱。

文明的恋爱往往是恋爱双方既相互爱慕、亲近，又举止得体、相互尊重，绝不是在态度、举止、语言等方面的粗俗和放纵。恋人在公共场所出入时要遵守社会公德，不要对他人生活造成不良影响；恋人独处时也要讲文明、讲道德。遵从恋爱道德就是在现实生活中维护真正的爱情，这是保持爱情长久的秘密所在。

第四，大学生应有的恋爱观。

恋爱是人格再造的契机，很大程度上改变着人的思想、心理和行为。因为在恋爱过程中，双方都有一种取悦对方获得对方以深爱的积极心态，所以恋爱双方常常要主动改正自己的缺点、放大自己的优点，并设法迎合对方

and try to cater to the interests of each other. At this point, if their partners point out their shortcomings, they both are willing to try to improve themselves. If couples do this, then the process of love will not only make the flowers of love bloom more luxuriantly, but also create a new couple in another sense. College students should not mistake friendship for love, nor mislocate the status of love, nor treat love one-sided or utilitarian, nor attach importance to the process regardless of the consequences, nor lose the direction of life because of lovelorn.

Therefore，College students must deal with several pairs of relationships: The first one is the relationship between love and learning. Learning is the primary task of college students. College students should regard love as a motivation for study, and also consider whether it is conducive to promoting learning as an important and special criterion for measuring the value of love. The second one is the relationship between love and collectivism. Couples in love should not confine themselves in a two-person world. Being away from the collective and alienating classmates will hinder their overall development and progress. The third one is the relationship between love and caring for others and society. The meaning of love is rich and profound, it not only includes the love between lovers, but also includes the love to parents, brothers, sisters, society and the country. Only focusing on love for lovers and neglecting love for others and society will manifest selfish and vulgar personality; on the contrary, having love for others

的志趣。此时如果对方指出自己的不足之处，是很乐意设法加以改进的。假如恋爱双方都这样做的话，那么恋爱过程不仅能使爱情之花开得更茂盛，而且会塑造出一对另一种意义上的新人。大学生不能误把友谊当爱情，不能错置爱情的地位，不能片面地或功利化地对待恋爱，不能只重过程不顾后果，不能因失恋而迷失人生方向。

因此，大学生恋爱应处理好几对关系：一是恋爱与学习的关系。学习是大学生的首要任务，大学生应把爱情作为奋发学习的动力，还应把是否有利于促进学习作为衡量爱情价值的一个重要而特殊的标准。二是恋爱与关心集体的关系。恋爱中的双方不应把自己禁锢在两个人的世界中。脱离集体、疏远同学会妨碍自身的全面发展与进步。三是恋爱与关爱他人和社会的关系。爱的情感丰富博大，不仅有恋人之爱，还有对父母之爱、对兄弟姐妹之爱、对社会和国家之爱。只专注于对恋人的爱而忽视对他人和社会的爱，这样的爱情就会显得自私和庸俗；相反，对他人和社会具有爱心则会使爱情变得高尚和稳固。

and society will make love noble and stable.

2. The Moral Norms in Future Marriage and Family

The natural attributes of marriage and family are the natural factors on which marriage and family are formed, the social attributes of marriage and family refer to their essential attributes. The stability of marriage and family is the basis of social harmony.

First, college students should respect the old and cherish the young in their future marriage and family.

Since ancient times, China has advocated the tradition that "The old should be supported filially and the young should be raised carefully", which has formed a good family moral tradition of respecting the old and cherishing the young. Children must respect and support their parents and elders, and parents must nurture and care for their children. This is not only a moral rule that every citizen must abide by, but also a social responsibility and legal obligation that everyone should fulfill. We must protect the legitimate rights and interests of the elderly and children, and resolutely oppose the abuse and abandonment of such groups.

Second, College students should insist on gender equality in their future marriage and family.

Equality between men and women in family life is manifested not only by equality in the rights and duties of husband and wife, equality in personality status, but also by the equal treatment to their children. To adhere to equality between men and women, we must especially respect and pro-

2. 婚姻家庭中的道德规范

婚姻家庭的自然属性是指婚姻家庭赖以形成的自然因素，婚姻家庭的社会属性是指婚姻家庭的本质属性。婚姻家庭的稳定是社会和谐稳定的基础。

第一，尊老爱幼。

我国自古以来就倡导"老有所终，幼有所养"，形成了尊老爱幼的良好家庭道德传统。子女要孝敬、赡养父母及长辈，父母要抚育、爱护子女，这不仅是每个公民必须遵守的道德准则，也是应尽的社会责任和法律义务。要保护老人、儿童的合法权益，坚决反对虐待、遗弃老人和儿童的行为。

第二，男女平等。

家庭生活中的男女平等既表现为夫妻权利和义务上的平等、人格地位上的平等，又表现为平等地对待自己的子女。坚持男女平等，特别要尊重和保护妇女的合法权益，反对歧视和迫害妇女

tect women's legal rights and interests, and oppose discrimination and persecution of women.

Third, College students should achieve harmony between husband and wife in their future marriage and family.

Husband-wife relationship is the core of family relationship. Harmony between husband and wife is mutual love, mutual assistance and mutual accommodation based on equality between men and women.

Fourth, College students should be diligent and thrifty in their future marriage and family.

Deligence and thriftiness are the guarantee of the prosperity of the family, manifest respect for parents' hard work and understanding of their efforts. Paying attention to thriftiness in daily life, and minimizing the burden on the parents and the family is the most practical contribution to them.

Fifth, College students should stick to neighborhood unity in their future marriage and family.

It is important to respect each other for neighbourhood unity, to respect others' personality, national habits, lifestyles, hobbies, etc., to achieve mutual understanding and mutual accommodation, help each other, kindly treat others, and be united and friendly.

的行为。

第三，夫妻和睦。

夫妻关系是家庭关系的核心。夫妻和睦是在男女平等基础上的互敬互爱、互助互让。

第四，勤俭持家。

勤俭是家庭兴旺的保证，也是尊重父母劳动所得，体谅父母辛苦操劳的表现。在日常生活中注意节俭，尽量减轻父母和家庭的生活负担是对父母和家庭最实际的贡献。

第五，邻里团结。

邻里团结重要的是相互尊重，尊重对方的人格、民族习惯、生活方式、兴趣爱好等，做到互谅互让，互帮互助，宽以待人，团结友爱。

Lecture Twelve
The Personal Moral Cultivation of College Students

Personal morality plays a fundamental role in social moral construction. In real life, social morality, professional ethics, and family virtues are ultimately based on the moral qualities of each member of society. The construction of social morality, professional ethics, and family virtues must be implemented in the development of personal morality.

I. Personal Morality and Its Function

Personal morality is a stable state of mind and behavior formed through social moral education and individual self-conscious moral cultivation. It is the result of an individual's identification and fulfillment of a certain moral requirement, which embodies the inner unity of moral identity, moral sentiment, moral will, moral conviction and moral behavior. College students must consciously implement personal moral requirements like patriotism and dedication, observing the law, being kind, hard-working and brave, then constantly improve their personal morality realm. Both social harmony and individual healthy personality depend on the continuous improvement of personal morality.

专题十二
大学生个人品德修养

个人品德在社会道德建设中具有基础性作用。在现实生活中，社会公德、职业道德和家庭美德状况最终都是以每个社会成员的道德品质为基础的。社会公德、职业道德和家庭美德建设最终都要落实到个人品德的养成上。

一、个人品德及其作用

个人品德是通过社会道德教育和个人自觉的道德修养所形成的稳定的心理状态和行为习惯。它是个体对某种道德要求认同和践履的结果，集中体现了道德认同、道德情操、道德意志、道德信念和道德行为的内在统一。大学生要自觉践行爱国奉献、明礼守法、厚德仁爱、正直善良、勤劳勇敢等个人品德要求，不断提升个人的道德修养和境界。无论是社会的和谐有序，还是个人的人格健全，都有赖于个人品德的不断提升。

1.Personal Morality Plays an Important Role in Promoting the Role of Morality and Laws.

Personal morality is the driving force which is conducive to the function of morality and laws. The requirements of social morality and laws can only become the normative force of reality by internalizing them into personal character. At the same time, the process of personal moral improvement is also a process of actively affecting social morality and laws, which can create conditions and provide motivation for the development and progress of social morality and laws.

2.Personal Morality is an Important Sign of the Perfection of Individual Personality

Personal morality is a very important part of an individual's quality structure. The improvement of other qualities such as intelligence and wisdom cannot be separated from the support of moral strength. On the one hand, personal morality determines a person's behavior in real life and social practice, as well as the coordination and handling of various relationships, which directly shows the personal realm and personal quality; on the other hand, personal morality points out the direction for the self quality cultivation, exercise and improvement, and provides guidance and control for personal growth.

3.Personal Morality is an Important Spiritual Strength in the Process of Economic and Social Development

Society is made up of social members connected through various social relations, and the

1. 个人品德对道德和法律作用的发挥具有重要的推动作用。

个人品德是道德和法律作用发挥的推动力量。社会道德和法律要求只有内化为个人品德，才能成为现实的规范力量。同时，个人品德提升的过程也是能动地作用于社会道德和法律的过程，它能够为社会道德和法律的发展进步创造条件、提供动力。

2. 个人品德是个体人格完善的重要标志。

在个人的素质结构中，个人品德是一个非常重要的组成部分，才智等其他素质的完善也离不开品德力量的支持。一方面，个人品德决定着一个人在实际生活和社会实践中的行为选择，以及对各种关系的协调和处理，直接显示出个人境界和素质的高低；另一方面，个人品德又为自我整体素质的修养、锻炼和完善指明方向，为个人成长提供指引和调控。

3. 个人品德是经济社会发展进程中重要的精神力量

社会是由通过各种不同的社会关系联结起来的社会成员组成

social morality is also manifested by the personal morality of each social member. The improvement of personal morality not only directly become an organic part of social morality, but also can pave the way and provide power for the better development and progress of social morality through its own influence and drive. In the new era of socialism with Chinese characteristics, the significance of giving full play to the function and role of personal is more prominent. As the foothold of socialist moral construction, personal morality affects the improvement of the socialist market economic system and the process of socialist democracy. The general improvement of the ideological concepts and moral qualities of members of society is the prerequisite and guarantee for the comprehensive construction of a well-off society and the realization of the Chinese dream of the great rejuvenation of the Chinese nation.

II.The Correct Way to Master the Moral Cultivation

Personal morality needs to be improved through moral cultivation step by step. As one of the important forms of human moral practice, moral cultivation refers to the practice process of individuals that internalizes the moral norms, standards and requirements of a certain society into intrinsic moral qualities so as to promote self-cultivation and self-improvement of personality. To strengthen moral cultivation and enhance personal morality, we should learn from various positive and effective methods put forward by thinkers in history, apply them to practice the needs of today's

的，社会道德状况也是由相互影响的每个社会成员的个人品德体现出来的。个人品德的提升不但直接成为社会道德水平的有机组成部分，而且可以通过自身的影响和带动为社会道德更大限度的发展进步开辟道路、提供动力。在中国特色社会主义新时代，充分发挥个人品德的功能和作用的意义显得更加突出。作为社会主义道德建设的落脚点，个人品德状况影响着社会主义市场经济制度的完善和社会主义民主政治的进程。社会成员思想观念和道德素质的普遍提高是全面建成小康社会、实现中华民族伟大复兴的中国梦的前提和保障。

二、掌握道德修养的正确方法

个人品德需要不断地通过道德修养加以提升。道德修养作为人类道德实践活动的重要形式之一，是指个体自觉地将一定社会的道德规范、准则及要求内化为内在的道德品质，以促进人格的自我陶冶、自我培养和自我完善的实践过程。加强道德修养，提升个人品德，应借鉴历史上思想家们所提出的各种积极有效的方法，并结合当今社会发展的需要身体力行。

social development.

1. The Method of Equal Emphasis on Learning and Thinking

The method of "thinking while learning" is to cultivate good virtue through modest learning, active thinking, right and wrong discriminating, learning kindness and prohibiting badness. In the process of improving personal morality, we must firstly do well in learning various moral theories and knowledge, especially socialist moral theories and knowledge. Secondly, we must think carefully, trying to organically unite the ways of learning and thinking. Confucius once said "Learning without thinking leads to confusion, thinking without learning ends in danger", only by adhering to the way of continuous learning and deep thinking, can we form a comprehensive and deep understanding of why morality is important, what kind of morality we need and how to develop morality, which will generate moral wisdom and we can thus lead a meaningful life.

2. The Methods of Introspection, Observation, Control and Treatment

The method of introspection, observation, control and treatment refers to discovering and finding out the negative tendencies in our thoughts and behaviors through repeated inspection, and suppressing and overcoming them in time. In daily life, we must always check and reflect in our hearts by moral standards, find out those bad faults, bad thoughts, bad ideas and correct them. Self-reflection is the premise to understand and correct our own mistakes. Zengzi once said: "Each day I

1. 学思并重的方法

学思并重的方法，即通过虚心学习、积极思索、辨别善恶、学善戒恶来涵养良好的德行。在提升个人品德的过程中，首先要善于学习各种道德理论和知识，尤其是社会主义道德理论和知识；其次要善于思考，并且把善于学习和善于思考有机地统一起来。孔子说"学而不思则罔，思而不学则殆"，只有坚持既不断学习又深入思考的修养方式，才能对人为什么要讲道德、讲什么样的道德和怎样讲道德形成全面深刻的认识，产生道德智慧，过有意义的生活。

2. 省察克治的方法

省察克治的方法，即通过反复检验以发现和找出自己思想和行为中的不良倾向，并及时对它们进行抑制和克服。在日常生活中，我们要经常在自己内心深处用道德标准检查、反省，找出那些坏毛病、坏思想、坏念头并加以纠正。自我反省，是自我认识错误、自我改正错误的前提。曾子说，"吾日三省吾身：为人谋

examine myself on three counts:whether or not I am loyal to those in whose behalf I act? whether or not I am trustworthy in my dealing with friends? whether or not I practise what is imparted?" Always reflecting on our words and deeds and overcoming mistakes, we can constantly improve our virtues.

3. The Methods of cautious Self-Discipline

The method of cautious self-discipline refers to adhering to your own moral convictions without being known and supervised, and acting consciously according to moral requirements, and never acting deliberately when there is no supervision. The method of prudent self-discipline is not only a critical inheritance of Chinese traditional method of moral cultivation, but also a method of moral cultivation that needs to be adhered to in modern society.

The Book of Rites: "You cannot control the Word of Nature. Those bondages that can be left cannot be called Tao. In other words, there are two kinds of things that constrain my nature. One is that you cannot leave at all times, and you will be lost once you leave the nature; the other is that you can leave." This kind of constraint that can leave cannot be called the Tao. Noble people can be cautious in doing things where no one can see them, and they can also be wary and hold in awe in places where no one can hear them, and they can be cautious to demand themselves strictly in places where no one notice them. It can be seen that caution is a kind of practice about individuals who are good at being alone, willing to hermit, be careful

而不忠乎？与朋友交而不信乎？传不习乎？"善于反省自己的言行，并对错误加以克治，才能使自己的德行不断完善。

3. 慎独自律的方法

慎独自律的方法，即在无人知晓、没有外在监督的情况下，坚守自己的道德信念，自觉按道德要求行事，不因无人监督而恣意妄为。慎独自律的道德修养方法既是对中国传统道德修养方法的批判性传承，也是在现代社会仍需坚持的道德修养方法。

《礼记·中庸》中提到："道也者，不可须臾离也，可离非道也。是故君子戒慎乎其所不睹，恐惧乎其所不闻。莫见乎隐，莫显乎微。故君子慎其独也。""道"是不可以须臾离开的。品德高尚的人在没有人看见的地方也能谨慎做人处事，在没有人听见的地方也能有所戒惧和敬畏，并严格要求自己。可见，慎独就是一种关于个人善于独处、乐于隐处、慎于微处，于独处、隐处、微处中自觉坚守道德情操的修炼功夫。自律是"慎独"达致的一种自觉自为的修养境界。"自"即

about tiny aspects, and being conscious of their moral sentiments. Self-discipline is a conscious and self-cultivation state achieved by "caution." "Self" means autonomy and self-awareness, and "discipline" means measurement and restraint; self-discipline is a personal cultivation method of self-knowledge, self-restraint, and conscious control.

4. The Method of Unifying Knowledge and Action

The method of unifying knowledge and action is to unify the improvement of moral awareness and the moral practice, so as to promote internalizing moral requirements into individual moral qualities and externalizing them into actual moral behavior. Emphasizing the unity of knowledge and action is also an important feature of Confucian self-cultivation. Regarding the relationship between words and deeds, Confucius explicitly advocated "listening to one's words and then observing his deeds." He taught his students that it is inappropriate to judge a person's quality by just listening to his words, more attention should be paid on his actual deeds. He believes that the purpose of learning is to "practice morality" "the gentleman fulfill his morality by learning" and "present one's personal loyalty to obtain morality". Only by "deeds" can make "morality" become reality. It can be seen that moral cultivation is not self-thinking that departs from reality, but a self-reflection and self-sublimation of people on morality through associating with social practice.

自主、自觉，"律"为衡量、约束；自律即一种自我认识、自我约束、自觉控制的个人修养方法。

4. 知行合一的方法

知行合一的方法，即把提高道德认识与躬行道德实践统一起来，以促进道德要求内化为个人的道德品质，外化为实际的道德行为。强调知行合一也是儒家修身思想的重要特征。在言与行的关系上，孔子明确主张"听其言而观其行"。他告诫学生，衡量人的品德不能只听其言论，更应看其实际行动。他认为学习的目的在于"行道""君子学以致其道""行义以达其道"。只有"行"才能使"道"变为现实。可见，道德修养并不是脱离实际的闭门思索，而是人们联系社会实践在道德上的自我反省和自我升华。

5.The Method of Accumulating kindness into Virtue

The method of accumulating kindness into virtue is to accumulate, consolidate and strengthen kindness or virtue in order to gradually condense into good morality. Accumulating kindness into virtue emphasizes that moral cultivation requires persistent accumulation, and the achievement of an ideal personality relies on "accumulation", as *The Chapter Advice on Studying in the Classic Canon by Xun Zi*" states: "Unless you pile up little steps, you can never journey a thousand li; unless you pile up tiny streams, you can never make a river or a sea. The finest thoroughbred cannot travel ten paces in one leap, but the sorriest nag can go a ten days' journey. If you start carving and then give up, you cannot even cut through a piece of rotten wood; but if you persist without stopping, you can carve and inlay metal or stone." We should make efforts to persist in accumulating, "do not do evil things though they may be insignificant, do not give up good things though they may be minor matters", so as to polish our personal morality and improve our spiritual realm.

Strengthening personal moral cultivation cannot be accomplished overnight, let alone to make it once for all. Doing it in accordance with effective methods of moral cultivation, and persisting for a long time, you can continuously improve and perfect yourselves, and become a person of noble morality.

III. The Cultivation of Lofty Moral Character

Xi Jinping emphasized: "For ethics con-

5. 积善成德的方法

积善成德的方法，即通过积累善行或美德，使之巩固强化，以逐渐凝结成优良的品德。积善成德强调道德修养需要日积月累的坚持，成就理想的人格靠"积"，正如荀子《劝学》所说："不积跬步，无以至千里；不积小流，无以成江海。骐骥一跃，不能十步；驽马十驾，功在不舍。锲而舍之，朽木不折；锲而不舍，金石可镂。"我们应该注重平时的坚持和孜孜不倦的努力，"勿以恶小而为之，勿以善小而不为"，不断提高个人品德修养和精神境界。

加强个人品德修养不可能一蹴而就，更不可能一劳永逸。按照有效的品德修养方法去做，并长期坚持下去，才能使自己不断进步、不断完善，从而成为品德高尚的人。

三、锤炼高尚道德品格

习近平强调："道德建设，重

struction, it is important to inspire people to form good moral will and moral sentiment, cultivate correct moral judgment and moral responsibility, and improve their ability to practice ethics, especially their ability to consciously practice." To cultivate lofty moral character, college students must strengthen their moral cultivation in terms of knowing,feeling,meaning, believing, acting, etc., improve their ability to practice ethics, cousiously understand the lofty morality, abide by the social public morality, strict our own personal moral cultivation.

1.The Formation of Correct Moral Cognition and Moral Judgment

Morality is the product of human society's production practice and communicative practice. In different nations, different cultures, and different stages of social development, the basic requirements of morality have remarkable differences, so morality has historical, national, and epochal characteristics. In class society, morality is an important part of ideology with distinct class character. Facing profound and complex changes of the world, college students should focus on enhancing their ability to judge morality, learning to analyze morality, and thus forming correct moral cognition and moral judgment. The most fundamental thing is to treat morality by adhering to the basic principles of historical materialism. On the one hand, we must objectively judge the progress and limitations of ancient traditional moral concepts and modern capitalist moral concepts. Especially, we must have a clear understanding of the irrationality of con-

要的是激发人们形成善良的道德意愿、道德情感，培育正确的道德判断和道德责任，提高道德实践能力尤其是自觉践行能力。"大学生锤炼高尚道德品格，就要在知、情、意、信、行等方面加强道德修养，提高道德实践能力，自觉讲道德、尊道德、守道德，自觉明大德、守公德、严私德。

1. 形成正确的道德认知和道德判断

道德是人类社会生产实践和交往实践的产物。不同的民族、不同的文化、不同的社会发展阶段，道德的基本要求具有显著的差异，道德因此具有历史性、民族性和时代性的特征。在阶级社会中，道德作为意识形态的重要组成部分，还具有鲜明的阶级性。面对世界的深刻复杂变化，大学生应注重增强道德判断能力，学会理性地辨析、讲求道德。形成正确的道德认知和道德判断，最根本的就是要坚持以唯物史观的基本原理来看待道德。一方面要客观评判古代传统道德观和近现代资本主义道德观的进步性和局限性，尤其要清醒地认识到当代西方资产阶级道德观念的不合理性；另一方面要深刻理

temporary western bourgeois moral concepts; on the other hand, we must have deep understanding to the historical superiority and progressiveness of the times reflected by the morality formed on the basis of the socialist production practice with the public ownership of production materials as the main body, and firmly establish a socialist moral concept with Chinese characteristics.

2. The Positive Moral Identity and Moral Sentiment Stimulation

College students should inspire positive emotional identity in their moral cultivation. In general, they should pursue truth, goodness, and beauty, avoid hypocrisy, evil, and ugliness, experience pleasure of morality, and pursue noble happiness; truly internalize the external social moral norms into self-discipline rules of conscience by respecting for virtue. College students should inspire positive moral identity and moral sentiment in their moral cultivation. Specifically, they should consciously cultivate their affection for family members, care for other people and the collective, and enhance their sense of social responsibility, national identity, national belonging and epochal mission, cultivate moral sentiment, existing with the motherland, catching up with the nation, and connecting with the people.

3. The Strengthening of Firm Moral Will and Moral Belief

Practice is important to moral cultivation, but there is a phenomenon that some college students can gain knowledge but without real practice, that is, they can master a lot of moral knowledge, but

解以生产资料公有制为主体的在社会主义生产实践基础上形成的道德所具有的历史优越性、时代进步性，牢固树立中国特色社会主义道德观念。

2. 激发正向的道德认同和道德情操

大学生在道德修养中激发正向的情感认同，总体而言就是要亲近真善美，抵制假恶丑，体验道德的愉悦，追求高尚的快乐；通过对美德的尊崇，真正把外在的社会道德规范内化为心悦诚服的自律准则。大学生在道德修养中激发正向的道德认同与道德情操，具体而言就是要自觉涵育对家庭成员的亲亲之情，对他人、集体的关心关爱，增强社会责任感、国家认同感、民族归属感、时代使命感，在与祖国同呼吸、与民族同步伐、与人民心连心的高尚情怀中陶冶道德情操。

3. 强化坚定的道德意志和道德信念

道德修养重在践行，但有些大学生存在知而不行的现象，也就是尽管掌握了许多道德知识，却没有落实在自己的实际行动

they never implement it in their actual actions, which results in the disconnect between knowledge and practice. In the process of transforming moral cognition into moral behavior, moral will and moral belief are the key elements. Moral will and moral belief are people's perseverance in the process of overcoming all difficulties and obstacles by practicing moral principles and norms. Only through the persistence of moral will and belief can moral behaviors reflect permanence. College students need to understand the profound truth of "It is not easy to do goodness", develop moral will, strengthen moral belief, learn to overcome difficulties and frustrations in the study, life, communication and growth, stay away from interference, avoid slackness, and overcome temptation, move forward, forge ahead in hard work, and achieve perseverance in order to achieve a noble moral character. College students in the new era must have the feelings and responsibilities of struggling for the nation, devoting themselves to the cause of humanity, and relentlessly pursue the lofty moral belief and noble moral realm of communism.

IV. The Implementation of Personal Morality in Practice

"Knowledge derived from books, after all, is not perfect. If you want to understand the truth, you have to do it yourself." The formation of noble moral character lies in practice and persistence. College students devoting themselves to the moral practice of advocating morality and goodness must learn from moral models, cultivate the spirit of voluntary service, vigorously carry forward the

上，导致知行脱节。在道德认知向道德行为转化的过程中，道德意志和道德信念是关键环节。道德意志和道德信念是人们在践履道德原则、规范的过程中表现出的自觉克服一切困难和障碍的毅力，通过道德意志和信念的坚守，道德行为才能体现出恒久性。大学生需要明白"从善如登"的深刻道理，磨炼道德意志，坚定道德信念，学会克服学习、生活、交往、成长中的各种困难和挫折，远离干扰、避免懈怠、战胜诱惑，在砥砺中前行，在拼搏中进取，并做到持之以恒、久久为功，从而成就高尚的道德品格。新时代的大学生要有为国家民族奋斗、为人类事业献身的情怀和担当，不懈追求共产主义的崇高道德信念和高尚道德境界。

四、个人品德在实践中的落实

"纸上得来终觉浅，绝知此事要躬行。"高尚道德品格的形成重在实践，贵在坚持。大学生要投身崇德向善的道德实践，就要向道德模范学习，培养志愿服务精神，大力弘扬时代新风，强化社会责任意识、规则意识、奉献意识。

new style of the times, and strengthen the aware-ness of social responsibility, rules, and dedication.

1.College Students Should Learn from Moral Models

Moral models mainly refer to those advanced people whose thoughts and deeds can inspire people to continue to be kind, and they are respected and imitated by people. Moral models include not only characters emerging from certain social moral practices and conforming to specific types of moral ideals; but characters who can be felt in close proximity and have a positive moral impact in our daily life. Studying the high moral characters and advanced deeds of moral models is conducive to improving the moral quality of all members of society and the overall moral level of society. College students are supposed to follow the example of the moral models to be virtuous, learn their strengths, promote the truth, virtue, beauty, and spread positive energy.

Since the reform and opening up, a large number of moral models with advanced deeds and noble characters have emerged in diverse regions,industries, and groups of people,including models of helping others, models of bravery, models of honesty, models of dedication, models of filial piety and love and so on. Some of them help the poor with their ordinary actions so that many people feel the warmth of the social family, and they also played the main melody of social harmony with love and devotion. In the face of death and disasters, some are righteous though knowing the risks, leave the opportunity for peace and

1. 向道德模范学习

道德模范主要是指思想和行为能够激励人们不断向善且为人们所崇敬、模仿的先进人物。道德模范既包括在一定社会道德实践中涌现的符合特定道德理想类型的人物，又包括人们日常生活中能够近距离感受的具有积极道德影响的人物。学习道德模范的高尚品格和先进事迹，有利于提升全体社会成员的道德素质和社会整体道德水平。大学生要向道德模范学习，崇德向善、见贤思齐，弘扬真善美，传播正能量。

改革开放以来，各个地区、各行各业、各类人群都涌现出一大批具有先进事迹和高尚品格的道德模范，有助人为乐模范、见义勇为模范、诚实守信模范、敬业奉献模范、孝老爱亲模范等。他们有的用自己的平凡举动扶贫助困，让许多人感受到社会大家庭的温暖，用爱和付出奏响了社会和谐的主旋律；有的在死神和灾害面前大义凛然、知险而上，把平安和生的机会留给他人，用鲜血和生命将灾难和危机化解，

survival to others, and resolve the disasters and crises by sacrificing themselves, which shows the historic feat of the supremacy of the people others. Besides, some leave hardships to themselves and give happiness to others without any complaint, demonstrating the noble character of Chinese civilization passed down from generation to generation.A fine example has boundless power. Moral models interpret the meaning of morality and demonstrate moral power with their own actions.

Respecting and publicizing moral models and learning from them is what's the era demand and what the masses are appealing to. Moral models are good examples among the masses that deserve our respect and we can learn from them as well. College students learning from moral models is to learn their noble morality of helping others out, caring for others, sand create life value in this process. Learn the fearless spirit that being courageous to stand out when facing the problems and dangers. Learn the noble characteristic that being honest with others and keeping promises. Treat others sincerely, handle affairs seriously. Learn the professional integrity that being dedicated and hard−working. Love and polish jobs no matter what they are. Learn the sincere feelings of being filial to the old and loving relatives, with the blood dependent. Keeping a grateful heart, and showing gratitude to others. College students should follow the examples of moral models to do more good things whenever and wherever. Be observant when we are in public, get along with our neighbors, drive on the road, travel outside and so on, and

展现了人民至上、他人至上的英雄壮举；有的把困苦留给自己，把幸福送给他人，无怨无悔，彰显了中华文明代代相传的高尚品格。榜样的力量是无穷的。道德模范用自己的行动诠释着道德的内涵，展示着道德的力量。

尊崇道德模范、学习道德模范是时代的呼声，是群众的心声。道德模范是群众身边看得见、摸得着的榜样，是可以学、能够学的标杆。大学生学习道德模范，就是要学习道德模范助人为乐、关爱他人的高尚情怀，在关心他人、帮助他人的过程中创造人生价值；学习他们见义勇为、勇于担当的无畏精神，在危难和考验关头挺身而出；学习他们以诚待人、守信践诺的崇高品格，老老实实做人、踏踏实实做事；学习他们敬业奉献、勤勉做事的职业操守，干一行爱一行，钻一行精一行；学习他们孝老爱亲、血脉相依的至美真情，常怀感恩之心、敬爱之情。大学生要时时处处以道德模范为榜样，多做好事，在公共场所、邻里相处、行路驾车、外出旅游等不同的场合做到崇德守礼、遵规守法，养成良好的道德习惯。

develop good moral habits.

Excellent quality and royal personality will not be formed at once, while they can be accumulated gradually. The moral models not only do the things that normal people are willing to do and can do, more valuably, they take the initiative to do such things that most people don't want to do and manage them better. Some people may hold the idea that the we can't learn from moral models because they are so noble, even though they are respectable and lovely. In fact, the moral models are those who start from themselves, from the things around them, from the little things, therefore they have made great progress from the reality self to ideal self. In our society and our era, advanced people are constantly emerging, and their performance, spirit and quality are our inexhaustible source of strength. College students should gain momentum from the moral models and be protectors, active disseminators and practitioners of social conscience.

2.College Students Should Participate in Voluntary Service Activities

Voluntary service refers to the service that individuals devote their time and energy to improve society and promote social progress without asking for any material compensation. Voluntary service is an important carrier for cultivating and promoting the socialist core values. Relevant departments in various parts of China have organically combined voluntary service with the activities of learning from Lei Feng, which has formed voluntary service of Chinese characteristics, pro-

优良的品质、高尚的人格并非一蹴而就，而是逐渐积累的结果。道德模范不仅做了普通人愿意做和能够做的事，更为可贵的是，他们主动做了许多人不想做的事，而且把大多数人能够做的事做得更好。一些人认为，道德模范固然可敬可爱，但不可学，因为他们太高大。其实，道德模范都是从自我做起，从身边事做起，从小事做起，以此实现了由现实自我向理想自我的飞跃。在我们这个社会、我们这个时代，先进人物不断涌现，他们的业绩、精神和品质是我们取之不尽、用之不竭的力量源泉。大学生应积极从道德模范身上获取前进的动力，做社会良知的守望者、积极传播者和践行者。

2.参与志愿服务活动

志愿服务是指贡献个人的时间及精力，在不求任何物质报酬的情况下，为改善社会、促进社会进步而提供的服务。志愿服务是培育和弘扬社会主义核心价值观的重要载体。我国各地各有关部门把志愿服务与学雷锋活动有机结合，形成了志愿服务的中国特色，促进了志愿服务的制度化、常态化，推动着志愿服务队

moted the institutionalization and normalization of voluntary service, and promoted the continuous growth of the scale of voluntary service teams.

The spirit of voluntary service is dedication, affection, mutual assistance and progress. Among them, the essence is dedication. Participating in voluntary service activities, on the one hand, we can help others, serve the society, and promote the improvement of social morality; on the other hand, we also regard the service for society and others as obligations and glorious duties. We can achieve a sense of accomplishment and happiness by serving the society and helping others. The dedication of voluntary service for others and public welfare undertakings is conducive to convey social care, promote social integrity, and form a good social trend of goodness and mutual trust. The spirit of volunteerism and the spirit of Lei Feng are highly unified, they all manifest the socialist core values. "The spirit of Lei Feng can be learned by everyone; dedication and caring behavior can be done everywhere. Accumulating small goodness to gorgeous one, and that's real kindness. When someone is in need, everyone should offer their support and work together to make the society a better one."

Voluntary service has become an important stage for college students to participate in social practice and develop themselves, and it is an important way for college students to care for others and spread the positive energy of youth. Nowadays, voluntary service activities of college students have spread in different areas like rural poverty alleviation and development, urban com-

伍规模的不断壮大。

志愿服务的精神是奉献、友爱、互助、进步。其中，奉献精神是精髓。参与志愿服务活动，一方面，帮助了他人、服务了社会，推动了社会道德水平的提高；另一方面，把为社会和他人的服务看作自己应尽的义务和光荣的职责，从服务社会和帮助他人中获得成就感和幸福感。志愿服务所体现出来的这种自愿地、不计报酬地服务他人和参与社会公益事业的奉献精神，有助于传递社会关爱、弘扬社会正气、形成向上向善、诚信互助的良好社会风尚。志愿精神与雷锋精神在本质上是高度统一的，它们都是社会主义核心价值观的生动体现。"雷锋精神，人人可学；奉献爱心，处处可为。积小善为大善，善莫大焉。当有人需要帮助时，大家搭把手、出份力，社会将变得更加美好。"

志愿服务已经成为大学生参与社会实践、成长成才的重要舞台，成为大学生关爱他人、传播青春正能量的重要途径。当前，大学生志愿服务活动已经遍及农村扶贫开发、城市社区建设、环境保护、大型活动、抢险救灾、社会公益等领域。大学生积极投

munity construction, environmental protection, large-scale activities, rescue and disaster relief, and social welfare. How do college students participate in volunteer service activities? One way is to go to where they are most needed. Providing high-quality and efficient services in international and domestic large-scale activities, never fear hardships and hard work in disaster, help and offer support for education in poor and remote areas, take the lead in voluntary activities at the grass-roots level, community, and family, which are all important manifestations for college students to care for society and devote themselves. The second way is to help vulnerable groups. College students should pay more attention to the social vulnerable groups such as the empty-nest elderly, left-behind children, poor workers, migrant workers and their children, and the disabled in voluntary service activities, and give them warmth and have affection to them. The third way is to do what they can. College students should devote themselves to voluntary service activities and pay attention to combining their own abilities, professions, and expertise with practice to increase knowledge, strengthen skills, and increase talents. In particular, they must take active action to assist in education, science, technology, culture, health and other fields, and participate in activities of cleaning urban and rural environment, green travel, low-carbon environmental protection, and beautifying homeland.

College students should learn from Lei Feng to set examples, and spread the seed of Lei Feng's

身志愿服务活动有三种方式：一是到最需要的地方去。在国际国内大型活动中提供优质高效的服务，在救灾一线不畏艰险、奋力救援，在贫穷落后地区帮扶、支教，带头把志愿服务活动做进基层、做进社区、做进家庭，这都是大学生关爱社会、奉献爱心的重要表现。二是帮助弱势群体。大学生应在志愿服务活动中多关注空巢老人、留守儿童、困难职工、进城务工人员及其子女、残疾人等社会弱势群体，注重向他们送温暖、献爱心。三是做力所能及的事。大学生投身志愿服务活动，应注重结合自身的能力、专业、特长，在实践中长知识、强本领、增才干，特别要积极参与教育、科技、文化、卫生等帮扶行动，多参与城乡清洁、绿色出行、低碳环保、美化家园等活动。

大学生应带头学雷锋，做雷锋精神的种子，把雷锋精神广

spirit, disseminating it on our motherland; active-ly participate in voluntary service activities, and feeling the power of goodness in the practice of going deep into society, observing people's sentiments, caring for others, and being devoted to society, write the story of Lei Feng in the new era by actual action, and dedicate themselves for the realization of Chinese dream.

3. College Students Should Lead the Social customs

Good social customs is gradually formed in the practice of social morality. College students devote themselves to the moral practice of advocating morality and goodness, they must carry forward truths, goodness, beauty, and avoid fake, ugliness and evil. They should be models or leaders of socialist morality to promote social customs of understanding honor and disgrace, advocating uprightness, making contributions and promoting harmony.

First, college students should understand honor and disgrace.

The concept of honor and disgrace has a clear motive force, guidance and regulating effect on an individual's thinking and behavior. Social customs are closely linked to the concept of honor and disgrace, they can influence and interact with each other. What kind of honor and disgrace a society has, what kind of social customs it will generate; in turn, what kind of social customs a society has, the people who live in it will also form what kind of concept of honor and shame. College students should be guided by the correct concept of honor

播在祖国大地上；积极参加志愿服务活动，在深入社会、体察民情、关爱他人、奉献社会的道德实践中感受善的力量，以实际行动书写新时代的雷锋故事，为实现中国梦有一份热发一份光。

3. 引领社会风尚

良好的社会风尚是人们在社会道德实践中逐渐形成的。大学生投身崇德向善的道德实践，要弘扬真善美、贬斥假丑恶，做社会主义道德的示范者和引领者，促成知荣辱、讲正气、作奉献、促和谐的社会风尚。

第一，知荣辱。

荣辱观对个人的思想行为具有鲜明的动力、导向和调节作用。社会风尚同荣辱观紧密相连，两者相互影响、相互作用。一个社会有什么样的荣辱观，也必然有什么样的社会风尚；反过来，一个社会有什么样的社会风尚，生活于其中的人们也就会形成什么样的荣辱观。大学生应以正确的荣辱观为指导，坚定正确的行为导向，产生正确的价值激

and disgrace, be firm in their correct behavioral orientation, and generate the right value incentives to help the whole society to form a good moral style of understanding honor and disgrace.

Second, college students should advocating uprightness.

Advocating uprightness is to insist on truth, uphold principles, and fight with the evils. College students must have a righteous spirit to move forward without fear, so as to work resolutely for the country and society. To advocate uprightness, we must cleanse ourselves and be strict with ourselves in our daily life, staying away from low-level tastes; actively maintain social public order, resist bad behaviors and evils, dare to uphold justice, be brave, and resolutely fighting against all acts that trample on social morality.

Third, college students should make contributions.

The spirit of dedication is the concentrated expression of social responsibility. Society is a collection of individuals, without them, the society cannot work. People are required to take responsibility for the society. Responsibility means dedication. The spirit of dedication can transfer the warmth of the society, which can not only shorten the distance between people, but also establish harmonious interpersonal relations and stable social order to promote the healthy and orderly development of the society. Being public-spirited and doing charity, being warm-hearted is the spirit of dedication. Standing up in the crisis to sacrifice

励,助推全社会形成知荣明辱的良好道德风尚。

第二,讲正气。

讲正气,就是坚持真理、坚持原则,坚持同一切歪风邪气作斗争。大学生须有一腔浩然正气,这样才能无所畏惧地前进,才能不屈不挠地为国家、为社会建功立业。要做到讲正气,在日常生活中就要洁身自好、严于律己;自觉远离低级趣味;积极维护社会公共秩序,抵制歪风邪气;敢于伸张正义、见义勇为,坚决同践踏社会道德风尚的一切行为作斗争。

第三,作奉献。

奉献精神是社会责任感的集中表现。社会是由一个个的人所构成的集合体,脱离了人,便没有了社会。社会需要人们对其负起责任。有责任,就意味着要奉献。奉献精神传递社会温暖,能够拉近人与人之间的距离,建立和谐的人际关系和稳定的社会秩序,促进社会健康有序地发展。热心公益与爱心资助、心中有爱是奉献精神,在危难关头挺身而出、牺牲小我是奉献精神,以职业与事业为人生目标的爱岗敬业

is the spirit of dedication. Taking job and career as the goal of life is the spirit of dedication. Taking serving the national science and technology innovation and progress or defending national security as one's own responsibility is the spirit of dedication. To choose dedication is to choose nobility. "Those who are virtuous and generous will be respected", college students should actively contribute to the society to make our society a more beautiful and happy one.

Fourth, college students should promote harmony.

A society ruled by democracy and laws, fairness and justice, integrity and love, vitality, stability and order, in which men and nature can live with harmony, is an important guarantee for the prosperity of the country, the rejuvenation of the nation and people's happy life. For college students, promoting harmony means to promote the harmony between their body and mind, the harmony between individuals and others, the harmony between individuals and society, and the harmony between man and nature. College students should have a harmonious attitude towards practice, internalize advocating and maintaining harmony into their own ideology and behavioral habit, promote the harmony between different people and between people and society, to realize friendly symbiosis between man and nature.

The status of social civilization is an important manifestation of social customs. All kinds of activities of creating civilized cities, villages and towns, companies, families and campuses are aim-

是奉献精神，以服务国家科学技术创新进步或捍卫国家安全为己任是奉献精神。选择奉献也就选择了高尚。"德厚者流光"，大学生要在奉献社会中积极发光发热，使我们的社会更加美好和幸福。

第四，促和谐。

民主法治、公平正义、诚信友爱、充满活力、安定有序、人与自然和谐相处的社会，是国家富强、民族复兴、人民幸福的重要保证。对于大学生来说，促和谐就是要促进自我身心的和谐、个人与他人的和谐、个人与社会的和谐、人与自然的和谐等。大学生要用和谐的态度对待人生实践，使崇尚和谐、维护和谐内化为自己的思想意识和行为习惯，推动人与人之间、人与社会之间融洽相处，实现人与自然之间的友好共生。

社会文明状况是社会风尚的重要体现。各种创建文明城市、文明村镇、文明单位、文明家庭、文明校园的活动，就是要

ing to promote the formation of a social customs of unterstanding honor and disgrace, advocating uprightness, making contributions and promoting harmony in the whole society. College students are the backbone for national rejuvenation. Their moral cendition and spiritual outlook have great influence on the moral condition and spiritual outlook of the entire society in the new era. College students should hold the sense of being master to actively participate in the creation of various spiritual civilizations, to pursue happiness for the family, give warmth to others, and contribute to the society, continuously lead the social customs, and improve moral quality.

在全社会推动形成知荣辱、讲正气、作奉献、促和谐的社会风尚。新时代的大学生作为承担民族伟大复兴重任的中坚力量，其道德状况和精神风貌在很大程度上影响着整个社会的道德状况和精神风貌。大学生要以高度的主人翁精神，积极参与各种精神文明创建活动，为家庭谋幸福、为他人送温暖、为社会做贡献，不断引领社会风尚，提升道德品质。

后　记

　　改革创新是中华民族最深厚的民族禀赋。只要是同时利党利国利民利校利众利己的事物，我们都应该允许其探索改革发展。作为炎黄子孙的我们，作为从事马克思主义理论研究教学的马克思主义思想政治理论工作者，也遗传着列祖列宗的民族禀赋中改革创新的基因。现实生活和工作中从来不缺做事者，但却缺敢于、善于正向改革创新者。《思想道德与法治》的双语教育教学改革创新本就是高校思政教学改革创新的路径之一，不应该被视为思政课教学改革的异类而加以排斥，也不应该因为自己喜好或擅长与否而冷嘲热讽、无端指责，甚至无情压制。相反，根据马克思主义物质多样性统一的原理，我们都是为了中国的思想政治理论教育教书育人的事业，在这一共同目标下，我们可以有多种方式进行实践，根据实践成效进行审视。双语思政课教学改革创新作为思政理论课改革的探索，经历了从无到有的过程，也是一个不断丰富和发展的过程，还是一个不断被接纳的过程。在双语思政课的教学探索过程中也必然会出现这样那样的问题，遇到这样那样的困难。这主要体现为双语思政课教学的教材缺乏，教师缺乏，课件缺乏，经验缺乏，授课教师本身水平、授课对象层次不一，等等，因而难度大、要求高。尽管如此，双语思政课教学探索仍然是高校思政课教学改革创新的重要内容，而《思想道德与法治》双语教学改革创新就是其中之一。

　　从 2019 年底开始，在对 2018 版《思想道德修养与法律基础》进行编著的基础上，我们把教材体系转换为教学体系，再在教学体系的基础上进行编译。经过三年多的努力，我们编译出了《大学生思想道德教育双语专题十二讲》讲稿，并就每一讲制作了全英文的课件。随后，我们根据 2021 版《思想道德与法治》教材，又对《大学生思想道德教育双语专题十二讲》进行了编译。《思想道德与法治》双语思政课教学在实践中也取得了较好的效果，经调查，同意本课程双语思政课教学的大学生占 80% 以上，其他已经实践的双语思政课的同意率也在 80% 以上。在《思想道德与法治》双语思政课教育教学实践的探索过程中，我们发现双语讲义、课件以及教学实践中存在不少问题。当然，这是难免的，我们也在不断解决。经过两年多的反复修改、校译，作为《思想道德与法治》双语思政课教学参考用书的《大学生思想道德教育双语专题十二讲》编译完稿。细心的读者肯定会发现，该书仅对大学生思想道德教育进行了编译，而并没有涉及《思想道德与法治》中的"法治"部分。这正是下面笔者需要向读者交代的问题。

在多年的高校思政课理论研究和实践教学以及领导工作中，笔者发现《思想道德修养与法律基础》（现在改为《思想道德与法治》，但其中内容相差不多）中的第六章法律学理性阐述较多，而应用性法律较少。我们设置"法律基础"或者"法治"这一内容的初心是让大学生学法、懂法、守法、维法、传法。大学生毕业后会面临职业选择、职场劳动、婚姻家庭、个人与集体和国家关系的处理等，会面临很多现实的不可避免的诸如劳资关系纠纷、婚姻家庭纠纷等，而"法律基础"或者"法治"的内容显然不够让大学生在毕业后面对诸如此类矛盾纠纷时进行维权。因此，笔者将《思想道德修养与法律基础》（《思想道德与法治》）分成两部分进行双语教学实践。因此，《大学生思想道德教育双语专题十二讲》只是《思想道德修养与法律基础》（《思想道德与法治》）的内容之一。至于"法律基础"或者"法治"的内容，我们本着实用性、针对性的原则，进行劳动、婚姻、国家、军事、考试、民事等方面普及性内容的扩充。

该书的出版既有理论价值，又有实践意义。就理论价值而言，该书填补了《思想道德修养与法律基础》（《思想道德与法治》）双语思政课教学改革双语教学资料的空白；就实践意义而言，该书既可作为高校双语思政课教学的参考用书，也可作为政治英语爱好者学习的参考用书，为双语思政课教学改革实践提供依托。

当然，该书还有一些需要完善之处。首先，该书只是对大学生思想道德教育方面的部分重要问题进行编译。大学生思想道德教育内容其实很多，本书不可能将其全部囊括。其次，该书的内容结构还存在一些需要补充的地方：一是每讲后面没有 New Words and Expressions。如果能在每讲后面有选择性地附上本讲的生词和短语，会更便于学习者有针对性地学习，避免学习者忙于生词和短语的查找而影响学习效果。二是每讲后面对一些专业术语没有进行专门的阐述，不便于读者更好地了解有关专业术语的提出背景、过程、内涵等，拓宽读书的知识面，如"新时代""四个自信"等。三是每讲后面没有附参考文献。由于该书是作为教学体系的一个讲义编译而成的双语教学参考性用书，翻译任务繁重，翻译量大，出于出版经费和讲义内容繁多的考虑，本书将参考文献删除，同时将讲义原有的教学目的、重点、难点、内容摘要、问题导入等部分也全部删除。四是有些翻译还需要斟酌，如古文部分的内容及一些诗词的翻译等。最后，由于排版工作繁杂、耗时较多，部分专家的建议没能在这次的出版过程中补充进去，敬请谅解。

该书的编译和出版，得到广西壮族自治区政策研究室（改革办）陈牧主任和梧州学院马克思主义学院吴昊博士（特聘为广西大学马克思主义学院中国－东盟共同体研究中心研究员）的鼎力协助，得到了新华出版社相关工作人员为本书校译的辛勤付出，在此一一表示感谢。

由于双语思政理论课教学实践和理论探索是一项开拓性工作，国内尚无经验可以借鉴，加上相关研究资料有限、编译者时间仓促以及笔者编译水平不高，书中难免有不尽如人意之处，恳请各位专家、学者和同人包容、批评、指正。

编　者

2022 年 4 月 28 日于南宁